THE
COLD
CASE
OF
RIVERWOOD'S
SILENT
KILLER

CHRISTIAN CANDELARIA

CONTENTS

CHAPTER ONE

The Perfect Lie

A man walked into the diner, the bell above the door announcing his arrival. The subtle smile on his face faded as he abruptly stopped by the door way, surprised to find the usually active diner deserted. Perhaps if he had checked his wristwatch, he would have known it was nearing closing time. It was dead quiet safe for the soft clinking of dishes and the gentle hum of the espresso machine. Margaret, the middle-aged waitress, looked up from wiping down the counter, her eyes locking onto his. The lighting inside was dim and the ambiance was warm, much like he wanted. Outside, it was chilly and the night's last rays had dissolved and the town was settling into darkness.

The lingering scent of brewed coffee and baked goods escaped into the night, but James' thoughts were elsewhere. If the diner had been filled with customers, then Margaret would be so occupied she would not have the time to scrutinize the lady standing quietly by his side.

James Reed, a familiar face in the Riverwood, stood there forcing a warm smile considering the tension that seemed to accompany him. His brown hair, graying at the temples, was cut short, and his brown eyes held a hint of weariness. He had a face that blended into the crowd but his tailored suit, the designer shoes were the trappings of wealth and luxury. James Reed was the driving force behind Reed Corp, a global giant with interests in finance and real estate.

Everyone in Riverwood knew James Reed, it was a small town after all. He had grown up in that small town, built his empire from the ground up. He had made his millions in that small town. Married his high school sweetheart, Lucy, in that small town and raised a child in the same community that had nurtured him.

So who was the lady gliding effortlessly beside him? She was not Lucy nor anyone else familiar to the townspeople. Her curly brown hair fell to her shoulders. Her features were gentle, with a smattering of freckles across her nose. Her fitted navy blue dress hugged curves that didn't belong on the arm of James Reed. There was something about her elegant stride and poised demeanor that suggested a confidence that bordered on intimacy. When she absentmindedly wrapped her arms around his, Margaret felt the unmistakable air of couple hood. The gentle way James smiled at her, even though it was a nervous smile, the soft glance she returned, showed she was just not some lady he picked up, they were together. James knew this story would spread like a wildfire but did he really care.

Margaret's eyes drifted from the woman to James, curiosity and disapproval shining in her tired eyes. "James, honey, you know it's closing time," she said with a hint of reprimand. James flashed his warm smile. "Just a quick coffee, Margaret. We won't keep you."

As Margaret poured their coffee, she couldn't take her eyes off the lady. When her eyes met with James, he stirred with unease. The lady, Rachel, continued to chatter because she oblivious to the tension growing in the room. James cleared his throat and cautiously started a conversation with a forced tone to return normalcy. "Margaret, how's business been?"

Margaret's eyes narrowed slightly as she struggled to put on that mask of polite interest, "Oh, same old, James. You know how it is." She paused, then started again with an edge to her voice, "I didn't know you were... entertaining tonight."

Rachel's chatter paused, and she glanced at James, and a faint crease formed in between her brows. For an instant, Rachel's eyes betrayed a shadow of doubt, right before her bright smile reclaimed its place.

James's face remained impassive but she quickly noticed a discreet pinkish hue spreading across his cheeks. "Just grabbing a late coffee, Margaret. No need to fuss."

Even though she tried so hard, she could not avoid gazing at Rachel. She was a beautiful woman but who was she and why was she with James Reed? Her eyes stayed for a moment longer, before she nodded curtly and returned to her tasks. "Enjoy your coffee, folks," she said.

All that struggling to maintain a neutral face got Margret nothing because Rachel still saw right through her and knew there was something tense about how she flashed suspicious glances at James. The latter didn't help that he kept clearing his throat and adjusting his tie.

As Margaret busied herself wiping down the counter, James and Rachel settled into their conversation. Rachel's laughter was like a stinging echo, disturbing the stillness of the night and James smile began to return with genuineness.

Rachel had been curious all the while. That waitress, Margret had made James uncomfortable, or was it that they were not supposed to be in the diner. If so, they why did he bring her here? "Why are you like that around her? Does she know Lucy?" She could not hide her amusement. James thought she was as bothered as he was but when he looked in her eyes, he found a hint of probing under her nonchalant attitude.

James shrugged, trying to play it cool. "Everybody knows Lucy, it's Riverwood. Small town, no secrets."

"So why did you bring me here? We could have been watching the stars somewhere, together."

"I just wanted to a different scenery, I wanted us to stop hiding. But the fact that she's alone here make me uncomfortable."

Rachel's smile faltered for a while, she was an outsider. Moving into Riverwood was James's idea. For the moment, it was not as welcoming as she thought it would, but did she really expect to blend in so easily? "I'm not from these parts, remember. I only moved here for you." She whispered with vulnerability, to remind him of her sacrifice.

James's gaze softened as he locked eyes with her, he loved her and would never forget the chances she took to build their relationship. "I know, baby. I appreciate that."

"I guess she doesn't know who I am," Rachel said and glanced over at Margret who still couldn't take her eyes off them.

James's voice dropped low and husky, when he said with conviction, "Not yet..."

The pause that followed was heavy. Rachel searched for answers in James's face but it was so blank she could not make anything out. She wasn't sure if James was ready for the backlash their relationship would face. The whispers, the judgmental stares, the repercussions on his marriage and reputation. Not even James was certain of what his words meant, but he wear that straight face to keep her mind at ease. His mind wandered back to the night they met, outside the suffocating bubble of Riverwood.

It was at a lavish party in Manhattan, Rachel has been working as an escort for one of the city's biggest kahunas. It was her bright smile and quick wit that attracted James to her. He did not expect that she would have a degree, many women did not have one. James was invited to the party, he never said no to any party. Even if he had to travel out of the country. That day, he stood out among the crowd as a very important person, when their eyes met, he could not take his away. Time froze, even as she was walking past him, holding another man's hand.

He waited for the right moment and when he got the opportunity to get to her, he did not waste it. She was standing outside, by a pool and lighting a cigar. And when he joined her, she lighted his too even though he was not a fan of smoking. Their conversations flowed effortlessly for a while, they even danced. It was a connection James did not expect to make with another woman since he married the love of his life. Before the night ended, James requested for her contact information, and she did not hesitate.

Their secret meetings followed thereafter, each encounter deepened their connection. But James's marriage to Lucy loomed like a shadow. He loved both women equally, perhaps if he had met Rachel earlier. There was just something about her that made him feel at peace. She was the party goer, lively and intelligent. She was everything he wanted to be back when he was younger. But in Riverwood, such a life was frowned upon. To be too happy was considered a sign of frivolity and absence of seriousness. Every man must wear a stern expression like a badge of honor. And every woman must temper her smile with a little sadness. A lot of joy was seen as a distraction from the responsibilities that came with living in Riverwood. No one dared to defy that unspoken rule, lest they would be labeled soft or carefree.

Therefore, every child was taught from a young age to rein in their laughter, to quiet their excitement, and to prioritize soberness. Playfulness was tolerated, but only in measured doses. Everyone was expected not to get too carried away, at least not in Riverwood.

Women like Lucy had mastered this look and that's why James liked her from the start. Her smiles carried resignation and her eyes looked warm, yet it was a fading light. She carved Riverwood's expectations into her soul and that's why his family thought she was the true reflection of the town's reserved beauty. And if his family wanted her for him, he accepted her wholeheartedly.

But Rachel came into his life so unexpectedly, with her infectious laughter to disrupt his perfect life. However, he wanted this for himself. He was tired of the life in Riverwood, he needed a little more than it offered him. Her joy was unapologetic and untamed, quite foreign to the town's sensibilities. James knew that introducing her to Riverwood would be a risk, but he couldn't help himself. He wanted to share his world with her, even if it meant confronting his hometown and his family. But was he truly ready for it all, maybe it was too soon. *Too soon.* He thought right before her voice broke his train of thought.

"I think I've had enough of her nosiness," Rachel said a little peeved at Margret for not minding her business. "Where can I stay for the night?"

James nodded sympathetically. "Let me take you to the hotel down the road. It's the best place in town."

"Will you stay with me?" she asked him. But his eyes dropped, avoiding hers as he cleared his throat. "I shouldn't," he said quietly.

Rachel thought if she looked harder, she would find a glimmer of hope in his eyes but his expression did not falter, his mind was made up. "I have to get back home," he added as he finally looked up. Rachel nodded slowly, defeated, her eyes clouding over.

When they walked out of the diner, the midnight's cold air surrounded them. The street was deserted, its silence almost wearing him down. The soft sound of gravel crunching beneath his feet was rather irritating than helpful. He couldn't shake off the feeling of Margaret's piercing gaze, her eyes burning into his back. He knew that sensation would follow him into the night. He couldn't help but wonder if she'd watched them leave, he glanced over his shoulder, half-expecting to see her intense stare following them. But she was gone, perhaps she was really closing for the night. Margret barely had a home, so she could even sleep in the diner.

"It's too quiet, it feels like a horror movie..." she giggled as she sat in the car. James smiled, shutting her door with a reassuring chuckle. "Don't worry, Rachel, Riverwood's not that scary."

As he turned to head to the driver's side, a shiver ran down his spine. He felt eyes upon him, like there was a presence lurking just out of sight. James spun around, his heart thumping out of its place. But there was nothing.

Only the long streetlight stood behind him, its light blinking steadily like a mechanical heartbeat. James heaved a sigh of relief, chiding himself for his foolishness. *Must be the late hour.*

As he settled into the driver's seat, Rachel noticed he looked spooked, "Everything okay?"

James forced a smile. "Yeah, just a little jumpy, that's all."

As James pulled away from the curb, the streetlight's blinking stopped and from the diner's window, he found Margaret standing there, glaring at them with a fixed stare. Even through his rear-view mirror, she did not move an inch. *Crazy lady,* he thought to himself.

It was a chatty drive to the hotel, but it was not enough to take James's mind off the trouble he had created for himself. The darkness outside seemed to mirror the emotions within. It was between his loyalty to his wife and the growing affection he had for Rachel. She had introduced to a life he never got exposed to while living in Riverwood. And did not want to lose her.

At the hotel entrance, James handed her the room key, hinting at not getting in with her. "You'll be safe here," he assured her.

Rachel's smile was faint, she had accepted sleeping alone but she did not expect to not be accompanied into the hotel. "Thank you... James."

As he turned to leave, Rachel's hand grazed against his and he felt the burning desire to cuddle and settle in her warmth but he didn't look back.

"Goodnight," he whispered and got in his car, driving away. James felt a creeping sense of unease, as if a thousand unseen eyes watched him from the darkness, from the bushes, behind the fences, behind the wall, through the windows, just like Margaret did. He had been too confident with his choices, now he knew the extent of the grave mistake he made bringing Rachel to Riverwood. His conscience would bite down on him for a long, maybe until he braved himself to choose between his wife and his lover.

As he turned onto his street, his anxiety grew stronger. He was just seconds away from his home. When he squinted to see the windows, he prayed Lucy was not standing behind one of them waiting for him, staring like she did some nights. There was no one there, just the black window gazing back at him like empty sockets.

He switched the headlights off as he pulled to the driveway. And for a second, he prayed Lucy was fast asleep. With a deep breath, James stepped out into the darkness ready to face whatever was waiting for him behind the entrance door to his house.

CHAPTER TWO

Playdate Interrupted

Lucy Reed was popular for being unapologetically opinionated. For other women in Riverwood, a sharp tongue earned them a hard slap on the cheeks, but she was the exception to the general rule. She commanded respect from everyone in town, from the lowliest shopkeeper to the wealthiest businessman. She was not afraid to say her mind and her words always carried deadly weight.

But her influence and reputation weren't solely due to her marriage to James Reed, no, Lucy came from old money herself. She was a member of the aristocracy, and she carried herself with the confidence and poise that came with it. That's why everyone equally hated and revered her.

Though James was a hardworker, he might have owned a huge part of his success to her. Her inheritance had provided the seed money for James's growing business, and her connections had opened doors that would have otherwise remained closed. And as his company grew, her influence behind the scenes grew with it. She would often host parties and charity events outside town or at their estate to win potential investors and clients.

And despite being a stay-at-home mom, Lucy was a silent partner in James's company. She had no seat at the board but her opinions always mattered to him. James often joked that she was the real brains behind the operation, and while he was only being facetious, there was more than a grain of truth to his words. Well everyone knew it was true. That's why she was even more revered than her millionaire husband.

And while that generational wealth was now fully invested in James's company, she still held onto the past. She'd often remind James that she'd helped make him successful. In subtle ways, she would point out that she was the one who provided the foundation for his success.

Lucy would joke that she'd polished James, and taught him about the finer things in life and James would tease her about being his socialite wife but she knew that her influence was much more deeper than he made it look. Sometimes when she spoke about her family history, he would listen to her with admiration and a little bit of annoyance. Her pride was a double-edged sword because it had driven her to support him and build their life together, but it also made her fiercely protective of her family's legacy.

And as the years had gone by so quickly, she had grown resentful of him for not being grateful enough. She knew James was cheating on her – *not just financially, by hiding company income* – but also emotionally, with another woman. Of course there was another woman in the picture. How then did she find a red lipstick on the shirt collar, men ought to be more careful. When she confronted him about it, he denied and gaslighted her.

There were nights when Lucy would stand by the window, waiting for James to come home. He was always late and it had become a ritual that she had grown accustomed to. Every night, she'd tell herself that tonight would be different, that tonight he'd come home early, smelling of his own cologne, with a smile on his face and a joy in his eyes, because he would be happy to see her. She held on, believing he would truly change for her, like he promised he would.

But tonight was like all the others. When the car pulled up, when James stepped out of the car, scanning the street outside their steel fences before settling on the front door and walking in smelling of a female fragrance, she knew he would never change.

She was sadder than she was angry. As she looked at him, standing in the doorway with that guilty look on his face, Lucy knew that she'd been fooling herself. James had gone deep into that life he had chosen for himself and there was no coming back.

She crossed her legs while sitting there on a chair. "Welcome home honey, how was your day?" She started casually. But James was not having it. He noticed how calm she looked, she had never looked that way. Plus she was sitting instead of standing by the window, she had never done that before. Everything was unusual, something was terribly off.

"It was fine. Just busy with work stuff," he replied gently as he shut the door behind him.

She continued calmly, with her sweet soft voice which was meant to keep James at ease, but it was doing the exact opposite. "Oh, I'm sure it was. You've been working so hard lately," she paused, but her eyes never left his face. "I'm just glad you're home safe."

James was beginning to feel anxious, he had gotten used to being shouted at once he walked in at that late hour, instead, she was nice. But there was also a note of passive aggression or was it just his mind. "Yeah, me too. Thanks for…" his voice trailed off as he observed her intense stare. "…is everything okay, honey? You seem a bit… off?

Her smile grew wider, but her anger was starting to slip through. "Oh, everything's fine, James. Just peachy," she replied sarcastically. "…I was just sitting here, waiting for you, thinking about how lucky I am to have such a wonderful husband…" She shifted her legs, uncrossing them and re-crossing them in the opposite direction. "I mean, what's not to love? You get to leave me at home with our child, day in and day out, while you're off living your best life…" Then she began to sound bitter and her face started to contort with pain and disgust. "And when you do come home, you're always so present, so engaged…" She rolled her eyes and giggled. "…with your calls, with your work, with whatever distraction you can find to avoid actually spending time with us."

James was starting to feel defensive, he could not afford to stand there any longer without saying a word. "Lucy, that's not fair. I work hard to provide for this family and-"

She cut him off, "Oh, I'm sure you do. And I'm sure your… extracurricular activities have nothing to do with the fact that you're never here." Then she stood up, her face now red with anger. "But you know what? I'm done. I'm done being ignored, done being neglected, done being treated like an afterthought."

And that was when James realized where this was going. He had always known she was tired of their relationship but he didn't know she would be brave to go for it. Not in Riverwood, it was greatly frowned upon. Imagine the many people who looked up to them finding out they were not the perfect couple they were posing as. "Lucy, what are you talking about?" He asked with dread in his voice.

She smiled, "I'm talking about the fact that I deserve better. And I'm going to get it…" she walked over to the coffee table, picked up a folder, and handed it to James. "Here. These are divorce papers and a few other things. I want my share of everything; the house, the cars, the bank accounts by the end of the week."

He hesitated for a moment before he began opening reaching inside with trembling hands. Inside were the divorce papers, a handwritten letter, and photographs. He was in those images, with Rachel. Some were explicit, some weren't.

"How did you get this Lucy?" his voice quivered as he asked.

"Someone left it at the doorstep. They want money, go ahead and pay them. But I want everything I deserve."

"Lucy, you can't be serious…"

"Oh, I'm dead serious. And if you don't comply, I'll make sure the whole world knows what kind of man James Reed really is."

James instantly thought about it. Imagine what Riverwood would say when they found out about his secret life, his extramarital affairs, and the countless lies he had told to keep them hidden. James's reputation as a respected businessman and Riverwood's pillar would be ruined. He could already imagine the headlines in the Gazette,

"James Reed's Secret Life Exposed" or "Respected Businessman's Infidelity Scandal." That was no good for his strong image.

He had always known the townsfolk knew about his infidelity, but if it became official news, if the rumors were confirmed in black and white, it would be a different story altogether. The townsfolk would no longer be able to turn a blind eye or pretend that they didn't know. They would be forced to confront his infidelity, and James knew that he would be shunned and ostracized by the people he had grown up with.

He imagined all the connections he had made through Lucy, all the social and business relationships that had been facilitated by her family's influence. He thought about the deals he had closed, the high-society events he had attended, and the powerful people he had met, all thanks to her connections. He imagined how those connections would go with the wind once Lucy was no longer by his side. He imagined the awkward phone calls, the unreturned letters, and the polite but firm rejections.

And he panicked a little as he realized just how much he had taken Lucy for granted. He had assumed that she would always be there, supporting him and pushing his success. But now, he was not just going to lose her, but he would have to face his vulnerabilities. Lucy was not just threatening to divorce him, but to expose him to the entire town the secrets his blackmailer revealed. She was threatening to take away everything that mattered to him.

She was right to want revenge, he thought about all the times he had lied to her, and all the times he had put his own desires above her needs. But now, as he looked into her eyes, he saw that there was no change her mind. She was determined to leave him, for good.

For the first time, he realized that he had underestimated her, that she was not the weak and submissive wife he had always assumed her to be. She was no more the Lucy he married. The Lucy his family always praised. That Lucy belonged to someone else now. It belonged to the past him. He had changed, and she had changed too.

How time flies, just yesterday they met at the ball in school when he had no one to dance with. His date had ditched him and she happened to hear him screaming at his reflection in her car mirror when she left the hall to smoke. And she asked for a dance just so he could feel better. But they clicked instantly, and that was how a real relationship blossomed until they finally got married, surrounded by family, friends and well-wishers.

Everyone had been saying he was lucky to be her husband, but as the tides changed and he became a millionaire, their tongues switched and they all agreed she was the lucky one. Perhaps that was what got into his head, to make him think he could do anything and she would ignore him because she wanted to continue being the perfect wife Riverwood expected of her.

"Tomorrow, I'll be out of this house and out of your hair. You have only but a month to get my demands ready." She said finally before storming upstairs, leaving him there to think about his actions.

James looked up, sensing he was not alone. "How you stand there and watch your mother try to leave," he said. Little Ben's eyes shone from the hole in the staircase. That's where he hid to watch all their squabbles. He had been watching his parents' fights for as long as he could remember, and it seemed like a normal part of life to him.

His eyes dropped, and he looked down at his doll he had been playing with. It was past bed time already but he liked to stay awake for his mother. Just so he could make sure she wasn't crying. He didn't understand why they couldn't just be happy like the families he saw on TV. He didn't understand why his mother was trying to leave, and why his father was trying to stop her.

"Ben, come here, sweetie. Mommy needs you." Lucy's voice rang from upstairs and he knew he had to go. Slowly he stepped out, while avoiding his father's angry gaze. And as he ran upstairs, he realized one thing, everything was falling apart and there was nothing he could do to stop it.

CHAPTER THREE

Upside Down

Through the years of their constant fights, Ben had learned to tune them out and lose himself to the less hateful world of his toys. Where they would fade into the background, to be replaced by the soft hum of his imagination, maybe his life was a balance of both chaos and quiet and that was the only normal he knew. Other homes were too quiet to be called a home. He thought it was right for every child to be brought up with love and discord, because despite all the fights, he never lacked anything.

But this time, his mother was packing her belongings. When she kissed him goodnight, she looked very sad and almost helpless. She had never looked helpless before. Most of the time, she looked sad but once in every while, a faint smile would appear on her face.

In the morning when a pale light filtered through the curtains, his eyes barely stirred open when he heard stomping feet running down the stairs and something being dragged. He hadn't meant to wake up, not yet. It was 5:13 am on the dot, around this time, he was still burrowed deep under the covers. But the strange sounds, and the hushed familiar voices, with muffled sobs and his father's pleading broke that and his heavy eyelids shot open.

He sat up, heart thumping with unease. Was it best to walk downstairs or look through the window? A second passed and the front door slammed, bloating the voices away. He walked to the window, tired of straining his ears. His father must have been tired from pleading desperately as he just stood there watching his mother leave. A chauffeur had come to pick her up and she was prepared to leave.

In that driveway, his mother stood by the open door of the car, ready to get in. Dry tears stayed in her calm face, her hand clutching a small suitcase. She looked up at his window as if it was for one last time. With a look of regret, she gave him a small, watery smile and raised a hand in a wave. Then, the car pulled away as the taillights disappeared into the morning mist, leaving behind of the defeated silence of his father.

Ben stood frozen, he felt hollow inside, a strange feeling he couldn't quite name. In that moment, it was like his world had lost its color, everything turned dull, black and white. It appeared that he was alone. Not even his toys or friends could erase that lonely feeling.

A few days had passed and he had hoped she would come back for him. But until a week went by with no signs of her, doubt began to creep into his heart. And the reality of his situation hit him. He had been left behind. His mother was not coming back for him. The idea of life without her was unbearable. He wanted his mother's warmth like she gave him every night. He longed for her to tuck him into bed once more and kiss him goodnight, or whisper sweet nothings in his ears and read him stories. She used to tell him he could achieve anything he put his mind to, but now it had dawned on him that he was just a child. A helpless child whose world had shattered before his eyes.

The silence in the house had always been a peculiar thing. Not the comforting kind of quiet that settled over a sleeping household, but a different sort altogether. It was a quiet created by an implied arrangement where every corner of the house remained hushed. It was the same in many rich households, but here it was eerie. Even with his friends over, it was supposed to be quiet. The domestic staff, a motley crew of cooks, gardeners and housekeepers, used to whisper amongst themselves, but it was never loud enough to go beyond the walls. It was almost conniving, as if they liked the separation of Mr. & Mrs. Reed. Ben used to hear them sometimes when he wandered around the house. They would speak of his father's long absences, his mother's sadness, Ben's loneliness, the echoing emptiness of the halls of their mansion, the way the little life left in this place had completed faded into nothingness.

They were right after all. Lately, the silence had deepened. It wasn't just quiet anymore, it was cold, hollow and dead. Anyone could tell why this had happened.

Then, one afternoon, Mr. Reed arrived home early. For the first time in a long time. Never had he returned home before the sun had begun to set. But on this particular afternoon, his car pulled into the driveway with an unexpected swiftness. And he wasn't alone.

As he stepped out of the car, a lady alighted from the passenger side. She was young. Beautiful. She had a bright infectious smile across her lips, Mr. Reed seemed very comfortable by her side. As Ben watched them walking towards the house, the world began to slow down and almost completely stopped. She was not his mother. She was not supposed to be here.

The sight of them, so close, kept him In a frozen stance for a while. Who was this woman his father was walking hand-in-hand with? Her cackle was now the loudest sound in the house, it had been quite a while he'd been around anyone who radiates with happiness. Well, it would only be a matter of time until it fades like every other thing in the Reed mansion.

Maybe it hadn't occurred to Rachel but she arrived as an intruder, not the stepmother she thought she was going to be. When she stopped to stare at the red-faced Ben perched by the edge of the porch swing, she thought it would be a quick connection.

It would be easier to win the heart of a child than that of an adult. She'd always been good with children, a few playful words and gentle touch and they would bend to your will. But this kid… he was different. There was something in his gaze that seemed dark and unsettling. It wasn't the innocent curiosity of a child, but a cold hatred.

He reminded her of a cornered animal that could lash out so unexpectedly. Deep down, she knew something was terribly wrong. It wasn't just anger, it was a grudge, it was pure rage. It was as if he could see right through her, and she feared that if she held up that gaze a little longer, she could drown in it.

She offered a gentle wave, and tried to smile. But everything felt forced. He didn't even return her gesture, or look away. His eyes remained locked to her, like a predator sizing up its prey. That's when the dread came creeping in, the kind that made her skin crawl. Did Mrs. Reed somehow leave a piece of her with him? He was a child with the eyes of an old man. Was he bearing his mother's scorn and disdain for the woman who snatched her husband?

Just as she thought she couldn't take it anymore, James's hand rested lightly on her shoulder, as he spoke softly into her ear, "He's just… shy, sweetheart."

She looked up at him, unsure, "He's not shy, James. There's something…wrong with him."

James sighed heavily, "His mother moved out, what did you expect?" He said under his breath.

"Oh," Rachel giggled nervously.

James gave her shoulder a reassuring squeeze as it dawned on her, "He's just a child, darling. Sometimes children act out."

He turned to Ben and spoke gently, "Why don't you come inside, son? Let's go get you some cookies."

Ben didn't move, he rather shifted his gaze to his father. And James felt a bit of what Rachel had experienced. "Now, son."

Ben finally looked away, down at his little feet hanging above the ground, once more reminding him he was a powerless child. Slowly, he climbed down from the swing like a wounded animal. As he walked past her, she caught a glimpse of his face. His lips were drawn into a thin cruel line and his eyes still held something detestable, like a promise of His eyes, however, still held that unsettling glint, a promise of vengeance. She knew with certainty that this was far from over.

Ever since that fateful day, Rachel failed to bond with little Ben. What was wrong with him? Why was he so difficult? It was an unusual kind of torture, trying to act normal in social situations where Ben was present. His icy glares, the way he'd turn his nose up at her attempts at conversation, the deliberate avoidance of her gaze – it all chipped away at her easygoing guise.

Rachel had always believed her purpose in life was to be cherished and adored. In her mind, marriage was just the perfect achievement, the greatest of all successes. A billionaire, of course, was the ideal suitor. In the grand scheme of things, love was only secondary. It was about security and stepping into a life of luxury.

She had never really thought about the woman she was displacing. She was a phantom. Neither did she think of how her son would react. After all, James mentioned he was just a clueless kid and kids, in her experience, were very easy. Maybe he got his attitude from his mother, who knows what she told him before she moved out. Ben must be the material manifestation of that woman's wrath.

And the worst part was that Ben had never given her a reason to hate him. He was simply a victim of circumstance. However, if he was a little less silent, they would all be better off. Now, she would never be able to be his step-mother, the mother she could never become. It's not a bad thing for their marriage, James didn't want more kids anyway. She married him because he promised her the world. And she believed that with all that, and her beauty, her life would be a bed of roses.

But roses have thorns and every pleasure has its price. When James would sneakily tell Ben to smile at her, she hoped he would at least try. Even if he didn't mean it.

But as the days dragged by, Rachel started to notice that James was struggling to keep Ben in line. Ben would often ignore his father's requests and James would have to resort to bribes or even threats to get him to behave. It felt like Ben was pushing, seeing how far he could go before his father snapped.

Rachel had started to doubt herself. *Maybe I am way over my head.* If James, Ben's own dad, was losing control, what chance did she have? She felt like she was walking on eggshells, never knowing when Ben would lash out or refuse to cooperate.

One day, while entertaining some guests in the living room, she could swear she saw Ben outside tearing his doll apart. But when she reported that to his father, Ben provided an unharmed doll. Granted, he had a lot of dolls then and maybe she overreacted to the 'accident.' That's what Ben called it, an accident. It was possible that it was just an accident. Kids could be rough with their toys, and it's not uncommon for them to break or damage them during play. James had defended that Ben was a playful child, and that he often got caught up in the moment without thinking about the consequences of his actions. So, it was likely that Ben hadn't meant to damage the doll, and that it was just a careless mistake. Maybe all of Ben's strange behaviors could be attributed to the fact that he was adjusting to his new living situation. Or maybe he was just an angry child who had made up his mind to destroy things and never smile at anyone.

It wasn't until the day they returned from the town's council member's burial and found Lucy in the house, dressed in a burial attire as well, did Rachel realize that Ben could have been a happy child if he was given a chance to. She was amazed by his sudden transformation. Ben had been holding back, waiting for the one person who could bring out the best in him.

As she watched Lucy interact with Ben, a tear dropped from her eye as it dawned on her that she could never replace Lucy. Not even with Lucy dead or missing. In this house, she was just a spectator, and James' trophy wife. In fact, maybe she was just a spectator because who could explain the calls James had been getting from investors, lawyers and bankers. Maybe…just maybe she was wrong about the bed of roses to begin with.

CHAPTER FOUR

The Puppeteer

The rain hammered against the windows of his office, as he stared into the city lights blurring through the sheets. Many think the cities have it all, but it was overrated. The city was not fair for the weak and unsuspecting. It was not a place where dreams were made, rather it was for dashing of hopes, and anyone could be swallowed whole if they weren't careful. On the other hand, in the town, people looked out for one another. It was a place where you could be yourself without fear of being judged, and reach your goals at your own pace. Rachel had disagreed with him but that was the reason he chose Riverwood over the cities. This was the small town where he built his empire, where even the big leagues from the cities connected with him. Riverwood was simple, quiet and lacked distractions.

But now, that same quiet seemed to mock him as he was now watching his ambitions slipping through his fingers. He'd chosen Lucy, not just for love, but for her generational wealth and ambition.

Back then, she had been the perfect partner for his business. And after he had gotten what he wanted from her, he had discarded her for this much younger woman, Rachel. This Rachel may have been witty, but not for business. Now that everything had become bare, he saw the truth with a haunting clarity. Lucy was truly behind his success. She had made his empire and he had only taken credit for it. Now that he had severed ties with her, he had found himself adrift.

As James sat there in his office, staring out, he couldn't help but feel the doubt creeping in. It had been months since his divorce from Lucy, and everything seemed to be falling apart. His business deals were tanking, his investments were losing value, and his social calendar was empty. He had always thought that he was the one who had built his successful career but now he had realised that it was Lucy who had been the one behind the scenes, pulling the strings and making the connections that had made it all possible. She was the one to attend the charity events and most networking parties, she was the one to make the introductions and build the relationships that lead to many deals. He had always thought that she was just being a supportive wife, just enjoying the perks of being a wealthy man's wife. But now, he had realised all that she had been doing. Now that she was gone, that network was disappearing, and James was left to pick up the pieces. He had been so used to his ex-wife doing these things for him, that it overwhelmed him when all Rachel could do was stand next to him and smile.

Without Lucy's connections, his business began to struggle, and he was starting to feel like a man without a safety net. Was Rachel no good for his growth or was Lucy just too good? Maybe he was being unfair to Rachel by comparing her to Lucy. The former's greatest achievement was being a beauty queen in her college, while the later, was business savvy and had a high level of competence.

He had thought that he had moved on from Lucy, that he had found a new sense of purpose and happiness with Rachel. But now, he wasn't so sure. Was he just trying to replace Lucy with Rachel, or was he truly ready to move on and start a new chapter in his life? These questions, he knew he had no answers to. But if he was going to move forward, then someway, they had to be answered.

Just then, his phone rang. It was Rachel, checking on him for the first time while he was in office. And that's when he looked at the wall clock and realised she was only calling because he was late. He hesitated for a moment, but then, he picked up, and Rachel's cheerful voice filled the line. "Hey, how's it going?" she asked, and James felt a bit of guilt wash over him, perhaps he was being too hard on her. Maybe she was exactly what he needed, and he just needed to give her a chance. "It's going," James replied as he tried to sound more upbeat than he felt. "Just dealing with some business stuff. But I'm okay." Rachel's voice was soothing, and James felt at ease once more. He had been overthinking things, this is what happened for everyone after divorce. Or is it now? He just needed to trust Rachel like he did Lucy. Was it not the best thing to do?

By the time it was 10 PM on the dot, James decided to call it a day and head home. His chauffeur must have fallen asleep waiting for him downstairs. As they drove off into the night, the rain began to subside and all that was left was a foggy veil that covered the town.

Just around a bend, the chauffeur slammed on the brakes and the car screeched to a halt, narrowly avoiding collision with a person standing on the side of the road, clad in a wet and bedraggled raincoat.

When he wound down the glass to get a better look, he saw it was Margaret standing on the side of the road. She looked terribly shaken, her eyes wide with fear, and her voice trembled as she spoke.

"You closed early today?" James asked her, trying to sound casual, but it was just a mask for his lack of concern. After all, he had never liked that nosy woman.

"No customers," she replied, her voice barely above a whisper, "… and I hate sleeping there now since the council member's death." James tried his best to look sympathetic, and he tried to be kind, "… maybe I can give you a lift?" he asked, knowing that it was the least he could do.

Margaret nodded happily, and as joined him in the car, he settled back, a predatory smile across his face. James had always known that Margaret was a font of information, a woman who knew everything that was going on in the town, and he was determined to get her to talk. Working in that diner allowed her to know everything, and it was often said that she knew more than the devil himself. In fact, people would whisper that if the devil ever needed information, he would have to make a pact with Margaret, for she was the one who knew all the secrets and stories about Riverwood. He hated that everyone's business was her business but that night, he needed information from her. And the good thing about Margaret was that she was easy to crack, especially once you did a simple deed for her. This simple lift that would protect her from the rain was enough to get her to get the talk of the town from her lips.

As they drove through the quiet streets, James made small talk as he tried to put her at ease. All he had to do was listen. As they drove through the quiet streets, James turned to Margaret and asked, "So, how has business been since your boss's death? I've noticed that the diner seems a bit quieter than usual." Margaret's eyes clouded over, and she hesitated before responding,

"To be honest, it's been a struggle. Mr. Harrison's death has affected a lot of people in this town, and many of them are still in shock. His family and I are managing to keep the diner afloat. I hope the police find the driver who fled the scene."

James nodded his head in agreement, "Is there anything I can do to help? You know I'm always happy to support local businesses." Margaret's face brightened slightly, and she smiled. "Actually, that's very kind of you to offer. But I think we'll be okay. His family just needs to get through this tough time and things will get back to normal soon." James nodded even though he doubted every word. Mr. Harrison's wife was a stay at home mum, she was not buoyant enough to support a business like that. He knew it would only be a matter of time before the diner was closed.

They drove in silence for a moment, until he garnered the courage to ask her a question.

"You know, Margaret, you're always so well-informed about what's going on in this town. Have you heard from Lucy lately? How's she been doing after our divorce?"

Margaret's face lit up with a warm smile, and she replied, "Oh, Lucy's doing great, James. She's always been a businesswoman, and she's really flourished since the two of you parted ways. I'm sure she's doing just fine." James nodded once more. He was glad to hear that she was doing well, but a part of him still felt a little regret. Maybe in truth, he didn't like that she was doing well.

"But tell me, James," Margaret started with a curious tone, "...do you think Lucy's success is due to her own hard work, or do you think she had some help along the way?"

James shrugged and replied, "I'm not sure what you're getting at, Margaret. Lucy's always been a capable person."

"And do you think she's still in touch with any of her old acquaintances from your time together?"

James wanted to nod but his mind was being distracted by the thought of her questions getting invasive. "Could we just drop it?"

But Margaret's smile grew wider, "Do you think Lucy's new business ventures are a way of trying to prove herself to you, or is she just trying to move on with her life?"

James shifted uncomfortably, "Margaret, that's a pretty personal question. I don't think it's any of my business what Lucy's motivations are."

Margaret's grin turned soft as she asked slowly, "And do you think your new wife is aware of the fact that Lucy is still keeping an eye on you?"

"What are you talking about, Margaret? That's not true."

Margaret's smile turned playful, "Oh, really, James? Then why did Lucy call me last week and ask about your new wife's favorite hobbies?"

James sat up as he could no longer hide his unease. "Margaret, I don't know what you're trying to get at, but can we please just stop this conversation?"

Margaret's smile faded quickly as she saw he was just about to throw her out of the car. "Oh, never mind, James. I think we're getting close to my stop anyway. Why don't you just drop me off around the corner? I can walk from there."

That suggestion left James with a little bit of relief. He was more than happy to get rid of Margaret and her strange questions. "Okay, sure. We'll drop you off around the corner." As the car pulled up to the corner, Margaret gathered her things and prepared to exit the vehicle. Just as she stepped out onto the sidewalk, and as the door was about to close, she turned back to him and asked, "James, do you think you'll ever be able to fully move on from Lucy, or will she always be a part of your life?"

James wanted to get away from her but now being questioned with his own insecurities, he couldn't help but mutter, "Margaret, I don't know what to say."

Margaret sighed heavily and smiled, "…don't worry, James. I'm sure you'll figure it out. Goodnight." With that, she closed the door and disappeared into the night, leaving James with his uncertainty.

Why did Margaret have to be so…Margaret? Why did she have to have so many questions? Why so intrusive and nosy? What more could he expect from a woman like her? Was she just trying to stir up trouble, or was there something more to it? Maybe Margaret was just trying to get under his skin, to unsettle him and make him question his own relationships and motivations.

James sighed and rubbed his temples, feeling a headache coming on. He didn't know what to think or feel anymore. He wasn't sure how to calm down the do emotions starting to well up.

As the car pulled into the driveway, and he looked through the window at his home, he saw his reflection in the mirror glaring back at him. And he saw how he looked tired and drawn, eyes red from lack of sleep. He felt like he was losing his grip on reality.

As he walked into the house, he found Rachel in the living room, standing there, waiting for him. He knew the smile on her face was fake, like a show where she was playing her part. As for Rachel, deep down, she was angry but she thought it was best to replace it with a concerned smile. "Honey, you're awfully late. Hope there was no incident?" she asked, but James just shook his head, feeling like he couldn't talk about it. He collapsed onto the couch beside her.

"Honey…" she continued, and sat next to him. All she was trying to do, was ease James' frustrated glare. But she was failing Her concern was no good for him. He was mentally exhausted and didn't need anyone speaking around him. He couldn't make out what she was saying, and even if he could, he wasn't sure he would have cared. Only then did he realise that her voice had begun to irritate her. She was only feeding his frustration and she was not even doing it intentionally. But it just happened, she was suffocating him and he couldn't take it anymore. "Shut up…" he said quietly but she didn't hear him and just kept going. "I said shut up!" He yelled and she froze. "Shut up, just shut up! You have no idea what I'm going through, and you're just making it worse! You know what, you've ruined my life, Rachel! You've ruined everything!"

Rachel's jaw dropped in shock as his words sank in. She tried to stand up but her legs felt heavy. Regardless, she staggered her way up and only when she looked back did she see how regretted spitting out all that venom. But even his remorse could not calm the tears welling in her eyes.

He rose up quickly as he recognised the weight of his words. "Rachel, I'm sorry. I didn't mean to say that. I'm just really stressed out right now, and I didn't mean to take it out on you."

But Rachel was having none of it. She shoved him out of the way with all the strength she could muster. "Don't apologize to me, James. You've been wanting to do this for a long time now. I just want to remind you that I'm Lucy so don't expect me to put up with your mood swings and all your crap."

As Rachel turned to leave, James felt a presence behind him. He turned to see Ben standing on the stairway, watching the argument with a focus that made James' skin crawl.

"You must be enjoying this," James said. But Ben said nothing in return. He just kept watching, his eyes fixed on James. For the first time looking at his own son, he felt uneasy. He had never been so fond of Ben but he had never felt strange about him. This was the first time. James felt a shiver run down his spine as he realized that Ben had been watching them again, just like he had the last time they had argued. It was like each time Ben watched himself argue, a piece of him died. And now, all that was left of Ben was a faint outline of a person.

What was this kid's problem? Why did he always seem to appear at the worst possible moments? "This is exactly why your mother left you...you creep." He said before storming off. And all Ben could do was just stand there, after all, what more could a child do? Maybe Ben did really enjoy watching his father suffer. After abandoning his mother, why wouldn't he? Again, he was already used to taking the blame for just watching.

It was not his fault James was a serial cheater. Neither was it his fault that sales were plummeting. It wasn't also his fault that James had begun to fall into addiction, making it easier for rich folks to avoid him. Where was James going with this life he had chosen for himself. Everyone watched him rise from grass and now he was falling back into it. His life was falling apart. The consequences started to show when he sold some of his cars, then let go most and then all of his staff. But then he still had two cars which he barely drove. How does this even happen? How can a man become nothing overnight? Where else can this happen other than Riverwood? Who else could it happen to, other than a man who chose beauty over brains?

That beauty had begun to turn into the beast and ultimately a nightmare when they moved out of the Reed mansion. No, this was not the life she envisaged. He could not even afford her regular salon visits that had kept her hands looking flawless. Neither could she afford to keep her hair rich. She was forced to use cheaper alternatives for skincare products and that was the biggest shame of it all. She was the talk of the town, many mocked her but had never been bold enough to say it her face. No, there were no roses in the first place. It was just an illusion. And she had learnt her lesson now. What to do? Run away? She could run away.

"Honey..." James called from the kitchen like he could hear her thoughts. She wanted to scream at him for blocking her thoughts but she just swallowed her anger. *Who's honey?* "Please, could you drop Ben off at school for me?"

Rachel raised an eyebrow, "...huh?" It was almost like his request was unbelievable. "No, James, I don't think I can. We can save gas if he walks to school."

James sighed, as he walked out. "Come on, Rachel, it's just a simple drop-off."

Rachel crossed her arms. "Kids his age walk to school, let the kid walk to school. He won't die of he walks with his legs."

If James could write a book about all the reasons he thought Rachel would understand, he would. But in the end, she didn't budge and Ben who had been standing there, was finally told ho pick his bag and trek to school. "I'll just stand here and watch him..." she said from the window.

Ben nodded and walked out of the room and she did as she said she would. As she turned back to reach for her cigarette, she heard James cursing in the kitchen when some plates fell and broke.

"What's wrong?" she called out, but James did not respond. She hissed and looked back and that's when she realized Ben had disappeared. The only thing left behind was his jacket lying on the floor. "James…" she called out and he snapped. "WHAT?"

"Ben!" she said rushing out and he followed suit. Outside, they found some flowers neatly placed on top of it. Like a gift. Violets.

James's face went white as he scanned the street frantically. "Where is he? You were watching him weren't you? You said you would watch him!"

They thought he would be in school but he wasn't. Or even with Lucy but she was too busy living her best life. And with that, the search for Ben began, a search that would last for days, weeks, and months, with no sign of the young boy ever being found again. The violets on his jacket were the only clue, and a haunting reminder of the day Ben Reed disappeared and the beginning of terror in Riverwood. Because it wasn't just Ben, many more of all ages disappeared in similar way. There were no demands, no witnesses , no bodies. And they had been missing for years until the authorities declared them dead. But the scariest part was that the perpetrators were never arrested. Or rather, Riverwood's silent killer was never found.

CHAPTER FIVE

A Fresh Beginning

"It's been two decades since little Ben vanished, and the police are still scratching their heads," Alex said finally as he reclined in his chair. He crossed his legs, and watched everyone as the weight of his words settled over them. Riverwood's silent killer was never found, despite all that effort.

In the back, Tyler had been oblivious to the somber mood and he had been too busy looking into the largest book he had ever seen. He slammed the book shut with a loud thud and the sudden noise jolted everyone in the room, especially the girls who jumped, startled.

"Jeez, Tyler!" Alex exclaimed, "You scared the life out of them!"

Tyler grinned sheepishly, "Sorry, got carried away." He gestured towards the book. "I've seen a book this big, Alex. I'm sure your parents hire people to carry it around for them."

He grinned, expecting a laugh, but the room remained silent. Alex stared at him in disbelief. "Tyler, how is that related to Ben?"

"Tyler," Emily started, slightly peeved, "This isn't funny."

Tyler's grin quickly disappeared as Maya, his girlfriend locked eyes with him, and he could tell she was few seconds away from tearing him a new one. "Oh," he mumbled, finally noticing the serious expressions on everyone's faces. "Right. Sorry, I..." He backed away from the book and slithered to Maya's side, sitting closely.

"You think they'll ever find him?" Emily asked softly with a trembling voice.

Alex shrugged, "Who knows? Maybe someday. But after all this time..." He shook his head.

"It's not like he just disappeared into thin air," Maya added, "... someone took him. There was an urban legend about it, Riverwood's killer on the prowl, hide yourselves...not just kids, even adults were his victims. No matter the size or age, they disappeared without a trace."

"Hey," Tyler butted in hoping to lighten the mood. "Maybe Ben's not dead, he could be hiding in plain sight or living a normal life with a normal blue-collar job or you know? Working at the local diner, flipping pancakes under a fake moustache" His attempt at humour fell flat. No one laughed, he shifted uncomfortably and turned to Maya. "And what makes you think the killer is a guy anyway?"

"The usual suspects," she retorted, almost caught off guard. "Well, usually it is, isn't it? Most violent crimes are committed by men." She said glancing at the rest for validation.

Tyler shrugged, "And what about women? Are they incapable of violence?"

"No, of course not," Maya answered quickly, a little defensive. "But statistically..."

"Statistics don't tell the whole story," Alex interjected. "You can't just box people into categories. Women can be just as dangerous as men, if not more so."

"Men have always committed more crimes than women. It's just a fact."

"And what about those statistics?" Alex challenged, leaning forward. "How were they gathered? Were women given equal opportunities to commit those crimes? Were their voices heard and their experiences taken into account?"

Maya scoffed. "Come on, Alex. You're not seriously trying to argue that women are somehow inherently more law-abiding, are you?"

"I'm not saying that," Alex clarified, "But I'm saying that the current statistics are likely skewed. They don't show the true reality. Historically, women have been marginalized and oppressed. They have been denied power, resources, and the same freedoms as men. How can we expect them to behave the same way when they've been systematically disadvantaged for centuries?"

Emily shook her head is disapproval. "That's a lot of big words, Alex. But it doesn't change the fact that men are still the primary perpetrators of crime."

"But why?" Alex pressed on. "Is it because men are inherently more violent? Or is it because society has conditioned them to be that way? Because they've been taught that aggression and dominance are signs of strength?"

Emily opened her mouth to respond, but no words came out. She realized that Alex may have a point. Either that or she was not well equipped to defend his assertions. "You know," she said, "Maybe the real question isn't who commits more crimes, but who committed the Riverwood's crime? Who is the silent killer? Who took Ben Reed?"

"So let's find whoever it is," Ethan blurted out and all attention turned to him. There was a brief quiet as they blinked at him like he hadn't been standing there for a long time. "What?" He asked as he put his phone in his pocket and leaned against the wall. Ethan was the definition of a human chameleon, every now and then, he keeps to himself despite being in the midst of close friends. Tyler gasped dramatically, "Ethan! You speak! About time. We were starting to think you'd morphed into your devices."

Everyone cackled as Ethan joined them and they formed a small circle. He blushed red like a pony, "Sorry," he mumbled, burying his face in his hands. "I... I just... I thought we should do something."

"Do something?" Alex echoed, "Like finding the killer? What are we going to do? Hire a private investigator?"

Ethan wiped his face as a faint smile appeared on his face. "Or maybe, hear me out, you know, ask around?"

"Ask around?" They asked, their voices dropping low.

"Yeah, ask around."

"I don't know Ethan, that's unlike anything we've done before." Emily scratched her head nervously.

"I mean besides this boring town, what else is there to do?" Ethan leaned forward, "Look, the police might have already closed the case. It's been twenty years already and no one has ever been caught for those murders. It wasn't just Ben, there were more. We owe it to them, at least."

"Owe it to them?" Tyler scoffed, "I didn't know any of them."

"Well," Ethan rolled his eyes, "we don't know them but-"

"I think what Ethan is trying to say is that maybe, just maybe, there's more to these cases than meets the eye," Emily finished and gave Ethan a nervous glance. Then continued. "Maybe beneath the surface of all that cold town, lurks a sinister secret society, a cabal of masked murderers!"

Tyler snorted. "Oh come on, Emily. You're watching too many true crime documentaries."

"Wait-" Emily held out a finger with mock indignation. "Just hear us out Tyler. I agree with Ethan. Besides, wouldn't it be exciting? Imagine, us, a bunch of kids, uncovering the truth about the Riverwood's silent killer."

Alex chuckled. "Okay, maybe not a secret society of masked murderers. But there's definitely something strange about that town. Too many coincidences, too many unanswered questions."

"Like what?" Tyler asked, skeptical.

"Well," Alex cleared his throat. "They never found out who sent those pictures of James and Rachel. Lucy suddenly disappeared after mourning her son. Get that?" He said with a bit of emphasis in his tone. "She vanished without a trace."

"Do you think she died too?" Maya asked.

"Maybe she just moved," Emily suggested.

"Maybe," Alex conceded, "but somehow, I don't think so. I think one of them knows what happened to Ben."

"You're not trying to blame Lucy for her son's death?" Maya groaned.

"No, I did not…" Alex replied with his arms up.

"Look, guys," Ethan cut in. "All those questions will be answered the moment we investigate it ourselves."

Tyler shuddered. "Okay, I think I've heard enough. This is exactly how horror movies start. Young people do not know where not to poke their noses."

"Oh come on Tyler, what's the worst that could happen. It's been twenty years, the perpetrators might be dead already."

Tyler sighed heavily and shook his head. "I need a breather. In my own space."

"It's only past ten," Maya protested and the others joined in as Tyler got up to get ready to leave. Suddenly, they froze at a sound. A floorboard somewhere groaning under unseen weight and a distant thump, then a slow, set of footsteps descending the stairs. Tyler turned to Alex as they fixed a glare at the door. "Didn't you say you're home alone tonight?" he whispered.

Alex nodded without taking his eyes off the direction of the sound. "The cook got the weekend off too." Their hearts hammered against their ribs as they exchanged terrified glances, their eyes wide with fear of the growing dread.

The doorknob rattled, then slowly turned. And as it creaked open, they got ready to scream their lungs out. That's when the figure standing in the doorway walked in with a casual grace and while their eyes were trying to adjust to the dim purple light, with a flick of the wrist, the harsh brighter light was switched on. They groaned with shock as it hit their eyes.

"Mum?" Alex heaved a sigh.

"Oh thank goodness," Tyler nearly stumbled as the relief washed over with a strong wave, and his shoulders sagged with exhaustion. "Mrs. Jenkins…"

Mrs. Jenkins smiled as her eyes scanned the orderly basement expecting to see something out of place. Surprisingly, there was none. Despite her attempts at a nonchalant demeanor, she was clearly flustered. She'd never imagined Alex would bring his friends down here, where his father considered sacred, and a place he could tinker and simply be. "Well, it seems we've disturbed your father's workshop," she said with a voice carefully modulated with concern and annoyance. "Perhaps we shouldn't be in here."

Alex tried to open his mouth but no words came out, he smiled, unable to articulate the unease that had gripped him. His mother was right, they shouldn't be in the basement. But if his parents had stayed out of town like they said they would for the next two days, maybe he wouldn't be in this situation right now. "You came back... what a surprise," he giggled as he rose up. The others followed as well, nervous smiles etched on their hesitant faces. Mrs. Jenkins began to usher them towards the stairs. "Come along, boys and girls. It's getting late."

"We were just on our way out, Mrs. Jenkins. Also you have a lovely basement, and one hell of a big book," Tyler.

Mrs. Jenkins froze mid-step, her hand hovering over the doorknob. "Big book?" she repeated, her voice tight. She turned to look at Alex, a forced smile on her lips. Her eyes say, *friends did not touch things in the basement.*

Alex giggled. "Tyler didn't mean it like that, mum. He was just, you know, exaggerating."

Tyler, realizing he'd put his Alex in the hot seat, finally mustered the courage to speak. "Yeah, sorry, Mrs. Jenkins. Didn't mean to offend." He gave Alex a sheepish grin, hoping to deflect some of the heat.

Mrs. Jenkins, however, remained unconvinced. Her gaze moved from Alex to the book, and back again, as if trying to decipher their intentions.

Seeing the storm brewing in her eyes, Maya decided discretion was the better part of valour. "Come on, Tyler," she said, grabbing his arm. "We should really be going."

Tyler readily agreed. "Yeah, see you later, Alex."

With that, they hurried upstairs until the sounds of their feet walking out the doorway faded with the thud of the second door.

"Mum…"

"You shut your mouth, Alex Jenkins. What has gotten into you?"

Alex shrugged as he glanced back at the room, hoping everything was truly in order. This would not have happened if Tyler didn't open his big mouth. The basement wasn't the typical dusty, cobweb-filled room with old belongings. Instead of overflowing boxes and forgotten junk, it was a properly arranged space. There was a little chandelier above that changed colors with each switch, different colored dull glows and one radiant light for study.

Rows of tools were thoroughly arranged along one wall, and beside it was an old workbench, scarred from with the marks of countless projects. An antique furniture, covered in clean white sheets, perhaps from the past era or based down from generations. A large piano, its keys slightly yellowed from years of use. But it was the bookshelves that truly set the basement apart. They stretched along the walls, most volumes hemmed in leather and bedecked with gold leaf. History books, volumes of philosophy and art, novels, encyclopaedias, you name it. It had it all. This wasn't just a basement; it was a library, and a sanctuary for Mr. Jenkins who very much appreciated the beauty of the written word. And they had been in it, not because they loved to read. But because it was the warmest place in the house. It wasn't their first time in it, but it was their first time getting caught.

"I'm sorry..." he said without daring to look up.

"No, you're only sorry because you got caught." Mrs. Jenkins shot back in a low growl from suppressing her anger. He could practically feel the heat emitting from her, she was hot tempered and that was why he feared her the most.

Then they heard the distant rumble of car engines, fading into the distance as cars drove out of the compound. His friends were leaving, finally. Maybe they got tired of trying to eavesdrop. Now he had realized his mistake, if they had left the two doors open, perhaps they could have heard the sounds of his mother's car pulling up in the driveway. Lesson learned.

He looked up, finally, to face his mother's wrath. "I'm sorry, Mom," he said, his voice sincere this time. "I'm really sorry."

She smiled sadly. "It's alright, maybe I won't tell your father," she said as she climbed the stairs. Alex followed her closely, shutting the door behind him.

"These kids…" Mrs. Jenkins shook her head, frustrated that they had left the entrance door open. "We always shut the doors," she said as she went to shut it. Alex went upstairs without saying anything. He hadn't seen his father but he didn't bother to ask, they had ruined his night and now he would have to sleep alone. It was supposed to be a sleepover, with his friends and some weed.

The dark shape moving under the door to his parent's room, hinted at his father's presence. He was home after all. He could be in the house and no one would realize, except of course he was having breakfast.

As Alex walked into his room, he slammed the door shut and locked himself in. Moonbeams pierced in with dust motes that seeped through the window pane. He flopped onto his bed, exhausted with regret. One thing that stuck from his little meeting with friends was that Riverwood's silent killer was never caught. How does he do it? Taking the victim and leaving their clothing or a piece of it behind, with violets buried in them. Perhaps the killer had a garden where they planted all sorts of flowers. Or it could be a florist or just a roadside vendor. Or not. One thing was sure, the killer did love those flowers.

It's easy to wonder why they didn't catch that killer back then. It wasn't like they were looking for Bigfoot. This was a serial killer, terrorizing the city. You'd think the cops would be all over it, Ben was the first victim, and many other victims came after him.

But maybe... maybe they just got unlucky. Maybe the killer was too smart or too careful. They might have been a loner, someone who blended in with the crowd, no real connections to tie them down.

Maybe if these occurrences happened in the 2020s, the police might have done a better job. Back then, the police force wasn't exactly known for their cutting-edge forensics. No fancy DNA testing and no massive databases. Maybe they just didn't have the resources to properly investigate.

Plus, the fact that people were scared. But fear can also make people close up. Witnesses might have seen something, but were too afraid to come forward. Maybe they didn't trust the cops, or maybe they were worried about retaliation.

It's frustrating to think about, all those years that went by, and the killer just walking free. Maybe they got away with it. Maybe they're still out there, somewhere. Or not, I mean not after all these years.

Then his train of thought got interrupted by some sound outside his window. The rubber tree that scraped against the fence, with branches that could reach his window if it wasn't always trimmed down on the instructions of his father began to rustle violently. His heart leaped as he sat up, were his friends back? Had they somehow snuck back into the compound, it's not like they wouldn't dare. Tyler could convince the smartest person on earth to do something stupid. He scrambled to the window, peering out into the darkness. But it was not the tree moving, in fact it was quite still. Even the leaves didn't budge.

But something continued to rustle. When he moved his gaze to the other side of the fence, he realized it was the mango tree with branches over the fence. Instead of the faces of his mischievous friends, he saw the strange figure huddled under the branches. A lanky man, his face obscured by a tattered red cap with the shape of a dog imprinted in the face, was shaking the branches with surprising ferocity.

"Hey!" Alex yelled, "What are you doing? You're gonna break that tree!"

The man was a little startled and turned his head towards the window. With wide bloodshot eyes that shone under the moon's light.

"Mind your own business, kid!" he snapped. "Just want some mangoes."

Alex sneered. "Mangoes? It's the middle of the night! And you're shaking the tree like it owes you money!"

The man let out guttural sounds, his eyes bulging like a frog's as his face contorted with rage. He flailed his arms wildly, his hands shot out like pistons, and he nearly lost his balance. He stumbled backwards and kicked at the air. With the way his legs were trembling with fury, it was clear that if he weren't careful, he'd be having a full-blown temper tantrum right there on the spot. With a thick local accent, he cried "Don't you see? I'm hungry! And these mangoes, they look juicy. So, I'm gonna get 'em, whether you like it or not!"

Despite trying to look tough and confident, Alex felt a bit of panic. This man looked like trouble, he was desperate as a cornered wild animal. "Look," he stammered, "just go away. Or I'll call the police and have you arrested."

The man burst into laughter, "Arrested? For what? Wanting to eat? This country is finished, boy. Everyone's hungry. Even the trees are afraid." He shook the branch again, and a shower of ripe mangoes rained down.

With a look of defeat, Alex retreated from the window. He sighed, *just let the man have some mangoes,* he thought to himself as he slumped back on his bed. With those crazed eyes, the man was capable of doing anything. Best not to provoke him so he doesn't climb one of those trees into the compound. Not even the big for nothing fences could stop him.

As for his friends, a sinking realization had hit him, they were not coming back. They had probably given up on their daring ideas, even if they didn't, everyone would forget about it.

He closed his eyes, trying to shut out the sounds of the night, the leaves still rustling outside, the distant barking of dogs, the man's angry muttering. Finally, he drifted off to sleep without tucking himself into bed or shutting his window, as he should have. His mother had always warned that he had no sense of security and he had proved her right.

The next morning, he woke up to the sound of someone barging into his room. By the time his mind reminded him, *you didn't shut your window,* the person was already pushing the curtain aside. The bright sun filtered through nearly blinding him. "Alex Jenkins Junior, what did I tell you about this window...?"

He wiped his face, a little disoriented, "...right, mum. It's you."

"There are fallen mangoes scattered everywhere, someone was here last night. Now imagine what would happen if he crawled into your room. You probably wouldn't have stood a chance. And from what we know, you interacted with him last night. Why didn't you tell us?"

He sighed heavily, "...they're just mangoes mum."

"Just mangoes you say? The police were here a while ago and looked through our surveillance."

"Wait, mum," his eyes widened as he finally made sense of what she was saying. "Did you say the police looked through our surveillance?"

"Someone found his cap," she continued, her gaze fixed at the tree, "by the dumpsters. Can you imagine?"

Alex threw out his hands, confused. "So what?" That tattered old thing, he must have had enough of it and decided to throw it away.

She turned to him. "They're calling it a murder Alex. It wasn't the cap that was the issue here. It's what they found inside it."

Alex felt a shiver in his bones, despite the summer heat. "What? Violets?"

"No, of course not Alex… thank goodness it wasn't violets. It was all his fingers, and… ears." She whispered and shuddered with disgust. "At least it's not that sick bastard who terrorized Riverwood. God no, he better not find his way into our quiet and peaceful Sunset Ridge. I'm sure the police will find the killer in no time. Also the police will be back later to have a word with you." She said with a pleasant smile as she walked out of the room like it was not a big concern.

Alex sat there, almost seeing it. The display of the man's fingers and ears inside his cap. His mind went back to the previous night, to the brief argument they had. And just like that, he was dead. He could be alive, maybe he was owing some people and they decided to teach him a lesson. But who could possibly lend money to a homeless guy. No it wasn't it. Could it be the silent killer, but with a different signature? Or was it just a copycat, or some serial killer who wants to become a legend like the silent killer.

He glanced at the window, and many thoughts ran through his head. If it was the silent killer, then Sunset Ridge was in danger. If not, Sunset Ridge was still in danger. A killer was roaming the town like casually. Hopefully, it would end with this one kill, unlike the horror show in Riverwood.

CHAPTER SIX

Sunset Ridge

Sunset Ridge was just a small town but it was home to many wealthy and influential families. Unlike Riverwood, where wealth was concentrated in the hands of a select few, fortune in Sunset Ridge was more evenly distributed. Doctors, lawyers, successful entrepreneurs, they all called this town the peaceful corner of the world home.

Life in Sunset Ridge moved at a leisurely pace. During the day, children played in manicured lawns, and the occasional chatter of neighbors catching up over garden fences. It was a place where many dared to leave their doors unlocked, children roaming freely, unlike the city life they had willingly escaped.

The town had always prided itself on its quietness. Crime was practically unheard of. Petty theft was the most serious offense residents could recall in recent memory. In fact, it had been close to a decade since the last murder had occurred within the town limits. A decade of peace, a decade of quiet contentment.

Up until now that the police just finished debriefing with Alex. It had been short but it was an eye opener. Tyler was right, it was only rational to keep away, despite this not being related to the Riverwood murders. But they were oddly similar, how else would the police explain the homeless man going missing and his body parts left for an unlucky passer-by to find. Was it really a good thing body parts were left behind instead of violets? After all, murder was murder. So why did this case not spook him out enough? Not even his mother was very bothered. Maybe that's how everyone felt about it. It was as if the town had collectively decided to bury their heads in the sand, and refuse to acknowledge the signs before them.

He couldn't understand it. Where was the outrage or the fear that followed? Maybe people were trying to gaslight themselves into accepting it was an isolated incident, a freak occurrence that wouldn't happen again.

Riverwood should tell them otherwise. The police didn't put much thought into Ben's disappearance until more people went missing and more violets kept appearing. Had the Riverwood killer returned, but to Sunset Ridge and with a different MO? If this was anywhere remotely connected to Riverwood, the police were grossly underestimating the killer. They were treating it as a simple burglary gone wrong, maybe because a homeless man was the victim.

Now would it be better to keep his eyes and ears open, to watch for any signs, any clues that might help the police protect the town from more tragedies. Or would it be better to ignore like Tyler warned?

"Hey kid," a hoarse voice said from a distance. And when Alex looked, this tall man with an imposing gait was asking across the street towards him. He looked quite rugged in his leather jacket and pair of scuffed jeans. If anything, he looked like he was out for trouble. "...You must be Alex," he said and reached out for a handshake to which Alex didn't dare reject. "I need to ask you some questions," the man said, but it was not a request.

"I just talked to a police officer," Alex said, trying to sound calm. "I don't know if I can tell you anything else."

"Sure you can!" The man answered quickly with a fake smile that faded as quickly as it came. "It's just a few...questions."

"Well...what is it?" Alex replied, ready to cooperate. Seeing that docile gaze in Alex's eyes, the man settled in. "I'm Jack Harris, private investigator. Here to ask you questions regarding that dead man. You may have been one of the last people to see him alive? How does that make you?"

Alex shrugged, "...awful, I guess."

"Yeah…" Jack's voice almost trailed off, "...it can be awful." Then he stepped closer and Alex froze. There was something about Jack that made him feel like he was being backed into a corner, like he was being intimidated.

Jack sneered, as his eyes shone with a hard, aggressive light. "You know kid, you can trust me. The cops don't know what they're doing. They're just a bunch of bureaucrats who don't care about getting to the bottom of things. But I do. And that's why you should trust me enough to tell me everything."

"What do you want to know?" Alex asked, hoping the quicker he answered, the quicker he could disappear into the building. He feared Jack might follow him if he decided to head in. Jack leaned in closer, now, his face was inches from Alex's. "I want to know what happened when you saw the homeless man," he growled. "I want to know what he said to you, what you said to him."

Alex tried to take a step back, but Jack's eyes stare held him in place and he just stood there, feeling threatened.

"Come on, time is money kid." Jack reminded him when it felt like a cat had got his tongue.

"I...I told him to leave the mangoes alone," Alex stammered. "He was picking them from our tree, and I didn't want him to get in trouble."

Jack shifted his gaze, sceptical. "That's it?" he said, and looked back at Alex. "That's all you told the police? Or...might you be hiding something?"

"Why would I do that?"

But even Jack didn't have an answer to that. Instead he leaned back and wore a bright smile. "I'm sure the police will get to the bottom of this Alex, you have nothing to worry about. Whoever killed that poor man will face the law soon. You can bet on that."

Alex nodded slowly, a little confused at the way the man switched so suddenly. "And you should be more careful," Jack said, looking away. "...you don't know who that crazy bastard could get next." He added with his back still turned to the street, not bothering to check for oncoming traffic.

Just in the middle of the road, a car came speeding around the corner, horn blaring. Jack threw his arms up in a reflexive gesture, and for a moment, it seemed like he was going to be hit. The driver slammed on the brakes, and the car skidded to a stop just inches from Jack's body.

The driver had a look of outrage on his face, he leaned out the window and shouted, "What the hell is wrong with you, man? You just walked right out in front of me!"

Jack turned to face the driver, a sneer on his face. He raised his middle finger and said, "Go screw yourself, pal!" And walked off casually like he did nothing wrong.

As the driver continued to complain, Jack turned and crossed the street, still muttering to himself. Alex watched him go, his mouth hanging open in shock. Who was this psycho of a man? He seemed to have no regard for his own safety, or for the safety of others. And what was with the aggressive behavior?

As Jack got into his car and drove away, Alex couldn't help but replay their short conversation. Why did he let the man walk all over him? Why was Jack, a private investigator interested in the case? Then someone would have paid him to look into the case? Or was he doing it for himself? Settling for the former, if someone had paid him to do this, who's to say a curious teen could not carefully poke nose and get away with it?

It would take a lot of balls to go down the path of poke nosing but he had chosen this path and it would more than scary deaths to get him out. A psycho was in town, it was not just the job of the police to fish them out. Jack was right, the police were bureaucrats, and who said an eighteen year old couldn't get things done.

So he took out his phone and texted Emily. *I'm heading to the corner bar where it happened. You should come with. Meet me there in ten.*

Without wasting any more time, he grabbed a car key. His mother wanted to speak to him but it fell of deaf ears. "I'll be careful mum." He shushed her before driving off, leaving her where she stood, by the doorway. Had it been back when he was sixteen, she would have followed him, but she had learned to let him make his own decisions.

The Corner Bar was one of the shadiest spots in town, it didn't get a lot of visitors because the people of Sunset Ridge had not accepted that way of life. It had a reputation for being a haunt for troublemakers, but it only came alive at night. During the day, it was a more laid-back place where young people like Alex could hang out and have a good time. But when the sun went down, the bar would completely change. It was a place where people went to get into mischief, but only under the cover of darkness. Despite its questionable reputation, the bar still had its fans, but only among a certain crowd. That's why it was easy to believe that one of those not-so-respectable patrons may have hurt the man and did away with him.

When Alex got there, there were no signs of Emily and when he tried to reach her, the call did not connect. So he went in alone, hoping he could achieve something before she arrived. Just as he walked in, what he met was an empty bar.

"Minors aren't allowed in here…" a voice said as a woman appeared from the back room, her bright green eyes gazing into Alex's soul as she walked across the bar. She was a small, dark-haired woman with a few tattoos on her arms and a small scar above her left eyebrow, which she got in a fight a few years ago. Ruby, the feisty waitress. Everyone knew Ruby for her sharp tongue that could calm down even the most heated situations. She had been working at the Corner Bar for a while, and moved into the town from the city because she wanted a much more peaceful life.

"…I'm not a minor," Alex finished and held back a little to show he was mature enough to control his emotions, but deep down, he was tired of people always treating him differently because they assumed he was a minor.

Ruby stopped to look at him and it was as if she was searching for any signs of deception. Then, to his surprise, a small, wry smile played on her lips, and she nodded slightly, as if acknowledging his claim.

"Okay, kid," she said, a little softer. "But what's a guy like you doing in a place like this? You're not here for drinks, I can tell."

As she spoke, she began to wipe down the bar with a dirty rag. Alex watched her, quite fascinated by the way her presence commanded the space around her. She was not the prettiest but she had an aura that set her apart, one that could draw people in and make them want to know more about her. He found himself wanting to open up to her, to tell her about his reasons for coming to the bar, but something held him back. Maybe it was the way she saw right through him, or maybe it was the fact that he wasn't entirely sure himself why he had come to this place.

"I'm sure you're aware something happened just outside the bar, so we're closed for now."

Alex joined her but still couldn't say a word. As she finished wiping down the bar, she leaned in closer to Alex, and tried to sound serious even though there was a mocking tone to her voice. "It was very scary…"

"What was it?" he asked in a whisper.

Ruby eyed him a moment, then glanced around the bar as if ensuring they were alone. "There was a… incident," she hesitated. "A man's parts were found dead just outside the bar. The police are still investigating, but it's not looking good."

Alex's eyes widened as he felt a surge of curiosity. "What happened to him?" he asked, his voice a little louder now. Ruby looked into his eyes, and she seemed to study him for a second before responding.

"No one knows, the rest of his body is missing," she said, her voice matter-of-fact. "He might be dead, mutilated. He might be alive, locked away somewhere with his fingers and ears missing..." Alex thought he would get nauseous if he kept going but he was far too deep in now to stop. "Do they know who he was?"

Ruby nodded. "Yeah, they do. I do. He was a local, a regular here at the bar. His name was... " She paused, glanced around the bar again before leaning in closer to Alex. "But I shouldn't be telling you this. You're not even supposed to be in here, remember?" She smiled. Slowly, she reached out and gently touched his arm, her fingers caressing his skin. Her touch was electrifying, and he was startled at first but then he couldn't help but wonder if she was trying to get closer to him. Then, she pulled back, and her smile disappeared like it was never there. "I need to see some ID, kid," she said firmly. "I need to make sure you're legal before we go any further."

Ruby's touch lingered on his arm, even after she had pulled back. Was she flirting with him, or if he was just reading too much into the situation. Never had he experienced that with an older lady, talking more of a badass waitress. He hesitated a bit, unsure of what to do next, before reaching into his pocket and pulling out his wallet.

As he flipped through the contents, Ruby's eyes never left his face. Alex finally found his ID and handed it over to her, watching as she took it from him and examined it carefully. Then she glanced at him, she nodded and handed it back to him, a mischievous grin across her face.

"Alright, kid, you're legal. But don't think that means anything. What exactly do you want? Are you some undercover or something? Why are you interested in a murder, are you writing a book?" She leaned in closer to him again, "Are you a true crime enthusiast?"

As she spoke, Ruby's eyes glanced from his eyes to his lips and back and again, as if searching for something. He wasn't sure of what she was looking for, and at the same time, he was unable to look away. And Alex froze at the uncertainty of his fate with her acting like that. Without a reply, Ruby continued to speak, Alex felt himself becoming more carried away. She was telling him things she shouldn't, about the bar and the people who came here, and he was listening. Maybe she was just talkative or she saw something there that made her feel like he wasn't a stranger at all. Something that made her trust him.

"The man who was murdered," Ruby started. "His name was Jeremy. He was a regular here. I don't know who could have done such a thing. And he was not homeless...he was just a hippie."

Now Ruby's face was inches from Alex's, and he could feel her warm breath on his skin. No matter how hard she tried, he couldn't get his eyes off hers. And then, so suddenly and almost involuntarily, Ruby's lips brushed against Alex's. It was a soft, gentle kiss, but it made him quiver. He thought held melt into her, as if he had been longing for affection for so long. He didn't plan to come into the corner bar to kiss this woman but somehow it happened. And he didn't resist, didn't even think about resisting. He simply let himself go.

But the moment was short-lived. Just as things were starting to get heated, the door to the bar burst open and someone walked in. An average blonde, Emily, who had rushed to meet Alex in ten like he had texted her.

"What the...?" she started to say, at first surprised but then anger took over as she saw the look on their faces.

Ruby pulled back from Alex, wiping her lips.. "Emily, I...," Alex stuttered as he nearly stumbled from shock, but Emily just shook her head.

"I think I'll just go," Emily said coldly. "I didn't realize I was interrupting anything."

As Emily turned to leave, Alex called out after her. "Emily, wait!" But Emily just kept walking, out of the bar.

Alex turned back to Ruby, a look of confusion on his face. "I don't know what just happened," he said. "I don't know why that happened."

Ruby just shook her head, still feeling the effects of their kiss. "I think it's because you wanted to know the dead guy," she answered without an ounce of remorse. "Now you've paid the price..." she added and started cleaning some bottles. "If I were you, I would run after her..."

Without thinking, Alex is just that. He spotted her walking down the street, her blonde hair bobbing up and down as she moved. He quickened his pace, calling out to her, but she didn't turn around.

"Emily, wait!" he shouted, but she just kept walking. When he eventually caught up with her, grabbing her arm to spin her around. But as he looked into her face, he saw only anger and hurt.

"Leave me alone, Alex," she spat. "I don't want to talk to you right now."

Alex tried to think of something to say to make it right. But Emily just shook her head, and pulled her arm free.

"I saw you kissing that...that woman. What is wrong with you?"

Alex finally felt the shame building up, but he couldn't explain what had happened. He didn't even understand it himself. All he knew was that Ruby had looked at him with those piercing eyes, and he had been lost.

"Emily, please..." but she just turned and walked away, leaving him standing alone on the sidewalk.

As he watched her go, his mind circled back to the moment that ruined his friendship with Emily. Was it worth it? Learning about the murder victim? He had never meant to hurt her, and now he wasn't even sure if he could fix things between them. How did he let this happen in the first place? This has topped all other mistakes he had ever made. And what did it all have to do with the dead guy anyway?

CHAPTER SEVEN

Dinner and Darkness

Emily White only started Midlands Community College because her parents wanted her to, not because she cared much about it. It wasn't that she was incapable, far from the case. Emily was, in fact, quite bright. She had a sharp mind, a keen eye for logic, and an almost uncanny ability to understand the emotions of those around her. But as for school, she considered that a chore. It was necessary evil to appease her venerated medical professional parents who expected nothing less than academic excellence from their daughter.

While this expectation was well intentioned, it had a paradoxical effect on Emily. It stifled her natural curiosity and replaced it with a gnawing anxiety. There was so much pressure to succeed and live up to their high standards, and she nearly lost herself to it.

She feared falling short, and had begun to doubt herself so much. She had always liked Alex but a part of her would always remind her that she was not good enough for him. Every now and then, she thought she was on the verge of losing him and losing her mind to her parents' constant scrutiny.

Her cautious nature worsened the problem. And that's why she hated confrontation. Disagreements, even the slightest discomfort, always made her quiver. Confrontation was her enemy. She couldn't imagine arguing with a teacher, challenging authority. So, she often chose to remain silent, blend in and avoid drawing attention to herself. This, of course, did little to improve her grades.

While that side of her life may seem like she lived in misery, her social life was quite different. Among her close friends, Emily had a great time. With them, she could be as witty and insightful as she wanted. They accepted her for who she was, flaws and all.

But even within the safety of her clique, she still felt inadequate somewhere. Her friends had their futures all planned out. Alex would obviously succeed his parents' company, Ethan would toe his father's line in the tech industry, his father had made a name for himself in the government too, Tyler is studying so much to make something out of himself and pursue his sports career, and Maya, let's just say that Maya could be anything she wanted because she had many family connections in all the arms of the government and sundry industries. While she was just feeling adrift. She had not big ambitions, no burning desire to achieve a particular field of study and the idea of joining her parents in the medical field was a dream she had thrust in the bin where it belonged. College, to her, was simply a way to appease her parents, so she could have time to think of the next big thing.

But even now, everything was spiraling out of control. A killer was on the loose and anyone could be next, hell anyone could be a suspect. Even that lady at the bar with the tattoo trying to kiss Alex. She had put that behind her as just an encounter Alex had no control of, the lady in question as perhaps desperate to get laid. But now, looking back, maybe she'd seemed a little off. A little too eager to get close to Alex. Why did she do that? And why did Alex let her? A seductress no doubt, no wonder she worked in the bar.

After that incident, she had walked away from Alex and had avoided him from then on. But the thing was, she was not certain she could keep that up. It was hard to avoid him, her friends were his friends. And with them around, she didn't have to worry about looking over her shoulder. When she was alone, her anxiety made her glance around the crowded diner. Everyone was suspicious. The gruff-looking biker nursing a coffee, the elderly couple sharing a quiet breakfast, the young mother nervously juggling a crying baby. Were any of them the killer? Was the killer watching her right now, observing her reactions, planning their next move?

She thought she was out of her mind when her hands trembled slightly as she picked up her coffee from the table and the liquid scalded her fingers. Why did that just happen? Was it because she was afraid for her life or was it anger? The anger she had held back in.

She knew she had to get out of the diner when a man in a red cap walked in and their eyes met. That victim was wearing a red cap and his fingers had been left in them, how cruel of the killer. She didn't see the man before he was murdered, but she had seen pictures of it online. It was crazy.

Now, this man just trotted in like he owned the place, a frown on his face. He could have been an innocent bystander like her, after all, the victim was wearing a red cap, not the killer, but why wait to find out? Her phone buzzed with a string of missed calls and unanswered texts. Alex was probably worried sick, she had been ignoring his calls for two days straight. And when they converged with friends, he never dared to ask her why she wouldn't take his calls. He had been ashamed of what he had done and would not appreciate the others finding out.

Then the news started. First, it was a red cap, and now it was the news. Someone had seen a man lurking near the scene of the crime. She got up quickly and left without caring to know what news the anchor had to deliver. When she walked past a quiet street, there had been a drawing. A simple sketch of a finger pointing. She saw it on a flyer plastered on a telephone pole, unsettling. Later that day, she was walking down the street when she saw a butcher come out of his shop, his apron splattered with blood. She nearly dropped her purse as her mind conjured up all the gruesome details of the murder. It was everywhere, lurking in the shadows, whispering in the wind. She was constantly on edge. She wondered what she could have done had she lived in Riverwood when those murders were constantly happening. Now this murderer that just came out of nowhere where was in Sunset Ridge. How more troubling could her life get?

The killer was out there, and she was starting to believe that she might be next. She knew it was ridiculous to think this way. Absolutely absurd. Sunset Ridge was filled with thousands of people. Why would the killer choose her? What made her so special? No matter how irrational her fear was, she could not ignore it. Every unfamiliar face in the grocery store could be the killer.

She'd always been a cautious person, but this was different. This was a primal fear, the kind that had nothing to do with logic or reason. It would seem that some few days ago, she was not intrigued by the idea of finding out what happened to Ben in Riverwood. But really, all she wanted was that do their investigations at a safe distance, and she only said with the belief that the killer was probably no more. After all, it was twenty years ago, if they were still here, they would be old and weak. Who would imagine this happening the night after their small get-together? Perhaps they jinxed it, they brought the killer back to life with their loud mouth and nonsense imaginations. The reality of the situation was far more terrifying than whatever she thought it would be. The thrill of the idea had vanished and all that was left was a paralyzing fear that she couldn't get rid of.

Why was she suddenly such a coward? She tried to rationalize it away. It was the unknown, the uncertainty of it all terrified her. The feeling of being completely out of control, why was she more afraid than everyone else?

Sunset Ridge had suddenly become a dangerous place. She was a coward, there was no denying and she hated herself for it. She longed for the carefree days of her childhood, back when Sunset Ridge was a safe and predictable place. Now, it only filled her with nothing but dread.

Being alone in the house was also a torture. When her house creaked from aging, it always sounded like she was in some horror movie. One time she doing herself checking locks, and another, peering out windows. Did she have to choose to stay in this dead quiet house, be around her mom in the pharmacy or stick around her friends even when she didn't want to see Alex's face.

Her parents were very dedicated to their work. The hospital and pharmacy were their lives. Emily rarely saw them, except for those "family dinners" where she was questioned about her performances.

So when Tyler called, suggesting a get-together at his house, Emily jumped at the chance. It didn't matter that she'd rather spend the evening pulling teeth than endure Alex's insufferable company. It didn't matter that the thought of going out into the street filled her with apprehension. It was just the prospect of escaping the suffocating silence of her own home and being around other people, even if they were mostly annoying, was too tempting to resist. Besides, what choice did she really have?

As she prepared to leave, she paused at the front door, perhaps to reconsider. Was it safer out there than in her comfortable home? She leaned against the doorframe, exhausted already, her heart beating like a drum. Deep breaths, she reminded herself, just deep breaths. It was just a little party, a chance to socialise and forget about her fears for a few hours.

She took a shaky breath, unlocked the door, and stepped out into the twilight. The party at Tyler's house might not be exactly what she wanted, but it was enough distraction.

As she walked down the street, the sound of her own footsteps echoing behind her gave her the creeps. Before now, she had never really paid attention to it. Now she realized how still and quiet Sunset Ridge could be at that time of the day. Safe for the few cars that would drive pass now and then, there was not a soul around her. Not that she wanted anyone around her, at least not anyone she didn't know.

When she go to Tyler's house, she tried to maintain a safe distance from Alex, but it didn't work. He was always in her space, stuttering, trying to apologise, this and that. Yet, when she tried to hide in the comfort of others, they would carefully move away from her. She knew there was something wrong by the way they looked at her, their forced smiled, their coded glances. They knew. How clueless could she be to think that Alex would not expose everything to them, this gets together at Tyler's was all planned to get them to make up. But she wasn't having it. Had she calculated properly earlier, she would have declined.

Maya sighed and put her hair behind her ears. "It's really hot in here, isn't it?" she said, fanning herself with her hand.

Emily shook her head lightly, "I don't feel hot at all." Ethan, who was sitting on the couch, nodded in agreement. "Yeah, me too, I feel the same way."

"Maybe we should open a window or turn on the air conditioning?"

But before anyone could respond, Tyler suddenly jumped up from the bed. "I'm going to go get some water from the kitchen," he said, already heading for the door. Ethan and Maya quickly followed him, pretending they hadn't heard Emily's suggestion. "Yeah, I could use a drink too," Ethan said, while Maya chimed in with "I'll come with you, I need to grab something from the kitchen."

As they filed out of the room, Emily followed them, "...yeah I could use another drink." But they were too quick and before she could reach the door, Tyler turned around and gave her a sheepish grin. "Sorry, we'll be right back!" he said, before shutting the door in her face.

Maya chuckled and leaned against the wall. "I bet she didn't see that one coming." Then turned around and found a door. "Oh Emma... why she join the party?"

Before Tyler could say anything, she grabbed the door knob and found her way in. "You can't just-" Tyler wanted to protest but stopped when she or Ethan weren't paying attention.

"You two are weird for barging into someone else's room like that. She's not even my friend or anything," he said, standing at the doorway.

"But she lives here, doesn't she?" Ethan asked touching a picture frame of Emma sitting on a table. "I bet she dreams of having you when you flash those muscles at her…" Maya stated casually as she walked around as if looking for something.

Tyler rolled his eyes. "We can't be in here guys."

"Is she like obsessed with flowers or something?" Maya asked and lightly tapped one of the blooms.

"I guess she's into it professionally…" Tyler replied.

Ethan remained at a place, staring at a picture on the wall. It was of peony single dead flower that stood out in winter. The environment looked cold and grey. The flowers' big blooms were wilted and brown. Its petals were curled and fragile, with a dark center. The snow around it was untouched, making the flower look lonely and sad.

"What an odd painting," Ethan sighed and moved towards a flower vase by the window. "Emma loves her flowers."

"I'm sure she does. It smells like paradise in here…" Maya agreed.

"Alright, alright, can we go now?" Tyler desperately chimed in, cutting them short. Maya turned to him with a look of annoyance, "what's the hurry, Tyler?" Then she glanced behind him, just towards Tyler's room. "I wonder what's going on in there."

"They're making up of course," Ethan answered walking out of the room. Maya followed immediately. Tyler who was starting to get sweaty, heaved a sigh of relief.

Back in Tyler's room, it had been awfully quiet. Alex had been trying to speak to her all night and now that they were in the room together, it seemed a cat got his tongue. Emily has tried to get away but she had been locked in there with him and there was no way out. All she could do was roll her eyes and grit her teeth, "it's not like it's hot in here or anything," she said.

She was left standing alone in the room, facing Alex's guilty expression. She tried to speak too, but her voice caught in her throat. Alex, on the other hand, had been struggling to find the right words. He opened his mouth to speak, but all that came out was a faint whisper. "I...I can explain..."

But she wasn't interested in hearing his excuses. She turned her back on him and walked over to the window, staring out at the town below. It was a deafening silence indeed, she thought she could even hear his thoughts.

"Don't bother," she breathed.

"Don't you want to hear what I have to say?"

"You're sorry, that's all you can say. Because…" she turned back to face him and his eyes dropped. "…you have no excuse for letting it happen. So you're sorry and that's that."

Then she turned back to the window "Tomorrow, we'll go back to the bar. Finish your conversation with that lady, because it seemed I interrupted…"

"Did you forgive me though?" he asked.

But she only took a deep breath, no words. He stood where he was, his eyes fixed on her back, he truly he could go back to the past. He took a step forward, then hesitated, unsure of what to do next.

She didn't react, as he slowly approached her. He stopped a few feet behind her. He raised a hand, then let it fall back to his side, that was the best he could do. Stand there in regret, hoping that somehow, someway, she would forgive him.

***

Ruby had just finished her shift at the bar, and decided to leave the bar that night. She was heading home, alone, just like she did every other night. The darkness never bothered her; she had grown accustomed to it over the years. Her feet knew the familiar path by heart. But lately, things had changed. Since finding those body parts, her mind hadn't been at rest. She had always been a sound sleeper, but now she found herself lying awake at night.

To calm her nerves, she had started having a drink or two before bed, accompanied by a sleeping pill to help her drift off. It wasn't the healthiest habit, but it was better than lying awake all night. She was almost home, just a few more turns and she would be safe behind her door.

As she approached the bend in the road, a dark figure suddenly walked out in view. It was standing in her way, with a dominating presence that filled the entire sidewalk. If she didn't know any better, she would say that the figure had been waiting for her. Her heart skipped as she found herself slowing down, her eyes on the figure. It was hooded, the face obscured by shadows, which made it impossible to discern any features. The way it stood motionless and silent, gave her creeps. Her instincts told her to be cautious, to cross the street and avoid the figure altogether. But her feet wouldn't obey, she was unable to move, frozen in uncertainty.

The figure didn't move either, neither did it speak. It just stood there, glaring at her menacingly. Ruby found her thoughts jumping from one worst-case scenario to another. She tried to tell herself that she was being paranoid, that the figure was probably just a lost tourist or a drunk who had stumbled out of a nearby bar. But the way it stood there watching her, made her feel like she was in grave danger. She took a deep breath, trying to calm herself down, and slowly began to back away. But as she did, the figure took a step forward in an eerily silent move. Ruby stopped, ready to arm herself with her pepper spray. She was completely alone, with no one with help. What's the worst thing that could happen now?

Slowly, the figure staggered across the street and down the sidewalk. She breathed heavily and nearly sank into the street flowers but she caught herself. She quickly found her foot and continued the path home. She had managed to compose herself and was now focused on getting home as quickly as possible.

She had failed to realise that she her back turned on the figure. She didn't hear the soft footsteps tagging along quietly, their pace now matching perfectly. There was no way she would see it coming.

CHAPTER EIGHT

Dead End

It seemed that with every murder, the town got quieter, colder and more intriguing. It's crazy how people claimed to be terrified of the silent killer and affected by the increased number of missing bodies. Yet after every murder, the town's folks moved on almost immediately as if nothing had happened. They swept every sign of sympathy under the rugs, the news went round and passed by and they left the slate clean for the killer to strike again. You can't blame them though, they had seen too many deaths and it became normal, just another sad incident. The only people that ever mourned the deaths are the victims family and close friends. The rest of the town just prayed they would never cross paths with the killer. No one bothered anymore; who is he? Is it even a he? Where he came from or why he killed all those people? Does he pick them at random or maybe those people did something terrible to him? Was he on a quest for revenge or is he a psycho that just loves to murder people for fun? The town's people are not bothered by these thoughts anymore. They had long held on to the hope that he would one day be caught and brought to justice but that had seemed impossible so now, they just hope they don't become a victim.

"I can believe this happened again." Emily's eyes were dull and she had a dull tune to her voice. She had been right about a murder spree. Killers like these don't rest after one kill. That stressed the hell out of her .

"Don't beat yourself over it Em, this is bigger than us." Alex replied, trying to make her feel better. They both strolled down the cracked sidewalk, their steps slow and lingering as they had no destination in mind. Alex had convinced Emily to leave her house. He has been worried sick about her. Emily had let the deaths get to her head, getting too scared and paranoid especially with all the findings she's made so far. Alex needed to distract her a bit. The truth is their life now revolved around the murders and finding out who was behind it but they still needed to be in control of how they felt and handled themselves.

"Someone needs to do something or at least try. The cops in this town can't do shit. I bet they're scared."

"Everyone is scared." Emily suddenly stopped and locked eyes with a guy who was coming towards her riding a bike. He looked homeless with dirty layered clothes. He rode past her, the both of them stared at themselves till he rode by. Alex noticed the strange encounter and tapped Emily.

"You ok?"

"Yeah, I'm fine." Emily replied, a mixed look on her face.

"What was that?"

"No idea, Riverwood is really home to the strangest things." Emily said and turned back one more time to see if he was really gone.

"Come on." Alex said and gestured her into a bar they had stopped in front of.

They sat at a table close to the window. Emily's eyes flashed around the bar and out on the streets, she startled at every little noise.

"What the fuck Em, you need to relax."

"I can't. I haven't slept in days Alex, I feel eyes staring at me."

"No one is staring at you, it's in your head." Alex signaled for the waiter to come and he ordered a cranberry juice for the both of them. "Hey…" Alex reached for her hand. "…you can stay at my place, as long as you want."

"Thanks."

The waiter approached their table with a tray of their orders, dropped and left. Alex's eyes followed him and trailed to the far end of the bar. His eyes widened as he saw a woman at the far end of the bar.

"Emily…" he leaned and whispered to her. "…look." He glanced at the lady and Emily followed his eyes.

"Who's that?"

"Must be an officer or something."

"Do you think we should work with her, tell her what we know?"

"No one would want to work with teenagers on a serious case like this and perhaps she looks mean."

"Alex, if we want a chance at getting this killer, we have to work with an officer of the law." Emily convinced, eager to go meet the detective. She kept looking back, trying to get a good look at the detective who was seated on a stool at the counter minding her business with a drink in her hand. She suddenly looked back and their eyes almost met. Emily averts her gaze in a sudden move and ended up hitting her drink which spilled across the table and onto her dress.

"Shit." She cursed. "I think she saw me."

Alex took some paper napkins from the box on the table and dabbed the spilled drink. The napkin didn't really do much as it soaked the drink and melted into it. A figure appeared before them and handed Emily a towel.

"Oh thank you." She said as she looked up and right in front of her stood the detective. Alex had already seen her and stared at her in shock. *What the hell is she doing standing right in front of us? Oh my God did she hear our conversations or maybe she needs our help?*

"Come with me, both of you." The lady said with a stern face.

Alex and Emily stared at each other while they tried to process what was happening.

The detective turned to leave and noticed they were not responding to her. "Now!" She firmly said and walked out. The two hurriedly followed her outside the bar and saw her already standing beside her car holding the door open. "Get in."

Alex and Emily stared at themselves, a little bit hesitant. They probably contemplated whether to obey or object.

"chop chop ladies." The detective urged.

They both gave themselves a look, shrugged and got in the car. She shut the door and got in herself.

"Where are we going?" Alex broke the silence.

"To the station."

"Are we under arrest?" Emily inquired.

"It depends."

"What, we haven't done anything." Alex chipped in.

"Are you sure about that?" The detective snapped back.

Alex and Emily looked at each other, a confused look on their faces. Their furrowed brows asked more questions than they did. They haven't really done anything wrong apart from poking around and looking for information on the silent killer. They hoped they had not stepped on any toe in the process. If the silent killer had any accomplice, he would not like a gang of kids sniffing around to fish him out and might try to harm them if they did.

Maybe Emily's paranoia could be justified after all. The kids never thought about where their curiosity might lead them to. What if they ripple still Waters in the process. They never knew who kept an eye on them, who was evil and who was good. The silent killer might have been some random dude, that sweet neighbor, the mail man, the person that people never expected at all. It could be someone people saw everyday. Serial killers always turned out to be the socially awkward kid who was bullied or the social butterfly who smiled all the time and never got angry.

They got to the station which wasn't far from the bar. It was about a thirty minute drive. The station was quiet as usual apart from the chit chats and radio sound. Not a lot of crime was committed in Riverwood. The silent killer sort of took over.

She led them to her office which looked more like a storage room, super small with loads of files on the shelfs. She pulled open one of the cabinets and brought out a large file. She sat on a large untidy desk with her name inscribed on a little slab, Detective Dona. Some of the letters were faded which was odd considering the fact she's new.

"Alex and… Camilla?"

"Emily."

"That's what I said." The detective rudely snapped back.

The mist of confusion around Alex and Emily disappeared as soon as detective Dona started to pry them with multiple questions.

"So, the silent killer, tell me what you know?"

Emily opened her mouth to say something but before a word came out, Alex cut her off.

"Nothing. We don't know anything."

The detective's lips curved into a very intimidating smile. She turned the file to face them and flipped it open. Every page revealed an information related to the murders from the Reeds to pictures of the victims and their various body parts.

"You know the bad thing about being in Sunset Ridge, there's no such thing as privacy, you as much as sneeze, the whole town's gonna hear about it. The good part of it, information is free."

"If that was true, the silent killer would have been stopped a long time ago." Emily sassed.

"True and I intend on doing that but till then, I'm going to need you guys to tell me everything you know about him."

"What makes you think we know something?"

"It's a small town. People talk." Dona said with a scoff. "Apparently a bunch of teenage kids has been running around playing cop."

"People went missing and no one was doing anything about it. Someone had to step up." Alex retorted a hint of anger in his voice.

"And what has changed since you stepped up, huh!" Dona retorted. She took a deep breath and reclined back into her seat. "You know what, I'm not here for this. What do you know about the waitress."

"Not much, we weren't friends or anything." Alex responded.

"Yeah, we never really hang with her."

"Where were you guys the night she died?"

'Home." Alex replied first and Dona shifted her eyes to Emily.

"Same."

"Any alibi who can vouch for you?"

Emily and Alex turned in sync and stared at themselves. "We were together." Emily said with hesitation, a sign of doubt in her voice.

Dona scoffed and turned to Alex, that intimidating smile still plastered on her face. "Really, what were you guys doing together?"

"Nothing, we were just together." Alex replied unsure of what to say next. Emily had caught him unaware with her reply. She shouldn't have lied though.

A knock on the door distracted them but Dona didn't answer. There was a knock again and the door swiped and in came Jack. Dona rolled his eyes. "Not you again." She said quietly. "I didn't ask you to come in." She turned to Jack and said out loud.

"Whoa, little miss rude. I'm fine, thanks for asking." Jack jested in his usual manner.

"Look, ma'am, we don't have any information that'll help you find what you're looking for. Besides, we are just as confused as you are." Alex replied after seconds of silence. Emily on her own part was already filled with contempt for the detective.

"Alright ladies…" Dona continued and Alex's brows furrowed. She reached into her pocket and took out two of her cards. "Here, my phone number's on it. If there's anything you forgot to remember or you find out, do well to inform me first." She slams the desk with her hand and the two got up.

"Sure thing detective." Alex replied her and they both left. Their eyes met Jack's as they walked out the office.

"Urgh, what's her problem? She should be grateful, we're trying to help." Emily muttered after they'd left the room where they were interrogated. "Why didn't you tell her what we know, it might have helped."

"You can't trust anyone Em, she already suspects us and that's a bad start. We have to be careful who we work with."

Alex knew expertly well, how to be reticent when such a fierce and hot-headed person tried to question him.

"You gotta keep an eye on those kids, there are something else. So, how's my favorite detective?" Jack said in a corny manner and sat across Dona with his legs up in the other chair.

"What do you want Jack?"

"Oh nothing much, just a little information on our progress so far."

"Our?" Dona pointed out in annoyance. She took the file on the table and walked back to the shelf she took it from. "This is a very sensitive case Jack and it's my case not ours, I can't just give out information to any civilian."

"Ouch!" Jack snapped and dramatically put his hands on his chest. "civilian? I'm not gonna lie that one hurt me, right here." He pointed to his chest.

Jack is one person Dona desperately wanted to get rid of. He had become a thorn in the flesh and refused to be pulled out. Everywhere Dona turned to, he appeared. She hated the fact that he was overly invested in the investigation and might just know more than she did. One of the perks of being a private detective. You get to do things your own way even if it required an unorthodox method. The end result is you get what you want and it is a much faster process. Unlike the legal method where you can't harass a person for the truth even when you clearly know that person was hiding something. Sometimes you have to wait to get a warrant for a search.

All these protocols are exactly what made it possible for evidence to be tampered with.

She also hated the fact that Jack was steps ahead of her. He was clearly more experienced and knew how to maneuver his way around people and get information. She had at one time been denied some information because according to that person, she had already spoken to the police. So now he paraded himself as the police. Jack didn't even need a badge to do the work. From afar, you could tell he was an officer of the law. His physique sold him out and he just had the mannerisms of a veteran cop.

"Listen Jack, you can keep interfering with my investigation."

Jack lifted up his hands. "I didn't do anything."

"I'm dead serious right now. If I hear you messed with evidence or even talked to a witness, I'll arrest you." Dona dared.

Jack smirked. "Fine Princess."

"Detective!"

Jack smiled and bowed before her. "Detective." He got up and Dona watched him leave. "Talk to the witness, maybe she saw something." Jack said before he left. She knew he wouldn't drop the investigation but somehow hoped her threats would get him to back off.

***

Becky's eyes looked cold and lost. She stared into the distance, a half eaten burger in her hands. She's been extra quiet since she found the body parts. The silent killer had that effect on people. Dona slid into the seat across yet she did move. She knew she would find her here. Where else do teenagers go in this town?

"Hello Becky." Dona called out. She looked in her direction to see what she was staring at but there was nothing. She was just zoned out. "Becky?"

Becky turned to her quietly, her eyes told a sad story, one that was scary.

"Are you okay?"

"Why wouldn't I be?" She replied, her voice void of expression. She snapped out of her zone and started to eat her burger.

"Hey, uuhm, I'm detective Dona, I wanted to talk to you about the waitress you found…" Becky paused abruptly and continued to eat her burger. "…the other day. Do you remember any other thing."

"Do you think I killed her?"

"Oh course not. But if there's anything you know that can help me catch the killer, I'd appreciate it if you tell me."

"He's watching us."

Dona snapped her neck to the window and flashed her eyes across the room. She doesn't see anyone.

"Who's watching us?"

"Him."

"Who's him Becky, tell me."

Becky ignored her and continued to eat her burger. Dona looked around but didn't find anyone suspicious. She stared at Becky till she finished her burger and started to slurp her drink.

"Here." Dona slid her card across the table to her. "If you remember anything or you're in any kind of trouble, call me." She said and left.

Becky was greatly disturbed after she found the waitress's body parts. She hasn't been herself ever since and it dawned on her that it could be anybody and no one was safe.

Becky was Ethan's longest crush back in high school. Being the weird silly boy that he was, Ethan never had the courage to actually ask her

Christian Candelaria

out and each time he tried to, words got caught up in his throat, he either said something silly or didn't say anything at all.

It wasn't just about his relationship with Becky. Ethan struggled with social interaction and is always the odd one. His introverted nature made people underestimate him because amidst all this, Ethan had a brilliant mind and that was his superpower. It didn't help that his father was actively involved in politics and that made him known even when he didn't want to. The only place he was his true self was in the endless coded world of the internet. He could hack any software no matter how complicated. A hobby he had grown passionate about.

"Excuse me Miss, we're about to close." A waiter called Becky's attention. She had been there the whole day and stared out the window.

"I can't go home, I can't go home." Becky muttered to herself.

The waiter was impatient, he did not care to figure out what she was trying to say. "You have to leave, we're closed." he said and left her.

Becky picked up the card Dona had dropped. She thought of calling her to come pick her up but changed her mind. She mustered some courage and decided to go home.

115

Days went by and Becky felt less paranoid. She had settled back into her old normal life. Typical of the people of Riverwood. The death only shook them up as soon as it happened and everybody is so devastated you would think they would never move on from it. Give them a few days, hell the next day and everyone was back to default. That may be the main reason why the killer kept coming back. They never took measures to stay safe, they walked about freely at night and alone especially in lonely and isolated places. No curfew of any kind and either the cops were scared or they didn't do enough. No way one person terrorized a town for so long and got away with it. People got too comfortable and so did the killer.

Mr. Rooks whistled his heart away as he peed on the side of the road behind his bus. He stopped by the bar for a round with his friends as soon as he closed for the day. Once he had enough of the booze, he headed back home, don't want to be caught drunk driving. He wiggled his waist and zipped up his pants. He had gotten into the bus ready to drive off when he noticed something strange on the truck. Probably an animal left a dump while he peed. Disgusting, he thought. Rooks got down from the bus to get a good look and clean it up. His eyes widened in shock.

"Dear God."

The silent killer had struck again.

CHAPTER NINE

Shadow of Death

Maya kept stroking Ethan's hair. Ethan's quietness wasn't new but this was the longest he had been quiet. They hadn't heard him speak in fourteen days. It wasn't a hidden detail that Ethan had a crush on Becky but only his clique knew about it, even Becky was oblivious to the fact that she had a secret admirer. Ethan felt that maybe, just maybe he will have the best proposal or he could tell her when she was alone that she had crept into his world and built her home. He could remember it like yesterday, anytime she smiled he would have butterflies and most times, he couldn't get that feeling out of his stomach. Who knew Becky would become the next victim? This feeling was strange to him, the feeling of heartbreak, the fact that he would never see her again! Becky will be 6 feet below the ground, so close and yet so far from him. "Let's find him" Ethan said. There was a brief pause as everyone exchanged glances, for a moment there the entire clique was lost for word. The loss of Becky must have really hit him hard.

"From what we've gathered, it is likely the killer goes for the person who finds the body." Alex broke the silence. Emily looked at him and nodded.

Alex continued, "the uber driver that was to pick her up was the one who found the parts and from the trend we discovered, the person who finds the body becomes the next victim." Ethan placed his hands on his chin as he was about to say something when Tyler cut in. "We have tried reaching out to the driver but it has proven difficult and abortive getting to him. It seems to me that if we must have him surface, we will need to let him know that his life is in danger." "Well, I believe you, I am seriously doubting the methods through which you tried to reach out to him." Tyler looked at Emily with a mocking smile "I wonder when Jerry became less afraid of Tom." Emily removed her shoe and threw it at Tyler who docked to dodge, on raising his head he saw that gaze of Alex. The glare that said *speak to her like that one more time.* Tyler became serious and kept quiet.

"I will program a minicamera with a microphone that is attachable to the driver's clothes so we can monitor him or maybe it's better we have it in his car since he could always change clothes?" Alex put his hands on his chin as he fell into thought. "We cannot fully monitor him if that is the case, we can only actively monitor him in the car and if by chance he is away from it, we can leave the conclusion to his guardian angel" Maya said. "Alright then, I will leave everything tech related to you" Alex gestured towards Ethan. He then turned his gaze towards Emily as it revealed some level of gentleness. "We will see Dona, hope this particularly meeting turns out better than the last time." Emily looked away from him pretending she was not the object of his reference. Alex smiled understandingly following through with the act.

Maya was the first to stand up as she hugged Ethan, "you will be fine," she whispered into his ears only to his hearing. Ethan looked away and smiled towards a corner of the room his subconscious laughing at him as he knew his smile betrayed his thoughts. Alex patted Ethan on the back and he walked out of the room, Tyler walked up to him and casually said "I thought tech bros were the hard guys."

Thump!

"Ouch!"

Emily punched him from behind. "This is why you're still single" as she stormed out of the room. Ethan saw everyone out as he was back to solitude, the only friend he had ever known. It was alive before Ethan first cried; it watched as he was cradled in his mother's arms. It was the one that kept Ethan company when everyone else left. They probably did not know how much they meant to Ethan and he knew he could not lose them because they were the only friends he had ever really known. Everyone that came into his life was always quick to leave through the back door slamming it as hard as they could, to hurt him. Alex, Maya, Emily and Tyler, they took him as he was and never criticized him. Even the dead could feel the love these friends had shown to him.

"Another," Dona shifted the glass towards the barman who was obviously worried about her. "That is the twelfth shot you have had tonight; don't you mind hitting the breaks." She looked at him and smiled "I would like to make it a round figure today." Micah was at a loss for words. Dona had the habit of coming to the bar to drink but she usually had her limits and would not readily drink so much. Maybe being a detective had more downsides than he had initially imagined. He had worked in the bar for six years and within this period he had met characters and all sorts of people. The most people who frequented the bar were usually married men he thought to himself. He loved the job owing to the peace it brought to him. The pay wasn't bad which was a testament to his unyielding devotion in having to treat customers well. On several occasions, influential customers had stumbled on the bar and whenever they left, they tipped him generously. This was a hub of gossip; most people came here to discuss important matters over a few shots. He was the ears of the streets even the ground could testify to that, the bottles never lied.

"Hello Dona"

She didn't turn her face but she exclaimed, "Jesus Christ, talk about persistent." Alex shrugged, "we knew we would find you here." She looked at them with a mocking smile and replied almost instantly, "the last I checked, I am the detective and you...," she pointed to Alex and then turned to Emily who proceeded to bring her face down. "I know your intention and I am uninterested, go home and suckle on momma's tits." Emily's jaws drop as she doesn't let a word slip through. "I could say the shots have begun working, I wonder how you carry out your duty with this side of you" Alex smiled as he looked at her. Dona glared at him, "I'll be leaving I don't time to chitchat with you go home."

"Wait! Dona, please hold on, we have got a lead!"

"Nothing to lead," she cuts in and she stumbles out of the bar. Alex and Emily rushed out of the bar to meet her outside. "The only lead you both should follow right now is the lead to your houses, if you want to place house, ask the neighbour's kids and stay out of my business." She entered her car and when she was about to zoom off.

"The person who finds the body becomes the next victim," Alex screamed as she zoomed off. Alex and Emily stood there dumbfounded as they watched the car disappear into the darkness.

Dona looked at the side mirror as she thought to herself, "kids just don't know how to stay away from trouble."

"I can't believe she didn't even want to listen to us," Alex said. Emily patted his back as she said in a hushed tone, "she just sees us as kids and it is not far from the truth." Alex looked at her somewhat surprised. "Thought we were on the same team." She turned her face away and pretended not to have heard him.

He decided to walk Emily back home. The road seemed long, just traffic lights, street lights and trees. Aside their footsteps, maybe the loudest thing that could be heard was the silence between them. "I remember when I once got lost in the woods, mum screamed my name as they looked for me," Alex broke the silence. He paused like he was trying to remember a memory that was slowly fading away. Emily listened intently but held her tongue. "The police had to join the search, I don't remember how I got lost in it, but I most definitely remember the whooping mum gave to me" Emily giggled like a child as Alex turned to look at her apparently surprised. "It wasn't funny on that day. I was scared and I could have sworn I saw someone drag a dead body into the woods, but the police never believed me. They said I was hallucinating. I hid behind the tree with the green marking. That was where they found me."

"Is that what fascinated you with the murders?"

Alex opened his mouth but could not find a suitable defence to her question.

"I don't know if this is the right decision we have made, but one thing is certain. It is risky and I don't know if I am ready for it." Alex looked at her with a soft gaze and wrapped her in an embrace. "I know it is for the best," it looked as if she had what to say but held back. Would it change his mind? She thought to herself.

"Goodnight Emily"

"Goodnight Alex, thank you for walking me."

Alex blew a kiss to her as he began walking back home. On passing an alley, he saw a hooded figure standing right there, that was the middle of the road he thought to himself. He rubbed his eyes gently and looked again, he discovered the figure was gone. He continued going as he thought to himself,

"Do I really hallucinate?"

He continued walking and arrived at home. He turned around and was shocked by what he saw. That was the figure he had seen at the alley, so he was not hallucinating. He wondered how the figure had gotten to his house, he did not see anyone following and why was the figure staring at the house. The thoughts unsettled him, coupled with the fact that there was a serial killer on the loose.

The front door opened up and Alex's mum stared at him with a piercing gaze, "late again, are we?" he lost focus there for a second as he turned to face his mum.

"I am sorry mum, I had to see Emily off. There was a man…."

He turned around and didn't see the figure any longer.

"If you are going to start a sentence, learn to complete it," she growled as she walked back into the house, Alex followed suit and locked the door behind himself. He dropped his phone on the desk as he collapsed on the bed. The tried to piece everything together,

"Who is that creepy guy?"

Hmm!

The buzzing of his phones breaks his thought flow as he picks up his phone and sees it is a group call initiated by Ethan.

"Interesting," he muttered under his breath before picking up the phone.

"Hello" Alex said.

"You are the last to join the call Alpha duck," everyone laughed. "I just saw it," Alex tried to defend himself.

"Well, Ethan says he has something interesting to tell us," Maya quickly chipped in.

"Okay then Ethan, let's hear you."

There was a brief pause before Ethan said anything. "I cracked the police database..."

"Hacked you mean," Tyler butted in, "will you just shut up and let him finish! Christ" Emily scolded.

Ethan went silent for some seconds. He then continued. "The police discovered that the killer left parts of the victim's body. This was not how he usually operated; They also noticed that the parts they kept began to change." Ethan stopped abruptly. He was sad as he remembered the one, he loved. He failed to resume after some seconds as if contemplating the weight of the information.

"What are the changes you are talking about? I want to believe you also have that information"

"Well, yes I do," Ethan continued. "It was a genetic kind of change, not one that happens to humans just after they die." He paused again as if waiting for the new information to digest. "Just complete the story already, stop breaking it already." This time around nobody said anything because they all agreed with Tyler. For once, Tyler felt good about himself.

"Okay then, the body parts they found, which is Becky's, grew flowers destroying the evidence. As you all know already, the body parts grow violets; the killer's trademark."

Everyone was stunned at the information. Ethan quickly continued before anyone got the chance to say anything. "This is all the information I could get from the database before getting kicked out."

"Good job Ethan, this has given us a wider range and scope to deal with." Alex congratulated him. "How about the camera?" Ethan hesitated and then went on. "I have begun but I still need some time to complete it."

"Everyone has heard, we tried getting in on Dona, but she bailed on us we may probably need an alternative." Still on the call, Alex got up from his bed and headed for the window to shut it.

There he was again, the man he had seen at the alley. For a moment there he froze, why was he beside the mango tree, was this person after me? He thought to himself. He closed his window and kept looking.

"Alex?"

"Alex?"

They called out before Alex snapped out of his daze. "Oh, sorry guys just a minor inconvenience." He walked away from the window. "Is there anything you will like to add?" Tyler asked him.

"Not at all."

He hung up the call and went under the sheets. Sufficient was the day's problems, he would think about other matters on the morrow.

CHAPTER TEN

Deck in a Mess

A s usual, Alex's mother opened the window as the rays of sunlight washed over him. He tried to put the sheets over his head. Maybe by doing so he could deceive his brain into thinking that it was still night.

"Get up Alex, it is morning already." She walked toward the door, glanced towards the bed and shook her head before leaving. He could hear the sound of the TV from his room. His brain had fully woken up. Standing up the from the bed, he grudgingly dragged his body downstairs. His mum was so focused on the news so she didn't hear when he tried to call out to her. He also decided to take a peek at the TV maybe he could find something of interest.

This was the story of Riverwood, the same killer, the same pattern. This had already thrown the entire Sunset Ridge into chaos. The reporters had caught on, maybe Dona would have also stumbled upon the same information or so he thought. Was this the copycat or was it the actual killer? He switched his view from the TV to his mum, whose hands were shaking with the teacup in her hands.

"You okay mum?"

That was when she realised that her fingers were getting jittery.

"Oh yeah, I am fine."

She turned to face him and she pointed towards the TV, "...no more coming back at night. I guess the reports tell a lot." He opened his mouth but no words were forthcoming. She nodded at him, "I thought as much."

It was not like it is new information to them, but the sun just began to shine in Sunset Ridge when it was going down somewhere else.

Unlike in Alex, whose mother never let him sleep past 8:00 am in the morning, Tyler's parents never really bothered about that. Either they were in bed too, or they were out early for work. That's why he learner to cook and take care of himself earlier on.

Knock!

Tyler stirred on his bed uncomfortably, hoping the knocking would stop but it didn't. It was as if whoever was knocking meant to harass him out of bed that morning.

"Yes?"

Tyler replied from atop the bed. The knocking stopped for a moment and then continued. Annoyed, Tyler stood up from the bed and walked towards the door as he swung it open.

"Typical of you to reply that way," Emma said. Falling into a daze immediately she saw Tyler's well-built muscles. Did he not usually sleep without a pyjama or a T-shirt on.

Tyler looked at Emma and did not know how to react.

Gulp! She swallowed hard.

"You know, one night is not too much to ask. I mean, even bears hibernate. So why can't I get a good sleep?"

"Err....," she stammered before gaining her composure. "You see, mornings like this are usually the times when sleep is enjoyed the most." She paused before she continued.

"I would let you build castles in the skies but I realised that you would probably be gone in one of the dragons you create before I got the opportunity to see you."

She stared at him intensely as if she was waiting for something. She realised she couldn't get her eyes off his chest. For a second she pictured herself lying on his chest twirling the hairs there as he whispered beautiful words to her. She didn't know when a giggle escaped her mouth as she blushed.

"Emm…" Tyler cleared his throat as he looked at her dead in face.

As if jolted by electricity, she finally sighed in defeat as she asked, "can I come in or what?"

He pushed the door slightly as he pointed towards the room. She smiled as she walked into the room, heading straight for the bed. She picked up his pillow and hugged it tightly. "This reminds me of my teddy bear at home. I miss home." Tyler walked toward a chair, pulled it out from under the table where it was tucked and sat down.

"You said you had something to discuss?"

"Oh yes," she quickly responded.

She put down the pillow and with a serious expression, "you know why I am here Tyler, don't pretend you don't know."

Tyler looked towards the ground as he smiled in defeat.

"There really isn't much I can do for you. I tried discussing with my parents hoping they would change their minds but adults." He hesitated before he continued, "you know, they see the world in a different way."

"I feel they consented listening to your loan request because you pay the rent and they think you are responsible."

He opened his arms spreading them in defeat as if trying to tell her that what she had was okay and she should manage it.

Tyler could not understand why his parents refused to give her the loan. The idea was perfect or so he thought. Maybe because she was still a growing adult and lacking in experience that was why they were sceptical. He couldn't count the number of times she had done good deeds for him. Inherently, Emma was nice. She would help his mum with the chores, help her do the dishes and even tag along when they had family outings. At some point his mum had had referred to her as a daughter from another mother.

Tyler didn't frequent the house. This was one of those off visits he usually had and had intended to leave before she arrived. Just like she had rightfully said, maybe he really would have ridden one of his dragons away.

She looked at him with a pleading gaze hoping he would change his mind and before he could open his mouth to say anything, she said, "thank you" and hurried out of the room before he had the chance to say anything.

Immediately she left, his phone started buzzing. What a busy morning, he thought to himself. He picked up his phone and smiled after seeing the Caller ID.

"Hello love." He whispered into the phone.

"I thought the good morning text usually came from the guy and not the lady," the other party said.

"I think you're right but it could be both ways you know? I mean love doesn't have first or second choices."

It was quiet for a few seconds before the other party continued. "You're home, right?"

"Yeah," he quickly responded.

"Anything to sooth the atmosphere?" Tyler thought for a second before replying with a smile.

"Maybe pizza and your presence will do." The other party laughed.

"King of the Ps. Do your parent know you have unprotected sex?" Tyler suddenly felt violated.

"Hey! Hey! Just get here already." He hung up the phone as he smiled knowingly.

Some moments later, there was another knock on the door.

"Come in," Tyler responded.

Maya walked into the room with a box of Pizza. She carefully placed it on the table and planted herself in Tyler's embrace.

It was so warm, she really liked Tyler and didn't know why Emily didn't dig into it. Emily looked for every slight inconvenience to pin the blame on him. Tyler was a funny guy and although he had a history, he wasn't that dangerous. Tyler was the only one she found attractive in the entire group. Alex was too bossy, Ethan was too introverted and who knows, maybe he was probably scared. Then there was Tyler, the one who made the group laugh and always tried to lighten up the atmosphere whenever it seemed tense. He was like the rays of sunshine on a winter morning. Just being in his embrace illuminated her world.

"Didn't expect you to arrive so soon."

"I wasn't far........," she responded but before she could complete her statement, he drew her into a deep kiss as he pulled her top and tossed it towards the chair.

Without an iota of resistance, she also pulled off his shirt. He lifted and threw her on the bed, pulling her pants down. He planted a kiss on her belly button, gently caressing as he headed for her breasts. His lips rested on her breasts and she let out a soft moan. Wanting to pull his head away, she held it and brought it back as she also reached for his trousers, unbuckling his belt. He held her hands and whispered softy into her ears, "not so fast."

He kissed her intensely clearly losing awareness of his immediate environment as his door swung open. They both paused and looked towards the door. There she was, Emma was stunned. Her hands went straight to covering her mouth. She had confessed how she felt to Tyler and on several occasions, had tried to make advances but he never let her near him. Who was the woman on the bed who was naked? Why was she kissing him so intimately? Those lips were sacred to her and she couldn't imagine them dancing on what she would call the gutter of another woman. She didn't know when tears begin to crawl out of her eyes as it began its never-ending journey towards the bottom of her face. She turned around and bolted away.

"Emma!" Tyler tried to call out.

"Now, you've got some explaining to do." Maya looked at him suspiciously as she pulled the duvet to cover her open chest.

Tyler looked at Maya, searching her eyes like he was looking for a part of it that would trust him on what he was going to say but failed to find anything.

"She pays rent here. My parents accepted her. She has been here for a while."

Maya looked at him with a mocking gaze. "How does that explain the tears that she cried?"

Tyler smiled in defeat as he knew the battle was long lost before it even began.

"She has made moves on me on some occasions and has confessed her feelings to me but I told her it couldn't work." Maya looked at him intently as if waiting to hear more but nothing was forthcoming.

"Did you tell her why it could not work?," Maya chipped in. Tyler opened his mouth as if his defence army had arrived to save him from the fires of the dragon, but nothing came out. His warriors had starved to death before the battle begun.

Maya looked at him and shook at her head, typical of men she thought to herself. At least he had told her he wasn't interested or maybe that is just what she wanted to believe to make herself feel good.

"I guess that is it." she thought to herself. She stood up and put her clothes back on.

Dona scrambled through Becky's case file as she was up to something with the new lead. After all the turns, she had finally found the house of the Uber Driver that found the parts of Becky's body. However, she had visited him three times already and he was not never at home. She decided to pay him one last visit. On arriving the house, she hit the door bell and waited for the response but nothing came up. She hit the bell a couple of times and still got nothing. She went around the house to see if she could find any leads, instead she saw his car parked there, behind the house. He was a supposed Uber driver who should be on the road consistently, that was why she had excused his absence for the three times she had come here.

She walked toward the car to examine it. The more she examined the car, questions kept popping up in her head. She drew conclusions that from the fact that the tires were still clean, albeit dusty. It signified that the owner had washed his vehicle but never got the chance to use it she went on to look around, there was a bus parked beside the car. The door of the bus was left open. She looked at the door and discovered that someone must have come in here not too long ago. On entering the bus, she walked down as she headed towards the last sit. There was something familiar yet strange about the bus. That odor... *Smells like a crime scene.* She had solved too many cases to be eluded by it. The buzzing of flies confirmed her suspicions but she still couldn't hold her curiosity. She waltzed towards the last sits in the back of the bus and there it was, parts of the Uber driver that should have picked up Becky, she didn't need forensics to confirm these suspicions.

That was when she realized it. She remembered the case file, the person that saw Becky last was the Uber driver.

"Dammit," she raised her head up as she found a hooded figure staring directly at her through the tinted glasses of the bus. She bolted for the door of the car as the figure slipped into an empty alley and disappeared. She got down and frantically searched for the figure, but it was like the figure just disappeared into thin air. That was it for her and she tried to put pins into the case, thinking of who had information into the fact that whoever found the body would become the next victim.

CHAPTER ELEVEN

Dance of the Damned

You would think after all her years of being a detective, she would be used to seeing dead bodies. Well no. Dona was traumatized. If there's one thing scarier than investigating a murder, it's experiencing the murder first hand or being the first person to come across a dead body, unexpectedly. There's something about it, it messes with you and soon, you won't be able to tell between facts and fiction.

Flashes of the scene kept playing in her head. Although she wasn't there, she could hear the knife slicing through the flesh, she could feel the blood seeping from the cuts, it must have been a big knife, sharp enough to cut through the bones or maybe he broke the bones with his bare hands, that would make the knife easier to cut through. The victims must have been unconscious the whole time, no way he cut off a finger and the scream wasn't loud enough to get neighbours talking. The twisted mind of a psychotic killer is quite unstable and unpredictable. You can't tell their next move and just when you think you have it figured out, they strike right under your nose and slip right through your fingers. How the hell does he get away every damn time? The horror grew inside of her, her mind played tricks and she just made herself afraid.

She would hate for the kids to be right, not after she side-lined them for so long. Or maybe her instincts were right and one of the kids might just be it. They knew too much, things she wouldn't even figure out on her own. But they were just kids anyway. Their stories were based on hearsays and stuff they read on the internet and newspapers. No solid proof. Dona had to work with evidence, not hints and ideas from a bunch of teenagers. Now it could be more than that, she had seen the murders herself and the kids suddenly start to make sense.

She had detained them the night after she found the bus driver. It can't be a coincidence they somehow kept appearing at every murder scene.

If it wasn't for Jack, that meddling asshole, she would have gotten more information from them. Tyler had stuttered when she asked him of his whereabouts the night of the murder. Those kids might be telling the truth but they're not telling all of it.

"What the hell..." Ethan cussed out as Dona patted them down one after the other. She was probably looking for a weapon, a knife to be precise.

'Are you serious right now?" Maya objected. "You can't possibly think we have anything to do with the murders."

"Is this even legal? I want a lawyer." Tyler got defensive, unsure of what to do. He hasn't done anything but a police case was the last thing he needed.

"Shut up Tyler, we're not under arrest." Alex jeered.

"You will be if you don't keep your mouth shut." Dona scolded, eager to drag them into the interrogation room and make them admit they knew the killer. She couldn't take it anymore, these kids were the closest thing to the truth about the silent killer. "You, come with me."

Emily became uneasy, she turned to her friends and back to Dona. " Me? no way. I'm not going..."

"Shhh" Dona suddenly hushed her and all eyes turned to her. They traced her eyes and she was staring outside. A movement had caught her attention and she could swear she saw a shadow.

"... anywhere with you. You could be the killer for all we know." Emily kept yapping, unaware of the tension that just rose around them.

"Shhh!" They all shushed her. Dona reached for the gun strapped to her waist.

"Get down and don't move a muscle." She said and cautiously moved towards the door. She swiped it open and pointed the gun to her left and then to her right. She heard light footsteps and leaves shuffle. Her grip on the gun tightened and she walked towards the noise. Dona hid behind a wall and as the footsteps increased, she braced herself. Once she felt it very close, she jumped out and pointed the gun at the intruder.

"Whoa, Dona hey! it's me." Jack yelled.

"Jack? What the fuck! I could have shot you. What the hell are you doing?"

"I should ask you the same." Jack replied and gestures towards the kids who were trying so hard to get a peek of what was going on.

Dona marched towards the door. "Keep your head down or I'll blow it off." The kids quickly moved back to their positions, behind the desk and under the tables. "They know something."

"They're just kids Dona, what could they possibly know."

"More than you do, trust me. They've been to every murder scene left by the killer."

"They're just bored and I think they're actually trying to help."

"You don't involve yourself in a murder case just because you're bored Jack." Dona snapped back. Her demeanor had changed, first she looked desperate, now she's angry. She thought the kids are the reason she hadn't found the killer. Either they were involved or one of them is the killer.

"Listen Dona, I know how you feel but these kids are not the problem."

"How do you know that?"

"I've been keeping an eye on them, they're just curious that's all."

Dona heaved a defeated sigh. "Fine." She still doesn't trust them but then again, they're just kids and haven't done anything wrong… yet.

A moving car out the streets honked so loud and Dona jolted, her hands reached for the gun she always kept on her bed stand as the lights from the car flashed across her room and disappeared. She let out a heavy sigh.

"This God forsaken town, look what it has done to me." She muttered to herself and collapsed back on the bed. She sighed again and looked across her room staring into the still darkness. She stared at it for so long she saw it turn into a moving shadow. She swiftly turned to the side and switched on the bed lamp. "I must be crazy."

She flipped the blanket off her. Her wandering thoughts has made sleep impossible or maybe it was too much caffeine. She had promised herself to turn it down a notch. Not after what she saw on the bus, now she has to live on caffeine and booze if she wanted to get to the bottom of these murder cases with her mind intact.

She pushed open the windows and a cold shiver ran through her spine. The gentle night breeze kept whispering, something was wrong, it would carry the horror in the air, keep you awake and bothered but it would never tell you what went wrong. It's like the answers right in front of you, yet you can't figure it out. The daunting buts and ifs in your head, constantly looking above your shoulder, checking twice when you hear a knock, it's like someone's got us on choke and you don't need to be a victim to be afraid.

Dona wasn't one to panic, she's a detective for Christ's sake so tell me why the thought of the bus driver's body parts gave her the creeps. The only witness that could have given her an insight and then it hit her. *What if the killer comes for me next?* If the kids were right and the killer followed this pattern, she could be next.

The fear started to creep back in and Dona couldn't help but imagine what it feels like to be killed. Does he torture them first? Make it quick or slow and painful? Does he kill his victims before cutting them up or just keep them alive and watch them suffer till they bleed to death.

Nothing she wants more than an honourable death. It would be a shame to die in the hands of a coward who can't show his face. How do you fight what you don't know?

She needed to slow down the thoughts that ran wild in her head and most of all, she needed to be with somebody. Jack was the only person she could think of. She threw on her pants, a jacket and left.

Few minutes later, she showed up at his doorstep. Jack swung the door open after she must have knocked a few times. He didn't say a word as soon as he saw her but he raised a brow obviously wondering what she was doing at his doorstep as such an odd hour. Dona held up a paper bag with a bottle of alcohol she bought on her way. Jack stepped aside and she went in.

"There's a rampaged psycho on a killing spree and here you are, roaming the streets."

"That killer is the same reason I'm here."

Jack chuckled. "Couldn't sleep?"

Dona sighed and sat on the couch, her head tilted back as she stared at the ceiling. Jack went into the kitchen and returned with two glasses.

"You know a case always look impossible till you solve it." Jack said as he opened up the bottles and poured drink into the glasses. "Most times, it's not when you're looking you find clues, it's when you're not."

Dona took her drink and gulped it down at a go. "Whoa, easy detective." Jack blurts out.

"If I get my hand on him, I will make him suffer."

"Well someone's suffering right now I and it's not the killer."

"Whose side are you on?" Dona provoked.

Jack laughed out loud, he always knew what to say to get on her nerves and Dona would fall for it every single time. He was always one to make jokes in serious matters, still he had a keen eye for details and always figured out the most complex cases. Dona refilled her glass and gulped it down again. Jack took the glass from her.

"Easy there, tell me what happened."

"Someone must have seen something. He's not invisible, is he?"

"It's not his first rodeo Dona, he strikes when no one's looking."

Dona turned to him with a serious face. "If this was your case, how would you solve it?"

"I'd use myself as bait, he can't escape if he's standing right in front of me, right?" Jack replied with a smirk.

"You don't know who or where he'll strike next, that's impossible."

Jack stared deep into her eyes. "Is it? Follow the pattern Dona, that is the easiest way to nab a serial killer." Jack could see the fear build up in Dona's eyes. He knew what that means. She's on the verge of giving up. She must have used all the tricks in the book yet nothing seemed to work. It's normal with detectives, not every case is a walk in the park but he's never seen Dona this scared. She has tried on several occasions to mask her fear with logic; *He's human after all. He'll eventually slip up and I'll be there to catch him.* But Jack knows, he could see right through her. If it was that easy, the killer would have been caught years ago. Maybe Dona is the breakthrough Riverwood needed, maybe she's not. Either way, every effort counts. Jack cups her chin, trying to calm her nerves.

"Learn to control your emotions, if there's one thing I know, your fears gives them strength."

"Jack, if the kids are right and the killer sticks to his pattern, I might be next."

Dona stared at him, their eyes locked and it got quiet. "let him come."

The mood got intense. Dona wasn't waiting for Jack to make a move, she needed the distraction.

And with a sudden move, she leaned in and kissed Jack. She paused and looked him deep in the eyes to make sure he wanted it too. Jack pulled her closer and they kissed passionately. Dona hoped on his body, her legs around his waist as they undressed themselves.

Getting laid was all the therapy session Dona needed, she didn't have it in mind at first but thank goodness it happened. Now all of sudden, her fears had vanished. She wondered why she was scared I'm the first place. She would eventually stand face to face with the killer if she truly believed she would catch him so why was she running from him when in fact all she wants is to catch up to him. *Fear is an illusion,* she said to herself, *a thought we create in our head.* Maybe Jack was right, I have to control my emotions. He gently strode her back, the back and forth was soothing for her and she didn't want it to end but she had to go. She suddenly feel silly for being scared in the first place.

Dona slipped from his arm, scanned the room for where he might have tossed her underwear and started to put on her clothes. Jack stared at her, not a word from his mouth.

"Don't look at me like that, we're not lovers." Dona jested.

Jack said nothing, s smirk grew on his lips and he just continued to stare at her. Dona threw on her jacket and headed towards the door. "Be careful."

"Awwn, you're sweet, aren't you?' Dona replied before shutting the door.

Dona got back to her apartment and felt the urge to check the rooms if there was any intruder. Maybe it was her security instincts that kicked in or she was in fact still scared. She kept repeating Jack's words in her head. Fear is an illusion. A heavy sign left her lips and she crashed on her bed.

It'd been almost a week since the bus driver went missing and not a clue as to where he could possibly be found. He was probably dead, none of the Killer's victims has even been found alive but deep down, Dona hoped she would find him and he would be the breaking point of her case.

A loud honk brought Dona back to reality. She had been daydreaming a lot and wasn't even aware she drove slowly in the middle of the road. It's been a long day and it was already late. "Sorry!" She yelled at the angry driver who drove past her. Dona stopped at a gas station, filled her tank and went into the store. "Can I use the restroom?" She asked the cashier who simply nodded with his eyes glued to the TV screen. She turned to leave and bumped into Emma.

"Detective?"

"Emma, hey. Shouldn't you be at home with your doors locked?"

"I can't isolate myself forever, can I?" Emma replied with a question.

Dona gave her a soft smile and nodded. "Stay safe."

She pushed the restroom door open and her eyes widened at the sight of Tyler and Maya. What the hell. Looks like these two were about to make out. They are both shocked to see her and a flood of embarrassment flushed their faces. Dona simply nodded and turned back out. She really did not want to know whatever it is that went on between them.

Maya giggled as soon as she left. "We should go."

"Yeah. That was close." Tyler added.

They walked back out to the store. Tyler flashed his eyes around to check if he would still see her. "I think she's gone." Maya said to him.

"Why don't you wait in the car, I'm gonna get some stuff. Want anything?"

"Nah, I'm good." Maya replied as she took the keys from Tyler and headed out. Tyler grabbed a few bags of chips and some soda and took it up to the counter.

Detective Dona caught his attention on the television which was on mute. She had a bunch of reporters around her with microphones and recorders. They all had one or two questions to ask and with the way she moved past them, it seemed like she didn't answer any. Probably used the old ' no comment' comment on them.

"Goodluck detective, you're gonna need it." Tyler muttered to himself. He paid for the chips and soda and left.

"That was quick." Maya said as soon as she saw him coming. Tyler took the car keys from her and got in the car. "I was thinking…'

"Aaaahhhhh!!!" A loud screeching sound grabbed the attention of Tyler and Maya and their expression changed into a shocked look. Tyler jolted out the car. He flashed his eyes around and settled on

Emma across the road. He ran up to her, Maya scurried right behind him. His face picked up the horror in Emma's eyes.

"What happened?"

Emma stood frozen, her hands pointed at what seemed to be a finger.

"Oh my God." Maya yelled and turned her face away in disgust. "That ring Tyler, that's…" Maya stuttered.

"Detective Dona."

CHAPTER TWELVE

Brewing Storm

There were days that felt like they told a mournful story. The whole day had not felt like it usually did, and as the sun was setting on this day, it felt like it was bringing to a close the energy the day had expelled. The sky was all shades of orange and pink, a beautiful sight that seemed out of place given the somber mood that had settled over the town.

What was going on was like a silent war. The town still reeling from the death of Dona and the beautiful display no one was seeking to catch.

Jack was standing in the opposite direction of Tyler's house, leaning on the wall of the building behind him. He has not processed his feelings concerning the Dona's death. He had mostly been numb and angry. He should have insisted she stayed longer at his place, maybe he would not have had to be here.

Dona's death had shaken the whole town.–For Jake, it had left a hollow in his heart. She was a pain in his ass but he would pick that over anything now.

His attention was drawn back to the house he was watching as a police car screeched to a halt. The back doors opened and a young guy stepped out. It was Tyler Martin. He was a college kid on a sports scholarship. Jack had done his research on Tyler and knew he was a popular kid who was well liked by his peers. He was also loyal to those he cared about.

The backdoor to the left admitted a young lady who quickly closes the door and walks round the car to the other side. He identified her as Maya Thompson. She had long curly hair that bounced with each step. Jack had learned that Maya was a creative person and also a college student with divorced parents. She was in a relationship with Tyler.

The police officer driving the car also got down and walked towards them. A young lady in her late 20s came down at the other end of the car as Tyler carefully took her hand. That was Emma, the person who first saw the remains of Dona. Jack watched as the police officer told them something he could not make out from his position. He watched as the officer patted a shaken Emma who nodded at whatever the officer was telling her.

He watched as the car drove off and he thought about what he had to do.

He had to question young adults who were college students mostly about a traumatizing experience they have had. He didn't like dealing with young people, but he had to do this. For Dona.

He took a deep breath and just as he was about to move, the front door opened and a middle aged couple came out onto the porch. Jack's eyes locked onto them and he thought about what he knew about them. That was Tom and Karen Martin, Tyler's parents. They ran a bunch of businesses and they were very comfortable. They were standing there, concern etched on their faces. He paused and almost swore. He had to get them away from the house to be able to face those kids. He reached into his pocket and pulled a business card from his pocket. He noticed that Tyler's mum looked past the trio as they approached the door directly at him. He stood upright and walked away calculatedly from the spot he was standing.

Emma, Tyler, and Maya were all visibly shaken, their faces pale and their eyes red from crying. Emma still had the blank horrified look on her face and Tyler's parents led them to sit and sat with them.

Nobody said anything for a while and suddenly a phone vibrated somewhere.

They all looked at each other and realised it was from Tyler's dad. He stood up and excused himself as he walked away from them and brought out his phone from his pocket.

"Can I make you tea, or get you water at least?" Tyler's mum asked.

Emma turned towards her and smiled, one that didn't reach her eyes and said, she was okay.

Tyler's dad walked back to the living room. " the call is from the office, they say its an emergency we need to attend to." Tyler's mum got up and patted Emma's hair. She kissed Tyler on his forehead and sent a smile Maya's way. Her husband was by the door and she knew that meant it was time to go. She got her hand bag from the dining table and stepped out after her husband. Tyler and Maya's eyes met, questions evident but they turned back to Emma who was still shaky.

They heard the car start in the driveway and the engine revving as Tyler's parents pulled out of the driveway to wherever they were needed.

Maya decided to bring Emma some water to help her calm her nerves. Just as she was about going to the kitchen, there was a knock on the door.

Their eyes turned to the door at the same time, confused, they were not expecting any visitor. The first thing anyone in their situation would think was, the killer had found them. But if the killer was truly behind that door, would he bother to knock? Emma held her heart in her chest as it threatened to thump out of its place. Her hands quivered as she held on to Tyler, voice barely audible when she said , " Are... are we expecting anyone...?" she stuttered, her voice breaking as she trembled. "Are you expecting anyone? Tyler?" she repeated.

Maya remained frozen where she stood, her eyes darting between Tyler and the door. If she had not cared so much for Tyler, would she be okay putting herself in this uncomfortable situation? She wouldn't do it for Emma, she never cared for her, after all, she used to suspect she was making a move on Tyler. She gesticulated with her hands to ask what they should do.

Tyler rose from the couch and walked towards the door. Though his weight felt heavy under his subtly shaking legs, he tried to look strong for the ladies. His heart thudded in his chest, and his eyes scanned the living room for a weapon, supposing it was who they thought it was. It was just the flower vase by the corner of the door, the one Maya gifted his parents. Would that be enough to slam the head of the killer with and buy them some time? What if he peeps through the peephole and a noose of the gun was staring back at him? No, it was not the killer's MO to kill with a gun. But...but how else would the killer get rid of three of them. *Oh*...his heart calmed a little as he remembered Emma was the person who found Dona first. If anything, she was in danger, not them. All he could do was try to save her, but he wouldn't lay down his life for her.

Maya sat by Emma, as they watched Tyler together. He was standing in front of the door now, ready to look through the hole. He hadn't used in a long time to know it was now obscured from lacking of cleaning. He sighed heavily and decided to open the door instead.

Slowly, just a crack, his head poking out to see who it was. The man he'd had a little memory of, familiar but his eyes sort of looked scary. "Can I help you?" Before he could land with his question, Jack did not wait for an invitation as he pushed the door open and barged in, his huge frame pushing Tyler out of the way.

"What the...?" Tyler trailed off, following Jack into the living room. He thought he should pick the vase, but he hesitantly shut the door instead.

"Don't so anything stupid," Jack warned as his he took a quick glance around the room, until his eyes landed on Emma who looked so stiff, like her bones would crack if she moved. He smiled and walked towards her, with a purposeful stride.

"Hey, I didn't invite you in" Tyler declared, trying to keep up with Jack. "What do you want?"

"Hey!" Tyler shouted again. " You can't just barge into someone's house like this!"

Jack ignored him, walking directly towards Emma. Tyler got to him and grabbed his arm and in a blink, Jack threw Tyler on the floor on his back. Emma and Maya jumped from their seats and instinctively run towards Tyler. They stopped in their tracks as Jack looked up at them.

"What do you want?" Maya cried, as Emma started wheezing with tears on her face. Tyler got up at that point and threw a punch at Jack but Jack's reflexes were faster as he caught the punch mid air and twisted Tyler's hand to the back.

"I'm going to call the police!" Tyler threatened, as he struggled to break free from the lock.

Jack smiled, a cold and calculated smile. "Go ahead and call them," he said. "I'd love to have a chat with them."

Tyler's face faltered, unsure of what to do. Jack released his hand just then and walked towards Emma and Maya. "Sit down," Jack commanded, his voice leaving no room for argument. Maya quickly helped Emma back to the chair and sat down beside her. "Emma, I need to ask you some questions," Jack said, his voice firm but controlled.

Tyler hovered over them, his face reddening with anger. "You do not have a right to be here, you need to leave. Now. Or I'll call the police."

Tyler hesitated, phone half-raised. Jack did not acknowledge him.

"Start talking," Jack said to Emma. "Tell me exactly what happened when you found Dona's body parts."

Tyler walked to stand between Emma and Jack, folding his arms " you do not break into my house and start asking questions like you own the place." Jack looked at Tyler and said nothing.

Jack turned his attention back to Emma. "So, Emma, can you tell me exactly what happened when you found Dona's body?" he asked, his eyes boring into hers.

Emma looked from Tyler to Maya and back to this man that has just barged into the place. She said a little prayer in her heart as she wished the last 24 hours could just be erased forever. This man they do not know is asking questions and she couldn't get her mouth to move.

Emma swallowed hard, her eyes darting nervously to Tyler and Maya before returning to Jack. "I...I was just walking out of the store, we were leaving for home and I stepped out first and I saw her. I didn't see anyone else around, and I didn't hear anything weird."

Jack nodded. "And what about you, Tyler? What did you see?"

Tyler set his jaw and said nothing. Jack smiled coldly, "...any one of you could be the next person to be killed, so you either start responding and let me take it from here or… you know..", he ran his finger over his neck.

Tyler hesitated and shuddered, glancing at Emma before responding. "I didn't see anything. I was just standing in the supermarket with Maya, we were about to step out and then Emma screamed." He took two steps closer to Jack and said " you really have to tell us who you are, are you from the police?"

Jack nodded, his eyes scanning the three of them. "I see," he said. "Well, I think it's time I introduced myself. My name is Jack, and I'm a private investigator. I was a friend of Dona's like you may have not thought and I'm determined to find out who killed her." Tyler slowly sat in a chair as Jack revealed who he was.

Maya spoke up, her voice quiet. "We have also been looking into this, there's a pattern where the first person who finds the last victim becomes the next. We have reasons to believe Dona found the Uber driver and that's why she is dead ."

Emma's voice trembled and she shuddered "I... I am going to be killed. They will find me…. I am going to be killed. Oh God!". She held on to her chest tightly and tried to breathe .

Jack leaned forward. " Hey, breathe, I'm here to help." Emma choked back a sob.

Jack pulled out a notebook, scribbling notes. "Walk me through everything you can remember" he glanced at Tyler and Maya "and everything you have gathered." For the next hour, Jack methodically questioned Emma, then Tyler, then Maya.

The room went silent, the only sound was the heavy breathing of the three occupants. Maya spoke up and broke the silence "So what do we do?"

Jack's eyes hardened. "We keep her close. Protected. Until we understand what's happening."

Emma's eyes were wide with fear. "What can I do?" she asked Jack.

Jack's expression was unreadable. " I will do everything I can to protect you, Emma."

The teenagers exchanged nervous glances. The game had just changed, and they were now players in a dangerous investigation where the stakes were life and death.

"I'm going to keep you all under surveillance," Jack said finally. "I want to know everything you do, every move you make."

"You're going to stay with me for a while, Emma. Until this blows over."

Emma's face went pale, and she looked like she was going to pass out. But Jack just nodded, his expression unyielding.

"It's for your own safety," he said. "And mine."

Tyler furrowed his brows and squinted, " what do you mean 'and yours'? Is there something we are missing?"

Jack did not say anything. Then after a moment he closed his notebook and looked up. " I don't need to be kept safe, I need to get to the root of this". He stood up curtly and turned to Emma. "You should get some of your things, we should leave right now".

Tyler stood up almost immediately and turned to Jack, " we don't even know if we can trust you, we don't know where you live or anything, why should we trust her with you?"

Maya and Emma also stood up confused at who to trust or stay away from.

Jack looked squarely at Tyler and said "...if I was going to harm anyone, none of you will be left standing." He turned towards the door. " We are fighting the same cause here but you don't have the strategy to keep her safe, I do. You have 10 minutes to meet me outside." Maya and Tyler looked at each other then turned to a scared Emma.

Tyler and Maya kept looking at the sedan as it sped down the road. Emma had packed a few things and followed Jack for protection.

"We have to tell the others what's going on," Maya said to Tyler. Tyler sighed and walked back to the house and Maya followed suit.

They walked straight to Tyler's room and got cozy in each other's arms on his bed.

Jack walked into the kitchen, where Emma was sipping coffee and staring out the window. "Morning," he said, pouring himself a cup.

"Morning," Emma replied, turning to face him. Her eyes looked tired, but she managed a weak smile.

Jack sat down across from her. "How are you holding up?" he asked.

Emma shrugged. "I'm okay, I guess. It's just weird being here, in your house."

Jack nodded. "I know it's not easy. But I need to keep you safe until we catch this guy."

Emma nodded, taking a sip of her coffee. They sat there in silence for a moment, the only sound the ticking of the clock on the wall.

It had been days since Emma had been staying at Jack's house. At first, she refused to stay in the room Jack gave to her and every morning, he would wake up early and find Emma sat at the kitchen table, a cup of coffee in front of her. She was mostly lost in thoughts and barely said anything to him. Jack liked it that way, he was not one for conversations.

As the days went by, Emma settled into a routine. She'd spend her days watching TV, reading books, or helping Jack with his investigation. Jack was starting to see a different side of her, one that wasn't so scared and vulnerable.

Jack appreciated how Emma had opened up to him. She shared her thoughts and feelings about the investigation, and they spent hours discussing what they knew. Emma was smart, and she had a way of thinking through problems logically. This made their conversations productive. They would go over each clue, each piece of evidence, trying to make sense of it all.

But there were still moments when the weight of the situation would hit her hard. Jack could see the fear in her eyes when she thought about the killer still being out there. He wanted to reassure her, but he knew he couldn't promise her safety. All he could do was keep her close and watch over her.

As the days passed, Emma started to feel more like herself. She laughed at Jack's corny jokes and occasionally shared tips from her course of study. It was nice to see her smile, even if it was just for a little while. Jack felt a bond forming between them, built on trust and the shared goal of finding the truth.

But as much as he appreciated her company, Jack knew it was time for Emma to return to her own home. He felt it was important for her to be in a familiar place, surrounded by the things that reminded her of normal life.

Finally, the day came when Jack decided it was time. He drove Emma back to Tyler's house. When they pulled into the driveway, Emma hesitated, her hand resting on the door handle. Jack turned to her, his expression serious. "You can do this, Emma. Just take it one step at a time."

Emma took a deep breath, her eyes fixed on the house.

Jack nodded. "It's okay to be scared. Just remember, you're not alone in this. I'll be nearby if you need anything."

With a small smile, Emma finally opened the door and stepped out of the car. Jack watched as she walked up to the front door, pausing for a moment before knocking. The sound echoed in the quiet afternoon air.

He watched carefully as she stepped inside, the door closing softly behind her. With that, Emma was back in her own world, but Jack knew that their journey was far from over.

As Emma walked back into Tyler's house, she felt a sense of relief wash over her. She was finally home. But as she looked around at the familiar rooms, she couldn't shake the feeling that something was off. She felt like she was being watched, and the hairs on the back of her neck stood on end. She tried to brush it off, telling herself she was just spooked from her time with Jack. But as she walked upstairs to her room, she couldn't help but wonder if she was really safe. Tyler was at her bedroom door, waiting. She walked right into his arms and they stayed in each others arms silently.

***

Tyler slumped on his bed, staring at the ceiling. His room was a mess, clothes tossed around and sports equipment scattered everywhere. He felt restless, his mind racing with thoughts about Emma and everything happening with the investigation.

It had been two days since Emma came back from Jack's place. She had been quiet than usual and he knew there was little he could do to take away the fear that was in her eyes. He was not the one who was directly in line of danger but he was a little scared.

He didn't like Jack's approach but he was relieved that he was involved because he clearly was more guarded than they were.

Just as he was starting to relax, he heard his mom's voice calling out to him.

"Tyler, honey, we're home!" she exclaimed.

Tyler groaned, not feeling like talking to anyone. But he knew he couldn't avoid his parents forever. With a sigh, Tyler pushed himself off the bed and walked down the hall. He wasn't in the mood for a long conversation, but he knew his mom wouldn't take no for an answer.

As he entered the living room, his parents beamed at him. His mom rushed over to give him a hug.

"Hey, sweetie, we've got some amazing news!" she said, barely containing her excitement.

Tyler raised an eyebrow, curious despite himself. "What is it?" he asked grudgingly.

His dad grinned. "We won an all-expense-paid trip to Hawaii! Can you believe it?"

Tyler's eyes widened. "Hawaii? How did you guys win that?"

Karen clasped her hands together, her eyes sparkling. " Two weeks in Hawaii!"

Tyler's mouth dropped open. "Seriously? How did that happen?"

His mom waved her hand dismissively. "Oh, it was just a lucky draw at a luncheon your father attended. We're just thrilled!"

Tyler tried to ask more questions, but his parents just laughed and said they were just lucky. They seemed really excited, but Tyler couldn't shake off the feeling that something wasn't quite right.

As they continued to talk, Tyler's mind wandered back to Emma and the whole Dona situation. He couldn't believe his parents were so carefree, like nothing was wrong.

Just as Tyler started to tune back in to the conversation, his mom dropped a bombshell.

"We leave tomorrow, sweetie!" she said excitedly.

Tyler's eyes snapped back to his mom's face. "Tomorrow? That's really soon."

His dad nodded. "We know, but we can't pass up this opportunity. We'll be gone for two weeks."

"But—" Tyler started, but his parents were already lost in their excitement, discussing what they would pack and how they would spend their time in Hawaii. He felt completely left out.

As he stood there, feeling a sense of isolation, something nagged at him. The investigation into Dona's murder wasn't over, and he couldn't shake the feeling that the killer was still out there, lurking.

Karen turned back to him, catching his worried expression. "Tyler, you should be excited for us! This will be a great break for the whole family. Think of all the fun we'll have!"

"Sure," he muttered, forcing a smile. Inside, he felt a tight knot of anxiety. He wanted to be happy for his parents, but he couldn't help but worry about Emma and the danger that seemed to follow them all.

What if they left and something happened? What if the killer targeted Emma next?

"Tyler, are you even listening?" Karen's voice broke through his thoughts.

"Yeah, I'm listening," he replied quickly. "I just... I need to think about things. Can we talk about this later?"

Tom frowned, his earlier excitement dimming. "We just want you to share in our happiness, son."

"Right," Tyler said, his mind still elsewhere. He could feel the weight of the world pressing down on him.

"Where is Emma by the way? Is she better?" Karen suddenly turned to Tyler and asked.

"Yes, she's been in her room." Tyler responded in a low tone. He wondered if they actually thought about the things going on and how bad thing could get.

"Don't worry, everything will be sorted out. The police won't let anything happen to her," Karen smiled nervously and turned to Tom so they could mumble on.

As his parents returned to their planning, Tyler felt a sense of urgency. He needed to do something about Emma's safety, his and Maya's safety.

CHAPTER THIRTEEN

The Devil in the Details

It is said that the Devil is good at hiding in plain sight as people tend to overlook the details that reveal his true nature. A master of deception, a shape shifter, able to assume many forms, and his influence can be felt in every aspect of human life. But despite his evil ways, at least the Devil has a motivation, a reason for his actions. He seeks power, control, and chaos, and even though his methods are twisted, they are driven by a desire to achieve his goals.

But what about those who commit evil without motivation? What do you call someone who inflicts harm and suffering on others simply for the sake of it, without any discernible reason or purpose? Is it not more terrifying to think that there are individuals who can perpetrate evil without any motivation, without any desire for gain or power, but simply because they can?

This kind of evil is perhaps more insidious and disturbing, because it seems to defy explanation. It is a randomness and senselessness, that can be more unsettling than the most calculated and deliberate acts of evil. At least with the Devil, you know what you're up against. You know what drives him, and you can prepare yourself accordingly. But with this other kind of evil, you're faced with a void, an emptiness that has no bottom.

This kind of evil is a manifestation of the abyss, a void that stares back at us with no eyes, face and no drive. It shows us that evil can be a fundamental aspect of human nature, a part of us that can't be explained or rationalized. It's a darkness that lurks within, and it's a terror that can't be escaped, because it's a part of ourselves.

It almost makes the Devil with his motivations and desires appear more preferable to this other kind of evil that had not reason, purpose or end. Truly evil and take many forms, some of which are more terrifying than others.

The Riverwood's serial killer had been a puzzling case for the police, as they have tried to understand the motivations behind the disappearances. Similarly, the Sunset Ridge new killer. The police had found no connection between the victims, other than the fact that the victims were witnesses. How then the first kill begin? Did he witness something that drove the killer to find him by the bar and murder him?

Was it just a chance encounter that gave way for the killer's interest in the first victim? Did the killer see something in the victim that triggered a desire to harm him? Was the victim somehow connected to the killer's past, or was it simply a random act of violence?

It had been days since anything significant had happened. Dona had been laid to rest in a quiet ceremony. Tyler's parents had travelled, leaving him to care for their home. If it wasn't for the fact he would need financial assistance from them, he would have ran to the dorm, Emma had begun to show signs of recovery. She was no longer startled by every little thing that moved around her, and she had started to regain some of her old confidence.

Maya, too, had returned to her life as if nothing had happened. She had gone back to her routine, attending classes and hanging out with her friends, and it was as if the whole ordeal had been just a bad dream. The police still checked in on them from time to time, but it seemed that whatever the killer had been planning, it had been put on hold. Perhaps, Tyler thought, the killer had lost interest, or maybe they had been caught and had been secretly executed by the police. A town like this, had a lot of secrets.

But despite the calm that had settled over the town, Tyler could still feel something was off. He had noticed that people in college were looking at him differently, like he was a dead man walking. It was as if they expected him to be the next victim, or as if they thought he was somehow responsible for what had happened to Dona. Tyler didn't understand why they were looking at him like that, when he wasn't even the one who found Dona that day. He had been just as much a victim as anyone else.

As he walked through the campus, they would whisper to each other when he passed by, and some of them would even cross the street to avoid him. It all made his angry and frustrated. He hadn't done anything wrong, why was he being punished like he did. What about Maya? She was there too? Why didn't no one give her the stink eye? Not that he would want that for her, but what made him the odd one out? Or Emma... She was the target after all. She found Dona before any of them. How could she just move on like that?

But as he thought about it more, Tyler realized that his worry wasn't just about himself. He was more worried about Emma than she was about herself. She was taking everything in stride, like she was just waiting for the other shoe to drop. Tyler, on the other hand, was on edge all the time, waiting for something to happen. He would find himself looking over his shoulder, expecting to see someone lurking in the shadows.

It was ironic, she had been the one who had been through the most trauma but she was obviously handling it better than he was. He was the one who was supposed to be strong, but he was falling apart. And Emma, who had every right to be broken, was somehow holding it together.

Whenever their eyes met, he could see the pain and fear in her eyes, and it broke his hear that she had to go through that mental torture and would probably still get killed in the end by the psychotic killer. *Well let's hope it doesn't come to that…*

Tyler had finally realized that he was worried about Emma, and he didn't want to leave her alone. And that's when it dawned on him he had slowly started caring about her. This case, this whole horror show has changed him in a way. He was no longer the selfish, arrogant person who only cared about himself. It felt strange, but it also felt right.

Tyler thought about how he had always been the type of person who looked out for himself first. But now, he felt responsible for her. He felt guilty for not being able to do more, for not being able to make things better for her.

One night, he invited Maya over for a drink. She came briefly but she thought she could get away with giving a lot of excuses.

"As much as we want to get to the bottom of this, we are not the police. Remember, we do our investigations from a distance. They are watching Emma, we can't get in the way," she told him. But deep down, she was just scared. Anyone would be, even Tyler was.

But he believed it was the right thing to never leave Emma, keep her company even if they were not close. There were cameras in the house, which allowed the police to monitor the house. But nothing would be better then a human presence.

As Maya stood in the doorway, she gazed at Tyler with an expectant expression. "Hey, Alex said we could come over…" she said casually. "Want to come with me?"

Tyler hesitated, as he glanced at Emma's door and saw she was sitting on her couch, her eyes fixed at some distant point. Each time, she tried to hide the fact that she was breaking down inside, but it would slip out in some unconscious way. Like this moment where she definitely had no idea she was staring into the void.

"I don't know, Maya," he stuttered, still uncertain. "I think I'll stay here with Emma."

Maya's expression didn't change, but Tyler could see that she was a little disappointed. He could tell from the way her eyes shifted to Emma in the background. "Okay, suit yourself," she heaved, but it was not from a place of anger. Actually, she was happy to get as far away as possible from that house, from Emma. "I'll text you later."

As Maya turned to leave, Tyler felt a tempting urge to follow her. He could have easily walked out with her, but Emma's predicament held him back. Whether it was a genuine concern or his instincts telling him to stay home instead of heading out with Maya.

Emma could sense he was staring and turned to him with a weak smile planted on her face. "Hey, I'm fine," she said softly. "You can go with Maya if you want. I'll be fine..."

But Tyler shook his head. "No, I'm good, "I'll stay here with you."

Emma smiled again. "Thanks for staying with me," she told him coldly and then stood up to usher him in.

Tyler smiled back, "Anytime," he replied as he walked in, glancing around her room like he hadn't been in there a thousand times. And he found himself sitting comfortable on her bed, unlike him. He'd never been this relaxed around her, but since the incident, they'd grown less formal.

Emma got up and got a drink and two glasses, and joined him by the bed. As Emma poured the drink into the two glasses, she thought she felt something intimate in the air. That could have been because of the way he looked at her but made her feel a closeness to him. She handed him a glass and their fingers touched, and her heart skipped. Suddenly, she sat and tried to grab his face for a kiss but his phone accidentally dropped into the glass. He tried to save his phone and ended up dropped his cup. Liquid on his clothes and the bed. It was a chaotic mess.

"Oh no, I'm so sorry!" Emma gasped in confusion, as she quickly grabbed a towel to clean up.

"It's okay," he replied immediately, because he didn't know what else to say.

The room fell silent, the awkward kind. And Tyler found himself looking up to lock eyes with the camera watching them from the corner of the room. He let out a deep sigh, and Emma followed his gaze, realizing that their private moment was being recorded. Yes, she knew it was there but it escaped her mind. She hissed, a little uneasy. She wondered who could be watching them and what they were thinking. She tried to push the thought away, focusing instead on the man in front of her, but this man equally felt so uneasy.

"I forgot that was there," she giggled and tried to touch him, give him a little comfort and apologize again for her mistake. But he gently pushed her away.

"It's okay, Emma. It's just a phone. It can be replaced. Just want to keep you company, okay?" he said, and looked away.

"Oh, yeah..."she replied like she just remembered. But it was only coming from a place of disappointment and hurt. She knew that he was upset, and she didn't want to make things worse. So she nodded and backed away, giving him the space he needed.

To make matters worse, he got up smoothly and moved to the couch. What was going to happen now? Was he still interested in her, or had she ruined everything? She looked over at him, trying to read his expression, but his face was neutral, giving away nothing

As the minutes ticked by, Emma began to notice that Tyler had become a little too quiet. She glanced over at him, trying to read his expression, it was obviously her fault he felt that way. She had overstepped, trying to kiss him, and now he was pulling away. That was not her plan. She thought he wanted to stay with her because he had been feeling same way. She regretted her actions, coupled with the feeling of embarrassment building up within her. *No, best way to not feel embarrassed is to own the moment.* She could brush it off and it would haunt her then and forever, but if she embraced the embrace the awkwardness, maybe he would laugh it off with her.

"Uh...clumsy me..." she laughed, her best attempt at making the situation less tensed that it already was. And caught a glimpse of him chuckling silently. She got up from the bed and walked over to the table, where her laptop was sitting. She opened it up and tried to act like nothing had happened by scrolling through her emails. Tyler looked up at her, a questioning expression on his face. "What are you doing?"

Emma shrugged, playing it cool. "Just checking my messages," she replied nonchalantly.. "I have a few clients who have been trying to reach me, and I need to get back to them." She didn't look back at him, for fear of meeting his gaze. She didn't want him to see the embarrassment and regret that was written all over her face.

Tyler adjusted himself on the seat, finally feeling relaxed. He was sure that they were both feeling a little confused after what had just happened. He wasn't sure how to act. He wondered if it would have been better to just go with Maya when she had told him about Alex's invitation. At least then, he would have been able to avoid this situation.

But he had made up his mind to stay with Emma, and now he was stuck with the consequences. He didn't want to leave her now, not after what had just happened. That would be too weird, and he didn't want to hurt her feelings any more than he already had.

As he sat there, trying to think of what to say next, he suddenly had an idea. "You know, you should hang out with us sometime," he said. He didn't mean it, not really, but he was trying to make small talk, to fill the silence that had fallen between them.

Finally, Emma glanced back at him, a smile on her face, but he could see she was somewhat amused. "You mean after the killer has marked me, I don't think so," she replied, sarcastically. , her voice dripping with sarcasm. She pushed aside her laptop, shutting it with a snap, and walked back to the bed with her eyes fixed on his face.

Something lewd about it that scared him a little. But he believed he was overthinking, it was normal to feel that way after what he had just avoided. Imagine Maya walking in on them. The camera too. And maybe he was too disciplined to cheat on his girlfriend, maybe.

He felt a flush rise to his cheeks as it dawned on him that she has seen right through him. They were both making individual efforts to make small talk and pretend like everything was okay. She had called him out first. And he didn't know what to say next, so he just sat there wondering how he was going to act normal. He took a deep breath, as he tried to calm himself down. When he looked over at Emma, trying to meet her eyes. He realized she was still smiling at him, and he knew that he was in trouble.

He giggled, blushing red like a pony. He knew he wasn't supposed to be doing that, not when she just mentioned her fears. Which were very valid. However, she wasn't helping matters with the way her eyes were fixed on him, and her amused smile. He cleared his throat to push down the strong urge to cackle, one that would have betrayed how sorry he truly felt for her. "I just don't get it," He said, shaking his head. "Why would someone do something like that? It's just so senseless."

"I know, it's really disturbing," she replied. "But sometimes, these kinds of killers are trying to get attention."

"What kind of attention is worth an innocent person's life?"

She shrugged and slowly lay on her bed. She hadn't given up making him feel at ease with her. But he barely noticed, not while the topic of Sunset Ridge's killer is ongoing. "I've been thinking about that," he started. "Why is the killer always leaving these tokens behind? If they're a copycat, can't they just do what the original did. Leave just the flowers behind? Why must we get gruesome details of the body parts of the victims?"

She crossed her legs and grinned widely when she noticed he was barely looking at her. Then she sighed and sat back up, frustrated. Bored out of her mind, her eyes began to glaze over as she stared at the flower on her table, as her thoughts slowly drifted away.

"You know these things," she spoke so quickly, "the killer is trying to make a point. Life imitates art, death is the canvas. Flowers bloom from flesh to remind us that even in death, beauty still exists. It's all in the flowers darling." She jumped out of her bed and trotted to the flower on her table and inhaled it. Then she opened her drawer and pulled out a little bag that contained some seeds that she tangled before the mirror in front of her. Her reflection smiled back at her.

Tyler's eyes narrowed as he turned to the camera briefly and back at Emma. Her eyes were closed as she took out one of it and smelt it. A peaceful smile spread across her face. "Even the seed smells great."

He wondered if she was admiring the strange seed or reveling in the darkness that had created it. "What kind of flower is that, Emma?" he asked, his voice taking on a cautious tone. Emma opened her eyes and turned her gaze to Tyler with a chilling focus. "It's a genetically modified flower , violets though…" she answered and slowly put it back in the drawer. Then she pulled out a petal from the vase and began savoring it. "This violet has been made to only bloom under very specific conditions." She paused, and watched Tyler from the mirror. "It needs a certain kind of nourishment," she continued with a voice that dropped below a whisper, "... a certain kind of... fertilizer."

"What kind of fertilizer?" he asked, though he wasn't sure he wanted to know the answer.

Emma's smile grew wider, "The kind that only death can provide," she answered and her breath caressed the petal like a lover's kiss.

Tyler nodded slightly and turned his eyes away. And he became silent, like they weren't having a serious conversation. Emma didn't notice at first, too caught up in her own thoughts and the thing on her hand.

Tyler's eyes landed on the floor, the walls, anywhere but on her or the flower. He nodded again, an even more imperceptible movement, as if acknowledging a conversation that had already moved on without him.

When he shifted his eyes to Emma, she was staring at the flower and her fingers absently stroked the petal.

Tyler was acutely aware of every passing moment. He felt like he was drowning in the silence, his skin prickled with unease, his heart beat just a fraction too fast.

As he sat there, frozen in discomfort, his gaze began to wander. For the first time, he took in the details in the room. The plants and flowers which made sense since Emma was a botanist, but there was something off about the way they were arranged, or the types of plants she had chosen. Strange how he hadn't noticed that she had a weird fascination for twisted art.

On the walls, there were pictures of flowers and plants. But the quotes underneath them were what really caught his attention. One of them said, "The beauty of nature is often accompanied by a deadly price". It sounded like a warning, and it made Tyler hold his breath.

It was like he had stumbled into a world that was both beautiful and scary, and he wasn't sure what to make of it. He glanced at the camera again, as if subtly signalling whoever was watching. But he didn't see Emma smiling at him.

That's when he suddenly remembered. He had a project that needed to be attended to. It was due soon and he was already behind schedule. Tyler's eyes snapped back into focus, and he turned to Emma with a forced smile plastered on his face. "I'm so sorry, Emma, but I just realized I have something to do. I… I completely…. Forgot about it…" He stuttered as his words tumbled out in a rush. Slowly he rose, his eyes darting towards the door.

"So soon?" She asked without looking at him.

"Yeah, but I'll be back soon. You'll see…"

She sighed, "…don't keep me waiting, Tyler. You promised to keep me company.

"I will be back…promise." He replied as quickly as he could, as he made his way to the door. His fingers trembled a bit. She caught wind of it but she didn't react at all. Instead, her eyes remained planted on him through the mirror and he knew she was aware he was escaping her room.

As he walked out of her room, fear settled in the pit of his stomach. The conversation with Emma had left him with more questions than answers. It didn't make him wonder what she was hiding, it made him think about how blind they must have all been to ignore the clear signs.

He quickly made his way to his own room, his fingers struggling desperately to operate his phone, but it was glitching and unresponsive. Earlier, the drink. He hissed and cursed his luck. At least the screen flickered, but that would do no good. He tried to restart it, but it wouldn't budge. Defeated, he flung it aside to try and gather his thoughts.

He wondered if he made a grave mistake seeking safety in his room instead of bolting for the front door. *I need to collect my thoughts.* He locked the door behind him and leaned against it, trying to calm his racing mind. The image of Emma's smile and the way she had talked about the flowers kept playing in his head. He couldn't understand why she had brought it up, or what she had meant by it.

The flowers growing in the dead bodies were a detail that only a handful of people knew about. The police had kept it under wraps, and only his clique had managed to get wind of it through their own channels. It was a secret that only a few people were privy to. Yet, Emma had mentioned it so casually like it was common knowledge.

How did she find out about it? Or maybe she was the one who orchestrated it all. *No.* He tried to convince himself it was just one big misunderstanding. She was probably under the influence of alcohol. Maybe she was high. Or she thought it would be sexy to do that and get intimate with him.

Emma had been playing everyone all along. She was a good actress too. She deliberately dropped his phone, to cut him off from his friends. It was a clever move he never anticipated.

And then it finally hit him like a ton of bricks, Emma was not the first witness, he was. He had been the one to find Emma first when she screamed. She was only luring in her next victim.

Panic set in as he tried to leave through the window, but it was stuck fast. He remembered now that it had been permanently shut for their safety, a precaution taken by the police to prevent the killer from gaining access to the house through his room. He was trapped, with no way to escape.

His eyes scanned the room frantically, searching for a weapon or anything that could be used to defend himself. He knew he couldn't underestimate Emma, not after what he had seen her do. She was a frail lady, but she had taken down so many people. He had seen the news reports, what she did to those bodies. Or maybe she had an accomplice. Maybe her accomplice was in the house. Worse, accomplices?

He spotted a heavy lamp on the bedside table and grabbed it. He wielded it tightly as he backed away from the door. He knew it was a poor substitute for a real weapon, but it was better than nothing.

He held his breath and strained his ears to pick up any other sounds. He thought he heard the door creak but perhaps that was because he didn't shut Emma's door. How reckless of him.

With the lamp clutched tightly in his hand, he felt he could do anything. He was ready to protect his life with every ounce of strength he had. Despite being in the worst situation imaginable, his room began to have the sweet, floral scent like he was in some kind of paradise. Like it was Emma's room, but he didn't have time to appreciate the irony. His priority was to get out of the house in one piece, to escape the clutches of whoever was trying to harm him.

As he slowly opened the door and tiptoed out into the hallway, his heart thumped so loudly, it looked like it was banging on his chest to be let out. Perhaps no one was coming for him, perhaps he was just being paranoid. But he still felt it somewhere that he was being watched, that unblinking eyes were trained on him from the shadows.

He glanced over at Emma's door, and it was exactly as he had left it. She was still in her room, humming a soft tune that he could have sworn were mocking him. He knew she was in there, waiting for him, waiting for the perfect moment to strike. He turned away from her door and made his way towards the stairs.

About to make his descent, he suddenly stopped and gave the stairs a good look. The stairs appeared to be moving, twisting and turning in ways that defied logic. He felt wobbly, a little confused, and his first thoughts were the drink with Emma. She drugged me didn't she? No, I barely took a sip before she tried to kiss me and knocked the cup out of my hands.

But just as he was starting to make progress, he heard the door opening behind him and Emma's calm voice answering his thoughts. "No, it wasn't the drink," Emma said, giggling. He turned to see her walking out of her room, a gas mask covering her face.

"I know it smelt like paradise while you were hiding," she continued. "That wasn't normal, was it?"

He didn't reply, he just turned back and took one step down the stairs. But his foot seemed to slip out from under him, and he nearly lost control. He grabbed onto the banister, holding on for dear life as his body swayed precariously.

The lamp fell from his hand and rolled down the stairs, shattering on the floor with a loud crash. The sound startled him, and he imagined it could have been him falling like that. He froze a little, unsure of what to do next. But as he looked back up at Emma, he saw that she was still standing there, watching him with an unblinking gaze. He knew that he had to keep moving. He took another step down, his eyes fixed on the door at the bottom of the stairs. He could see the handle, a freedom that lay beyond. But it felt so far away from him, unreachable.

He looked back again and she was moving closer, that wasn't where she had been standing. He panicked and took another step, but the stairs were now missing. He crumbled, thinking if he laid low, the fear would go away.

"I really wish it hadn't been you who found Dona…Maya was right there but you had to be the man to save the damsel in distress, didn't you?"

As Tyler crawled down the stairs, a feeling of dread washed over him. Emma's words echoed in his mind as he wondered which way to go. "I knew at some point you would find out it was me…and I hate this whole situation just as you do," she said, and her hand slapped against the banister with a loud crack. Tyler glanced back quickly, she was closer now

He continued to crawl down the stairs, his hands and feet finding holds in the worn carpet. He was careful to avoid the missing parts, which were now everywhere. And Emma's words kept coming, each one a dagger to his heart. "No one ever appreciates my talents, not you or your parents," she spat.

"Speaking of your parents, I really hope they enjoy their trip. A few credit card scams can really do wonders in sponsoring trips, you know. You should try it. I'm glad they bought the fake website story..."

Tyler's mind reeled as he processed her words. She had been behind the fake website, the one that had fooled his parents into leaving town. But the anger building up within him was quickly replaced by fear. Emma's smile grew wider as she gazed down at him. "You'll be my best work of art," she said excitedly. "I promise. This is just because I really like you."

Tyler's skin crawled as he heard her words. He was almost at the bottom of the stairs now, a few more moves and he would be at the door. No matter how disadvantaged, he truly believed if he moved faster, maybe he would escape.

But when he got to the door and reached out for the door handle. As he grasped it, he realized it was locked. He pulled and pulled, but it wouldn't budge. His legs gave out beneath him, and he slid down the door like a flat surface. His body, now weak and helpless. Emma's maniacal cackle boomed through the room.

"I must have made it very strong," she said proudly, "You can't blame me, when you have all those muscles." She pulled out a syringe from her back, with a coloured liquid inside. "It's time for me to disappear, two of my pinkies and your ears will be enough to convince them the killer got both of us." Tyler's heart sank as he realized what she was about to do to him. He raised a hand, his last attempt to save his life. "No, please..." he said under his tired gasps.

But Emma was unmoved. She calmly pushed his hand away, and it landed on the floor with a thud. "The others didn't even get a chance to speak," she replied coldly. "If you don't struggle, it won't hurt."

She took the syringe closer and he shut his eyes to bear the pain of whatever was going to happen to him afterwards. She jabbed him on the neck with a force that made him jerk and struggle to free himself. But it was not enough.

Tyler felt a searing pain shoot through his neck. He tried to cry out, but his voice was muffled. Emma's face was inches from his, as she whispered, "This will make it all so much easier."

"Hey!" Someone called out loudly behind them.

"SHIT," Emma's heart dropped and she turned back quickly, hiding the syringe behind her back and letting out a loud innocent scream. "Someone's in the house, he got Tyler," she cried.

"Nice try…" Alex said as he charged towards Emma.

She looked confused when she looked down at his hand and he was holding a fire extinguisher. And in a quick move, she struck Emma. She crumpled to the ground, stunned. He aimed the fire extinguisher at her and pulled the trigger, releasing a blast of foam that covered her up.

As the fog swirled around them, Alex rushed to Tyler's side, helping him to his feet. "We need to get out of here, now!" he shouted. Still groggy from the sedative, Tyler stumbled forward, only relying on Alex to guide him through the fog.

When Alex looked by the stairs, Emma was lying there incapacitated. Maybe he had passed out, there was no time to find out. As they staggered out into the fresh air, they only stopped with Ethan pulled to the curb, stopping by their side. Alex's car was packed by the road, no wonder he or Emma didn't hear him coming. And he found his way through the back yard. The police were arriving as well, just in time to stop the madness.

"She's in there," Alex yelled, almost hysterically. "Call the ambulance!!"

When the police stormed in, they thought it would be the end of the nightmare in sunset Ridge. But you should have seen the weary looks on their face when they found the house very empty.

CHAPTER FOURTEEN

Message on the Wall

There were many things that fuelled the thirst for justice. Apprehending someone who has wronged you or a loved one, or the personality that just liked justice. Ethan had been locked in more than ever since Becky has been a victim, he just wanted to make sure the person who did it to her got put away. This time, he didn't know what to think with what almost happened to Tyler. He wondered what would have happened if they did not realise quickly that night. The signs were there, thankfully, the loopholes were found quickly. Now that Emma was at large, he knew they had to get to her first or the killer does.

His phone buzzed on the desk and pulled him from his thoughts. He grabbed it and hoped for a message from Tyler or Alex, but there was nothing. Ethan sighed and felt a knot tighten in his stomach. The silence was heavy, and the longer he waited, the more anxious he became. What if she came for any of them? The police had also found it hard to track her down.

Ethan looked through his notes again. He had written down everything about Emma he knew and what others knew. She was a professional botanist who was really interested in what she did. There was something he had not figured out and it bugged him.

Being the techie of the friend group, he had checked all hotels and motels where she could have been hiding but it had yielded nothing either. She left with nothing and her phone was not connecting so that was hard to track.

The police had started investigations since the same night Emma almost killed Tyler and there had not been much luck on their end too. The police investigation took a sharp turn after the discovery of Emma's background. The detective sat in the conference room, surrounded by case files and photographs. The team had dug deep into Emma's past, and what they found was disturbing.

Emma wasn't just a casual plant enthusiast. She was a professional botanist with advanced degrees and specialized training in rare and potentially dangerous plant species. Her academic records showed a particular fascination with toxic plants and their medical applications. The forensics team had been connecting the dots between the previous murder victims and the strange botanical growths found on their body parts.

"Look at this," the forensic analyst said and spread out several photographs. "The plant species growing from the previous victims match Emma's research papers from graduate school. She published multiple studies about rare plant propagation in unusual environments."

The detective leaned forward, studying the images. The connection was becoming clearer. Emma's extensive knowledge of plants could explain how the killer managed to create those botanical altering crime evidences. Her background in botany provided the perfect cover for someone with murderous intentions. If apprehended, they were finally able to put their boss' killer away.

The police search moved to abandoned buildings and off-the-grid motels where someone could easily hide. The first location was an old motel just outside of town. The paint was peeling, and the parking lot looked like it hadn't seen a car in years.

"This is exactly the kind of place she would choose," one of the officers muttered to his partner, Detective Rodriguez. He was the one who replaced Dona at the station. They walked through the empty rooms and looked for any sign of Emma's presence.

In one of the rooms, they found something interesting. A small notebook was hidden behind a loose baseboard. The pages were filled with detailed botanical drawings.. Notes about poison extraction methods were scribbled in the margins.

"This is getting creepy," Rodriguez said and bagged the evidence. "She's been planning this for a long time."

They checked three more motels that day. Each location felt more desperate than the last. Abandoned rooms with broken furniture, evidence of quick stays, but nothing concrete that would lead them directly to Emma.

By the end of the week, they had checked over twenty potential locations. Emma was still nowhere to be found. She had vanished into thin air, barely leaving behind any traces of her or her expertise.

The evidence mounted, but Emma herself remained a ghost.

Jack had also been frequent at the station. He was a little disappointed that the signs slipped past him. He had even shared some of his finding with her. He was at the station to get an update on their search and investigation. He told the detective, "Killers like this. They can't help themselves. She'll make a mistake eventually."

The investigation continued. Photographs, evidence bags, and maps covered every available surface in the police station. Emma's face stared back from multiple photographs, her calm expression hiding whatever darkness lurked beneath.

The copycat was still out there. Emma was still out there...

The hunt had just started.

Ethan stared at the points he had jotted down and back at his laptop screen. He knew there was something hidden in the surface and it infuriated him that he could not place his hands on it. Maybe he needed to go over the conversation with his friends.

He picked his phone and started a group call.

"This is new, what's up?" Maya's voice came on. There were clicks as others joined the call. Ethan told them there was something he could feel would lead them to where Emma was. " You hacked into something or what?" Tyler joked.

Ethan sighed and insisted they do what he asked. Tyler recounted that she was a professional botanist who knew about delicate flowers and wanted to start her own garden.

Alex reminded him that she had said there are a lot of dangerous flowers and that she had not seen a lot. She later mentioned that she has grown some she genetically engineered.

Emily impatiently asked him to say what he found out.

Ethan hesitated, then spoke. "I went through Emma's research work in detail, trying to understand the processes involved in genetic flowering. She had to be in possession of certain chemicals—ones that haven't turned up in any of the police investigations. It doesn't add up. If she was working on this, where are the chemicals? Why hasn't anyone found them?"

There was silence on the line, everyone digesting this new information. Maya cleared her throat and said , "You think she hid them?"

Ethan nodded. "It's possible. And if she did, it changes everything."

Alex leaned forward, his voice low. "We need to find them."

The static noise and breaths were the only sounds as they processed the implications.

"She said it was at her small garden…" Alex slowed down as they all realised.

Ethan's mind raced. "She loves the botanical garden. It's one of her favourite places."

"We have to get Jack," Tyler breathed.

"I will call him," Maya said. They agreed not to go to the location that night. Maya got across to Jack and filled him in on the situation.

She told him that they would need him for protection mostly and getting around but Jack said he did not have the time to play catch with little children. Maya told him they were up to something and persuaded him. He told her he was going to think about it and hung up the call.

Ethan was not able to get any sleep and was the first one at their meet point the next morning. The others arrived and Maya informed them that she was not sure if Jack was going to show up. Tyler said they could go ahead without him, adding that Jack was too full of himself. He directed them to a small shed she has been making use of to grow some flowers. He managed to drive them in one of the old cars his dad had.

"She has been making use of this place and she was planning to expand I think. That's why she asked my parents to invest in her business" Tyler explained.

When they arrived at the garden, the atmosphere felt different. The garden was a small one and it was a shed covered by trampoline material. There was a small slit that was an obvious entrance. There was a pause as they looked at each other and silently waited for who would venture in first. Ethan sighed and went in while the others followed. The flowers and plants in the shed were obviously untended. It was peaceful, yet the silence felt unsettling. The small shed was crowded by all five of them. Ethan walked towards a particular flowerpot that is by the edge of the shed to the left and squatted to get a closer look. "Does this look familiar to anyone?" Ethan asked. Alex moved closer to Ethan and his expression changed.

"Those are the flowers that has been growing out of the body parts left at the copycat's crime scenes." He breathed. The others stared at each other, a chill look passed between them.

"These are from the vase at the house," Tyler whispered but they all heard.

He said the police found a piece of it in her room when it was searched.

*Okay, there is nothing here, do you know anywhere else Tyler?" Ethan asked with a tone of urgency after a while.

They were soon packed in the car and followed another direction Tyler gave.

The new spot was a large empty building that obviously needed to be worked on before it can be used by humans. It was longer than it was wide and the roof were high. Their search yielded nothing either and Ethan was evidently frustrated. He knew he was really close and there was just a piece of the puzzle missing.

They drove back to Tyler's house as they had agreed to check Emma's room again to confirm if they or the police missed anything the first time.

As they walked into the living room, Tyler paused at the flower vase on the coffee table, his eyes fixed on the blooms. He bent down, his nose inches from the blooms, and took a deep sniff. His eyes widened, and he turned to the others.

"This is it," he said, his voice low. "This is the same scent I smelled that night. The one that made me weak."

The others exchanged a look. "Let's get to her room. We need to find out if we missed anything."

They trooped upstairs, their footsteps quiet on the stairs. Emma's room was just as they had left it, the bed unmade, the closet door open. Ethan stood by the door, taking it all in. He was studying the pattern of the design on the bed cover, his eyes tracing the complicated lines.

Suddenly, he gasped. "Guys, look at this," he said, his voice excited.

The others turned to him, curious. "What is it?" Emily asked.

Ethan's eyes were fixed on the bed cover. "This design... it's not just a pattern. I think it's a map."

Maya's eyes widened. "A map ? How is that possible?"

Ethan brought out his phone and showed them a digital map that indicated where the bodies had been found and pointed back to the bed.

"Where are the markings?" Alex asked, his eyes scanning the design.

Ethan pointed to several spots on the map and then on his phone. "These marks correspond to the locations where the victims' bodies were found."

The others leaned in, their eyes tracing the design. And then, Ethan's finger landed on a green mark.

"What's this?" he asked, his voice low.

Alex's eyes narrowed. "It is marked differently. That looks like the town's outskirts."

Ethan's eyes met Alex's. "It wouldn't hurt to check."

As they went back out, they saw Jack's car parked behind the one they have been using. Tyler rolled his eyes as they trudged to him. "i thought you said we were playing catch, why are you here?"

Jack does not respond, he ordered them all to get into the car and update him on the way. they all did but Tyler lingered. He gave in a second after seeing that the others were not in with him.

The drive to the outskirts of town was tense, the only sound was the hum of the engine. Jack asked and Ethan decided to fill him in on what they had done since the day started.

"I hope none of you touched anything in that garden, that will be contaminating a potential scene" jack said in a cold tone. They all looked at each other and there was the silent consensus that none of them touched anything.

As they turned off the main road, the trees grew taller, the plants thicker. They drove down a dirt road, the car bouncing over potholes.

And then, they saw it. A small clearing, hidden by tall plants and flowers. A few trees towered above.

They got down from the car and walked through the bushes to the clearing. There was a building that looked like a ban at the edge of the clearing.

The group exchanged a look, and Jack nodded. "Let's go."

Jack slowly pushed the door and it swung in. He stepped in first and the others followed. The space was dimly lit as the only source of light was the one from the door.

Ethan went to the right turning his flash on, the others went in the opposite direction, not sure what they were to look for. There were roughly folded sheets, there was a table with bunsen burners, pipettes, and a pH metre. Jack lifted a tarp that was placed roughly on the side of the table and there was a faded glove underneath.

Ethan on his end also saw tarps littered everywhere. He moved some out of his way and underneath one, there was a crate filled with glass bottles. He bent to take a closer look, there were different liquids in them. He quickly took a picture of the crate from the top and the side. He stood up and dropped the tarp.

As he stood straight, Ethan suddenly paused and stared at the far end of the wall, his phone torch pointed at the wall. He could not move or call but he heard the others come towards him.

They noticed he was not moving and they all followed his gaze.

The group gasped, their eyes fixed on the horror before them. Emma's body was lying on the ground, her limbs twisted at unnatural angles. Her skin was pale, her eyes open, staring up at the sky. Her chest is bare and there are cuts all over her chest and breasts. The bones in her hands were seen as it had been skinned too.

The wall above the body was smeared with blood and with a message that said 'Only One.'

This had just thrown them back to the beginning. Who killed the copy cat?

Jack's voice was low. "I need to call this in right now."

The others nodded, their faces pale.

CHAPTER FIFTEEN

The Fraying Edge

A little bit of this and a little bit of that, mixed together with a whole lot of crazy, and you had a toxic blend of obsession, madness, and murder that would ultimately lead to a devastating conclusion. Before the police could find the garden, they had all already disappeared into thin air like they weren't there at all. Jack had made the difficult decision to stay behind. He wanted to be there to face them.

Despite their reservations about him, he had been very helpful. They didn't get in his way and he didn't get in theirs. Maybe that could be the beginning of a new kind of relationship with him. Perhaps he would refrain from bullying them always.

Alex and his friends sat quietly in his room, each mind wandering beyond what could have been if Emma was not made. It was as if they were all trying to come to terms with what had happened. Just days ago, Tyler nearly lost his life. And he was back here, all smiles like nothing dangerous happened to him. It had been just like he said, young people never knew when not to poke nose. Maybe if they hadn't been too knee-deep into finding the killer, he wouldn't have been in trouble. Perhaps, it was what saved him. Now knowing where he stood when he realized it was Emma was the culprit. Would it have been different if they didn't start digging into the case? *No,* he thought. He would have found Emma screaming after finding Dona. He would have still believed she was the one in trouble, not him. In fact, if he wasn't always on the alert, maybe he could have ignored the signs. Who knew she was crazy, she was going to fake her own death, kill him, disappear, and perhaps continue her spree by killing whoever found Tyler. That would be Alex had he been late, wouldn't it?

So many other lives had been lost. Ethan hadn't gotten over Becky. Neither had Jack about Dona which was the only reason he accompanied them to the garden in the first place. They felt relief that Sunset Ridge would know peace once more. No?

In the end, it was Emma who had ultimately met a grisly end. The official report had listed it as a homicide, and the killer was still at large. *The killer?* There was time they were asking this question. So now there was a new killer... Maybe she was in fact not the copycat and she was killed for trying to copy the copycat. Or she was the copycat and was killed by another copycat. Or...she was killed by the original Riverwood killer. It was quite known that the Riverwood's silent killer somehow, always found it's copycats. But it was assumed that killer died long time ago, so who offed Emma? The previous copycats had met the same end with same message on the wall. Until new video evidence showed Emma was in fact a copycat. But the videos which were in her possession showed her how killed her victims. No matter how Ethan tried to find them through his channels, they were not uploaded. They had realised now that Emma had been playing with fire, and she had gotten burned.

The investigators were left wondering whether Emma's actions provoked the original killer into coming out of retirement? Or had the original killer been watching Emma all along, waiting for the perfect moment to strike? It was all too scary to even imagine. Maybe Emma's actions had been a mere imitation, to get the original's attention. Or maybe she truly believed she could outdo the master... she had so many improved antics. It was simple and plain, yet complicated at the same time. She had so many weapons to achieve her goals. Gas to throw the victim off balance, liquid to provide the body with the enough nutrients to grow the engineered seeds. Had Emma's actions been a mere imitation, a desperate attempt to get attention from the original killer? Or had she genuinely believed she could outdo the master?

They had been through so much, and they had come out the other side. But they knew that they would never be the same again. "It's strange to say this...but I'm glad some other killer got her..." Tyler said a heaved a sigh of relief.

The others nodded glancing at themselves, unsure if they should be agreeing or not. Emma's death meant there was another killer out there. "It's a vigilante, don't you know small towns have those things..." Maya added and looked around for validation. And they all nodded again, even if they didn't believe it either.

When Tyler had asked Alex how he knew he was in trouble, Alex had causally said, the surveillance was manipulated. Yes, Ethan had tapped into that too and they were watching. And when something seemed off, Alex stormed off and drove off in his car. The others chased after him, surprised he was going in alone. Before they could reach the police, they had already made their way to the house.

Tyler's parents had to cut their vacation short, and they returned home, happy to find their son in one piece. But that incident had strained their relationship with their son. That's why recently, if he wasn't in the dorm, he was in a one of his friend's home. Anything to keep away from them.

It had been weeks since the attempt on Tyler's life, and the town was still reeling from the aftermath. The police had been working tirelessly to uncover the identity of the person who had ended Emma's life, but so far, they had come up empty-handed. With no particular witness to the murder, the authorities had been left to rely on speculation and rumors, which only muddied the waters.

The town had slowly begun to put the murders behind it to move on. They had accepted that the killer was just one of them, one of the most innocent looking of all.

Everyone desperately wanted to believe her killer was not another psycho, but a vigilante. The idea had first been suggested by Jack, who had been pouring over the evidence and talking to people around town. And Maya had sided with his reasoning. It made sense that the killer had only targeted Emma to take great care to avoid harming anyone else. 'Only one?' Perhaps the killer was reminding the town that there should only be one silent killer who emerged twenty years ago. This town didn't need a version of that psycho. Yes?

It had to be a vigilante, they thought. It was the only explanation that made sense. They desperately needed it to be true, because the alternative was too terrifying to contemplate. If it was another psycho, then they would never be able to feel safe again. They would have to sleep with one eye open.

But if it was a vigilante, then they could finally start to feel some closure. They could begin to heal from the trauma of the past weeks.

But was there truly time for them to heal too? They weren't just anyone in the town who wasn't already invested as they were. It had become more than just a game; it was something personal now. They were no longer just searching for answers, they were searching for truth.

Ethan sat perched on the edge of Alex's desk, staring at the map of Riverwood that was pinned to the wall. His finger traced the streets of the town that had long become too quiet for anyone's comfort.

Maya sat cross-legged on Alex's bed, arms folded tightly over her chest as she stared at the array of notes scattered across the floor. She looked frustrated and could barely think.

Alex gazed nervously over her shoulder at the open window. The darkness of the night had become so unyielding. Down there was the mango tree where it all started. Despite trying to look strong, sometimes he would imagine what would have become of Tyler if he didn't make it there in time.

Emily was sitting on the bed, her eyes darting from one person to the other. She couldn't imagine losing any of her friends, and she was glad to be part of this team, though inexperienced, were ready to put in their best. She didn't believe in their efforts earlier, maybe now she could feel safe. Even if there was some vigilante killer out there. That was a good thing, wasn't it?

And then there was Tyler himself. Ever since the incident, he had changed. The shock was like it had cracked something open inside of him. He'd never been a stranger to darkness, but there was something different in his eyes now, a kind of intensity that hadn't been there before. He'd always been the one to deflect serious conversations with a joke, the one who preferred the carefree lightness of youth. But staring death in the face had stripped away that veneer. The frivolous had become insignificant. A new purpose had taken root within him.

"It's not right," Tyler finally said. "What happened to Becky, Dona, all those people… what almost happened to me… it's not right. We can't just move on and hope the police find this vigilante."

Maya nodded, her dark eyes filled with a quiet fury. "He's right. We can't just go back to normal. Not after… after everything."

Ethan tapped his fingers on the desk. "But what can we do? The police are investigating Emma's attack, and they haven't found anything yet. And Riverwood… that's been cold for years."

"My theory is that Emma's killer is same as Riverwood." They all turned their eyes to her, Maya agreeing with her.

"Maybe we're looking at this wrong," Tyler said and all attention went to him.

Maya raised an eyebrow. "What do you mean?"

"We've been so focused on Sunset Ridge, so caught up in the person connected to it, we've forgotten our original plan." His eyes darted to Alex. "You saved me. You gave me a second chance at life, and now, I need to find out what happened in Riverwood. We all do."

Maya frowned, standing up. "You're saying you want to help? After everything? I mean I think we should back off now…"

"Oh come on now Maya, let's not do this…" Ethan told her.

A ripple of agreement went through the room. They were too young, with no special training or investigative skills. But they had something the police didn't: a freedom to think creatively and explore unconventional theories. They were not bound by the same rules and procedures that governed the police department. They were able to approach the case with curiosity and openness that might not be possible for more experienced investigators.

Tyler continued. "We need to find out what happened in Riverwood, then maybe we might get the answer that will finally give us a clue about who really killed Emma. Might be the original Riverwood serial killer, might not."

"God I hope not!" Emily blurted. A nervous smile escaped Alex's lips as he briefly stared at her. Then he nodded in agreement with

Tyler. "I think we can do it," he said. "We've already proven that we can make a difference. And if we can uncover the truth about Riverwood's killer, maybe we can bring some closure to the families of the victims. It's crazy we're not detectives, we're just us," he added.

Seeing the look on their faces, the kind of look that showed they were agreeing with Tyler, Maya shot back hoping to get their senses back to them. "I don't know, guys. This is a big risk, we could be putting ourselves in danger again. Who knows, we might start something we can't finish."

Alex chewed on his lip, his eyes drifting back to the mango tree. "If we can find Sunset Ridge's killer... maybe we can find Riverwood's serial killer. Maybe Emma's killer is connected to Riverwood, maybe they're not, but we have to try. For everyone who's been affected."

Maya picked up a paper from the floor, holding it up for everyone to see. The headline was 'Sunset Ridge's botanist went crazy.' "Look, if we go down this road, we need to make sure we're ready. We're talking about something bigger than we've dealt with before."

Tyler gave her a firm look. "I'm ready."

Alex smiled at him, for the first time in a long time, he saw determination in Tyler, not just someone he'd dragged along on this wild ride. He was in this just as deeply as he was.

"We all need to be ready," Alex said softly. "And that means we don't just look for answers. We look for the truth. The whole truth. No matter what it means."

Ethan nodded. "First, we need to gather information. Everything we can find about the Riverwood murders. Newspaper articles, police reports, anything."

Tyler rubbed his hands against his knee, still deep in thought. "You know," he said, "if we really want to find the truth, we should go to Riverwood."

Maya, who had been in the middle of taking a sip from her water bottle, choked. "I'm sorry, what?" she sputtered, coughing as she waved her hand in front of her face like that would somehow make the suggestion disappear. "Did you just say we should go to Riverwood? As in, physically take our bodies to the town where people have mysteriously died?"

Ethan shrugged. "Well, yeah. I mean, how else are we going to get the full picture? Looking at old articles can only take us so far. If we go there, we can talk to people, see the places where things happened. Get a real feel for it."

Maya let out a short laugh. "Ah, yes. Fantastic idea. Let's all pack a bag and take a nice little vacation to the town that had a serial killer. Should we book a hotel while we're at it? Maybe we should place a bet on who's most likely to be killed?" She crossed her arms and shook her head in disbelief. "Nope. Absolutely not."

Tyler had been watching her in amusement, and he finally sat up. "Maya, think about it. We can be careful. We don't have to go knocking on doors asking, 'Hey, did you murder those people?' But being there in person could give us clues we'd never get from a distance."

Maya held up a finger. "See, the fact that you even had to clarify that we won't be walking around asking suspected killers for confessions tells me everything I need to know about how bad of an idea this is."

Tyler rolled his eyes. "Come on, Maya. If we want real answers, we have to take real risks. We won't be stupid about it. We'll plan everything out."

Maya huffed and looked around for someone to back her up. But Ethan and Alex were both nodding to Tyler's words, clearly convinced. She glanced at Emily, the only other female in there for support, but she smiled and shrugged. It was four against one.

She groaned and hissed. "Fine! Fine. But if I get murdered in Riverwood, I'll kill all of you. Every one of you."

Alex grinned. "Deal. Now, let's start planning. We need a solid cover story, a place to stay, and most importantly, a way to not end up in a missing person's report."

Maya muttered under her breath as she flopped onto the couch. "Great. A very well thought plan. What could possibly go wrong?"

Ethan smirked and patted her back. "That's the spirit." And Maya quickly shot him a glare. "Not funny, Ethan. Not funny at all.

CHAPTER SIXTEEN

A Town in Limbo

Before Riverwood became a town known for its disappearances, it was the kind of place where nothing ever really happened. It was hidden between endless miles of forest and softly rounded hills. It was even safer and quieter than Sunset Ridge. Many of its inhabitants had moved to Sunset Ridge leaving the town almost empty.

Riverwood had no chain stores or highways which cut through its center. It was just a collection of small shops, a single diner, and houses with front porches where families gathered on warm evenings. People greeted each other by name. The biggest concern most folks had was whether the high school football team would finally win a championship.

It wasn't perfect, but it was home for many families. And then, one day, Ben Reed disappeared. At first, no one panicked.

Riverwood was the kind of place where a lost dog got half the town searching. Kids wandered off all the time, playing too long in the fields or getting caught up at a friend's house. So when Ben suddenly disappeared from his family, leaving behind his clothes and a flower, they thought he was playing games on them. No matter how James tried to convince him that Ben thought that was Ben's way to get attention, he still believed something was wrong. He reported to the police and by nightfall, search parties were forming. People combed through the woods with flashlights calling his name. The sheriff's office set up a command post outside the Reed family's home, and organised volunteers. Someone printed flyers with Ben's school picture and taped them up in shop windows.

At the diner, people talked about it over their coffee cups. At the gas station, they asked each other the same question: "Where could he have gone?" Because in a town like Riverwood, there weren't many places to go.

The search continued until there was no hope of finding him. No one wanted to say it out loud, but the truth was that kids didn't just disappear. Not from a town like this. James' enemies has finally gotten to him.

Riverwood had never known fear before. But now, it was everywhere. And then, six months later, someone else went missing. Daniel Whitmore was a mechanic, the kind of man who never left a job unfinished. When he didn't come home one night, his wife assumed he had lost track of time at the shop. Maybe he had taken a drive to clear his head.

But when morning came and Daniel still wasn't home, the fear that had spread after Ben's disappearance came rushing back.

His truck was found behind the shop, keys still in the ignition, driver's side door open. The police searched every inch of Riverwood, through the fields, forest, and riverbanks. Nothing.

Until one day, his jacket appeared on the porch with a violet on it. That was the moment people realized Ben Reed's disappearance wasn't an isolated tragedy. Something was wrong with Riverwood.

People stopped letting their children walk to school alone. Even adults were back in the homes before 7pm for fear of meeting the same date. Then Lisa Carter, a council member, disappeared. Next was Evan Brooke, a schoolteacher who left work late and never made it to his car.

One by one, people vanished without a trace. No bodies. No witnesses. No clues. It didn't matter who you were, young, old, man, woman. No one was safe.

Some people tried to leave, but Riverwood wasn't an easy town to escape. It was isolated, very much surrounded by large trees and winding roads that could be assumed to have no end at hindsight. The only thing that reminded them they were with the rest of the world was the city lights that they could perceive at night.

Since Riverwood was the kind of place where people stayed because they had nowhere else to go. And so they stayed.

And they waited. And they wondered who would be next. The final breaking point came one bitter winter night, when a fire broke out of the diner. It started in the dead of night, the flames climbed high into the sky. Anyone could see the billowing smoke from miles away. And by the time the fire department arrived, the fire had already spread across town.

The fire department didn't stand a chance against the angry flames that raged everything Riverwood built. By dawn, the town was unrecognizable.

When the fire finally burned out, the police hoped to find answers and so searched the wreckage. What they found were bones, charred and broken. It should have been the answer people had been waiting for. But it wasn't.

Because the bones were too old. Too scattered. Some from animals, others unidentifiable. There was no proof that any of them belonged to the missing. No proof that the fire had anything to do with them at all.

The police found nothing incriminating in the diner's ashes. No bodies or evidence. But by then, it didn't matter anymore.,

People didn't care if there was proof. They didn't care if it was just a rumor, if fear had twisted their minds into seeing ghosts where there were none. They were done waiting. Their town was cursed and they weren't sitting around to wait and see what other tragedies it had in store for them.

People packed their bags. They didn't care where they went, just as long as it was far away. Families abandoned their homes. Businesses closed. By the end of the year, half of Riverwood was gone.

Those who stayed did so out of necessity, or because they had nowhere else to go. But they lived in fear as they waited for the next name to be whispered among the missing. Riverwood would take someone else and they would not be able to stop it. One thing they were certain of, whatever had started with Ben Reed wasn't over.

Who would think that a place with a reputation would attract a bunch of kids who had been living a good life. That's why they didn't tell anyone where they were going when they set out. The road to Riverwood was just as they pictured, eerily silent. It felt longer than it should have. It was the kind of road that made you feel like you were the only people left in the world.

Alex sat in the passenger seat, his leg bouncing impatiently. He thrived on adrenaline, and the idea of stepping foot in Riverwood, where the infamous silent serial killer first started, made his blood rush with excitement. He was sure they'd find something -something big- and he was determined to be the first to figure it out.

Emily sat quietly in the back, her hands resting in her lap. Self-doubt gnawed at her. What if they were making a mistake? What if they were just kids poking around in something too dangerous for them to handle? She wanted to be brave, but the idea of walking into a place where people had vanished without a trace made her stomach twist with fear.

Ethan was sitting next to her. Social interactions were already hard enough for him, but going to Riverwood meant talking to strangers, maybe even officials, asking uncomfortable questions. He wasn't sure if he was up for that. He preferred facts, research, things he could analyze from a safe distance. But now, he was stepping straight into the unknown.

Maya had her arms crossed and an irritated look on her face. But inside, she was a tangled mess of nerves and curiosity. She didn't want to go, she'd made that abundantly clear, but she also couldn't ignore the thrill creeping into her bones. Maybe a part of her wanted to prove she was right about this being a terrible idea. Or maybe, deep down, she wanted to find something even scarier than her own fears.

Tyler was driving the car. Who would believe he would be the one leading them into Riverwood after the way he reacted in Alex's basement. He believed they were doing the right thing. Someone had to figure out what happened all those years ago, starting with the disappearance of little Ben. If there were answers to be found, he was sure they would find them.

The road signs counted down the miles. Riverwood was getting closer. Maya gripped the edge of her seat as she stared out the window. She had been anxious the whole trip, but now she realized they were nearer, her discomfort turned into something closer to dread.

"I can't believe I agreed to do this," she muttered under her breath and crossed her arms. "How are we sure this isn't one of those towns where people show up and never leave?"

Tyler smirked as he swerved around a bend. "That's kind of the point, isn't it?"

"I know you're trying to be funny but it's not helping."

Alex looked at her through the rear-view mirror. "Calm down Maya, everything will be fine."

"You don't say…" she mumbled, and finally the trees broke and there it was. Riverwood.

The first sign they had entered the town was the old, rusted road sign leaning to one side, half-swallowed by weeds. 'Welcome to Riverwood.' Someone had crossed it out in red spray paint. Below it, in jagged handwriting, someone had written; 'welcome?'

Maya swallowed hard. "Okay…so maybe they don't like strangers…"

"Most towns are like that." Emily answered. "Especially if they believe that whoever kidnapped their people was not from Riverwood."

It was clear that Riverwood was a place caught between two versions of itself, the past and whatever future it was trying to have. On one side of the road, homes sat abandoned with shattered windows and walls covered in vines. Some still had the scars of the fire that had torn through the town all those years ago. The mailboxes in front of them were rusted shut because their owners were long gone. No one had rebuilt them. No one had come back for them.

However, just across the street, freshly painted newer homes stood as if someone had tried to bring life back into Riverwood. These houses had manicured lawns, cars parked in the driveways, signs of people trying -desperately, maybe- to make Riverwood a home again.

"They actually rebuilt," Ethan murmured, almost in disbelief.

"Some of them did," Alex corrected. "But not everyone."

They passed what had once been Riverwood's main street. Some shops had been restored. Their windows displayed fresh signs of business, a bakery, convenience store, even a small diner. But others had been left to rot.

They had read about Riverwood. They had talked about it. They had imagined what it would be like. But now as they say right in the middle of it, surrounded by its remains, they realized the Riverwood didn't just have a bad past, it had never truly escaped it.

Slowly, they noticed the weight of eyes as figures began to be perceptible behind curtains. Those shadows shifting behind half-open blinds were people trying to see them. Then there were more people. Some standing on their porches pretending to be sipping their coffee but never actually drinking. Shopkeepers who stopped stacking shelves just to watch as the car rolled by.

No one waved or smiled or spoke to them. Maya sank into her seat. "This is literally the beginning of every horror movie ever."

Tyler kept his hands on the wheel. "Maybe they're just… not used to new people."

"They're looking at us like we're intruders." Alex watched the townsfolk carefully. Some looked cautious. Others looked suspicious. A few looked outright afraid.

They passed a gas station, where an old man in greasy overalls leaned against the pump, his eyes locked onto their car. He didn't move or blink. He just watched.

Then they passed the old diner that stood alone with its sign missing letters, and the windows boarded up. Maya shivered. "Is that... the diner?" she asked.

No one answered right away. They all knew the stories, the rumors that after the fire, people had murmured that the missing had been buried beneath the diner's foundations. Nothing had ever been found, but the legend had been enough to keep people away. It looked like no one had touched it since.

Alex breathed heavily, as they passed the diner. "We're really here."

"So... no one thought to just, I don't know, tear it down? Maya asked looking back at it.

Ethan shook his head. "Maybe no one wanted to touch it."

"Or maybe," Tyler added, "they were too afraid to."

No one argued. A block ahead, they spotted the new diner, Riverwood's attempt at moving forward. Unlike its predecessor, this one was bright and modern, with a red-and-white sign that read, 'Penny's Diner' in bold letters. The windows were clean. The lights inside shone warmly. It looked normal.

Tyler pulled into the parking lot and killed the engine. It was a little too silent in the car and Maya's breath shook. "This was a mistake."

Alex opened his door. "Too late now."

The moment they stepped out of the car, the town stopped. Conversations died mid-sentence. Forks froze halfway to mouths. People turned in their seats to look at the newcomers. It wasn't just curiosity. It was something heavier.

Maya felt the air press against her chest. "This is definitely the beginning of a horror movie."

Ethan adjusted his jacket, and pretended not to notice the way every single person on the street was staring at them like they had just walked out of a grave. Alex, on the other hand, didn't pretend. He met their gazes head-on. Were they unwelcome because they were strangers? Or because the town knew exactly why they were here?

They made their way toward the diner, and the bell above the door jingled as Tyler pushed it open. And Inside, the silence was worse.

A group of older men at the counter stopped mid-sip, with their coffee cups hovering. A waitress holding a tray of plates nearly dropped it before steadying her grip. A mother with a toddler in a high chair quickly pulled her child closer.

Maya's fingers twitched at her sides. "So this is the part where they all pretend they weren't staring at us, right?"

The townsfolk tried, some turned back to their plates, some went back to fake conversations. But it was clear that they were still listening and watching with sidd eyes.

Tyler took the lead, trotting toward the counter. The server behind it, a young woman with blonde hair tied in a messy ponytail, looked scared. She held onto the notepad like it was life, her knuckles appeared white. Tyler leaned slightly on the counter. "We'll take a menu."

She only stared blankly.

Ethan giggled. "Uh… do you guys not do food here, or is this, like, a 'no outsiders allowed' thing?"

The girl blinked, then opened her mouth and closed it again, like she didn't know what to say.

It was Emily who finally had enough. She let out a nervous laugh and shook her head. "Seriously? No offense, but we just got here. We didn't do anything wrong or whatever you all think we did. We just want food."

The girl looked like she wanted to say something. Maybe to deny it or to tell them to leave. Instead, she just nodded stiffly and slid a few menus onto the counter.

Tyler took one without his eyes leaving hers. "What's your name?"

The girl hesitated. Then, finally, she answered. "...Penny."

Alex jerked. "Wait. As in 'Penny's Diner' Penny?" The girl nodded slowly.

Tyler set the menu down and drummed his fingers lightly against the counter. "So," he said casually, glancing at Penny, "what's the deal with the old diner?"

The moment the words left his mouth, the atmosphere shifted. Penny stiffened. The notepad in her hands crinkled slightly under her grip.

Behind them, the quiet shuffle of cutlery on plates stopped again. Someone coughed awkwardly. A man in the corner suddenly found great interest in stirring his coffee.

Maya sighed. "Maybe not a normal question around here."

Penny glanced at the other customers, almost like she was looking for permission. But no one helped her. Tyler waited, but Penny said nothing.

It was sort of a dead end so Alex leaned in with an easy-going smile. "You know, we should probably introduce ourselves first. We're with a news station. Doing a little research."

Before he could continue, a voice cut through the air. "Aren't you a bit too young for that?"

They turned to see an elderly woman sitting at a booth near the window. She was small but not frail. Her posture was straight and her brown eyes were filled with something unreadable. Her silver hair was pinned neatly into a bun, and she wore a burgundy cardigan over a floral dress. A steaming cup of tea sat in front of her. Despite her age, there was something about her that felt dreadful.

Alex forced a polite smile. "Excuse me?"

The woman looked at them. "You don't look like any reporters I've ever seen."

For a second, no one spoke. Then Ethan, nervous and sweating blurted out, "It's a school project!"

Maya groaned internally. *Smooth.*

Emily fought the urge to face palm. Alex and Tyler just nodded along, like that had been the plan all along. "Yeah. School project."

The woman stared at them for a long moment, then she smirked.

"School project, huh?" She mused and stirred her tea slowly.

Maya gave her best attempt at an innocent smile. "Yep. History class. You know, learning about small-town mysteries, urban legends... that kind of thing."

The woman didn't look convinced. But, to their relief, she didn't call them out. Instead, she set her spoon down and folded her hands neatly in front of her.

"Well, what do you want to know?"

Alex took a breath, "What really happened to the town? The thing that started with Ben Reed."

The second his name was spoken, everything changed. The warmth in the woman's face drained instantly. It looked something colder and distant. She held her teacup slightly, and stared directly into Alex's soul. It had the kind of intensity that made the hairs on the back of his neck stand up.

Everyone in the diner appeared to be watching them too. Even Penny shrunk back like she had caused the trouble. Then slowly, the woman smiled.

It wasn't a warm smile. It wasn't even an amused one. It was the kind of smile that made you wonder if you're safe or not. The kind that made you wonder whether the person in front of you was happy to see you… Or if it was just another psycho to watch out for.

CHAPTER SEVENTEEN

Haters and Heartbreak

Margaret looked forward to that day. She knew sooner or later, people would want to know the truth especially after the rise in the number of deaths. It may have taken over twenty years and she may have convinced herself to move on but deep down, she missed the free life she used to live. She missed the peaceful town she once knew and she wanted to go back to it. It may not matter now that she was old, but she wanted Riverwood to go back to what it used to be way before the silent killer came to play. When she took the kids to her home, she did so not because she hadn't told many reporters about the town before. But because she felt this would be different. People who actually came to hear the truth, not the ones that media painted.

"I'm not surprised you guys are here. I've been watching the news and I knew sooner or later, someone would come knocking at my door." Margaret said as she welcomed them into her home. The old-fashioned living room looked small but had a sense of comfort and nostalgia. The kind that made one want to stay home and watch movie all day long.

Margaret settled into her cushion. "Come, come in. Don't be shy." She said with a smile as the kids slowly strolled in and made themselves comfortable on the sofa. Their eyes moved across the room and settled on every antique, flower vase and family photograph carefully curated around the room while they pondered at the back of their mind how she was able to isolate herself from society for all these years.

"We really need your help. We need to know how all these started if we want a shot at catching him." Tyler said to her.

"There's nothing I'll say you don't already know. What you don't know is the ripple effect Ben's disappearance caused. The town's people were so busy shifting blames they did little to find Ben."

"Why do they blame you for it?" Ethan curiously asked.

"Oh they don't blame me for it. They think I destroyed Riverwood."

"Did you?" Alex asked.

"Hey take it easy, she's doing us a favour." Tyler huffed, provoked at Alex's lack of empathy.

Twenty years. That's a really long time to be alone. Margaret had left her whole life behind, no friends or family, completely isolated from the world she knew and blamed for something that was entirely her fault. Tyler could feel her pain. All the people she knew were probably dead, those alive probably hated her. If there's anything worse than being dead, it's being in the midst of people who wanted you dead. It made her look over her shoulder each time she was out on the streets. She did not feel safe anymore. They sneered at her when she walked by and she also heard them talk about her. She always thought someone was after her, to be publicly hated like that, she had to walk on eggshells. It was tough to live like that so she did the only thing she thought was best for her.

"That's alright son." Margaret continued. "The fire was my fault anyway but I didn't do it on purpose."

"How did it happen?" Maya asked.

"I forgot to turn off the coffee machine. I hated myself for it, still do. The manager had called me around two at night, and said the diner was on fire. I left my home that night and before I got there, the diner was burnt down and the fire spread."

"Oh my God." Tyler whispered.

Margaret chuckled, marvelled at the disbelief. She too couldn't believe it. That such little fire could ravage an entire town. We were too busy saving ourselves, we couldn't save anything from our homes. Many died from the fire and a lot were injured. The fire department figured it came from the coffee machine, it got overheated and sparked. Margaret blamed herself for days. She slipped into depression and most times, she wished the fire had taken her too because the way the town's people treated her made it impossible to believe she was one of them. Riverwood wasn't the same ever since. The life that once bubbled in it was no more. They were a few people in it but it was dead, a zombie town.

"What about Ben's parents, what happened to them?"

"Oh dear Ben." Margaret began as she lowered her eyes and stared into the distance. "Whatever happened to that sweet boy. This all started with him. If only his parents… if only James had not…" Margaret teared up as she spoke and it streamed down her cheeks. She sat still, eyes wide open like she absentmindedly relieved the past. Tyler picked up the tissue box on the table and offered it to her.

"Oh thank you." She chuckled. "Look at me, doing the exact thing I despised others for doing to me, I'm shifting blames." Margaret said as she dabbed the tissue on her cheeks.

"You know, Lucy," she continued. "Lucy was an angel, at least to me. After the diner dwindled in business, the manager sold it, that was before the fire of course. I thought I was going to get laid off but Lucy said I could stay. Imagine my surprise and happiness when I found out she was the one that bought the diner. She paid me even when we weren't making any sales. She wasn't all those things people said she was and she definitely wasn't responsible for her son's disappearance. At that point in her life, she needed all the support she could get but what did people do, they blamed her, insulted her and cast her aside. People in this town, they don't like successful women. You are seen as a threat, something that's not supposed to be, especially when you're divorced.

"But the divorce wasn't her fault. I heard her husband was cheating on her."

"Yes he was. But no one ever blames the man. The only thing I blame Lucy for was not fighting for Ben. She should have taken him with her and maybe their destiny would have taken a different course. Oh that poor boy." Margaret teared up again and the room went quiet as the kids stared at her in silence.

"Forgive me," She sniffed. "It's just so hard relieving the past, even after all these years."

"Do you have any idea where Lucy could be?" Ethan asked.

Margaret scoffed as she turned to the him and gave him a look. "She disappeared just like I did. The town hated her so much she feared for her life. And they didn't just hate her for the disappearance of her son, they hated that she was so successful even after she divorced her husband. That woman James brought into his life was the start of his downfall. Only a fool would be stupid enough to leave a woman that contributed greatly to his success for one that came to drain it. Lucy didn't let the cheating scandal get to her. She was a strong woman. She fought for everything that belonged to her, took it and built her own empire. She invested so much in this town, bought a lot of business that was already closing up and breathed life into it. But this godforsaken town is filled with ingrates. Just a handful appreciated her. Others thought she was selfish for leaving her husband and her son. They said she was just showing off her wealth. Some said she stole from her husband. She couldn't take it anymore, she took what she could, sold some of her property and left Riverwood for good. Her son's disappearance was just what they needed to finally cancel her."

"Wait." Tyler cut in, his eyes brimmed with an idea. "The diner, it has a sprinkler right? It sets off an alarm in case of fire."

"Yeah." Margaret replied unsure of why it mattered.

"The diner is right in the heart of Riverwood. Someone must have heard it and called the fire department."

"The fire had already destroyed the diner before they got there. They couldn't control it."

"Tyler, where are you going with this?" Maya asked.

"A spark from a coffee machine couldn't have caused such a devastating fire." Alex answered.

"Exactly!" Tyler yelled as he slapped his hands and jolted up from his seat leaving Margaret startled. "Someone wanted that fire outbreak. It wasn't Margaret's fault."

"Honey, they found the source and it came from the coffee…"

"I need you to think…" Tyler said, he sat on the edge of the couch beside her and clasped his hand, his eyes focused on her face. "Did you really forget to turn off the coffee machine the night before? Think Margaret, you worked at the diner for a really long time. Would you really make such a clumsy mistake?"

Margaret's brows furrowed and her face was lost in thought, a confused though, her eyes zoned out as she tried to play the past in her head.

"Jeez, that was twenty years ago. How is she going to remember?" Alex interrupted.

"Even if she does, it's too late to do anything about it." Another added.

"It's not too late. We can clear her name and if we find out what or who really started the fire, it might just lead us to the silent killer."

"You think the killer started the fire? That's not his M.O, why would he do that?" Margaret asked, more confused than before.

"You said the town hated her for leaving her husband and she bought most of their property and business, what if the fire was an indirect attack on her. They wanted to take away everything she had. And right after that, her son disappeared." Tyler emphasized, he had a satisfied look on his face, one that was convinced, like he just solved the world's most complicated case.

The others stood there and stared at him, speechless. They wanted to back him up but they still had doubts and the full story hasn't been revealed yet. They couldn't judge a version if they didn't know the rest. Tyler's theory was somehow understandable. But then it's hard to believe that someone went through all that and destroyed a whole town just because they hated Lucy and wanted to make her suffer.

"How then do we explain the other deaths and disappearance that are not related to Lucy?"

"I don't know. Maybe the killer was hungry for more. He had a lot of copycats too so it's definitely not the same person."

"Let's say you're right," Alex continued. "It must have been someone close to her, someone with a motive, who would get away with it without being suspected."

"Could it be her husband? Maybe he didn't like how she moved on without him." Maya added.

"No. James wouldn't hurt his own son. He would never." Margaret replied, just then her eyes widened and she looked at Tyler.

"What?" Tyler noticed her expression.

"She never really got along with Ben, Rachel. She thought he was one of the reasons her relationship with James didn't work. Ben was quite difficult I must say especially with her. Their relationship was bliss when it started, James and Rachel, they seemed perfect but you can never compare it to what he had with Lucy. I think Rachel knew that and she hated it."

"We need to find her, Lucy too." Alex said.

"Easy to say. How the hell are we gon do that? No one's heard from them for what, twenty years."

"Margaret, if there's anything you can tell us." Tyler pleaded.

"I'm sorry hun, I wish I could help but I haven't heard or seen them ever since."

Tyler sighed defeatedly. "Fuck." He whispered.

"There goes our last hope."

Every time it seemed as if they were close to the truth, they would hit a brick wall. No matter how hard they tried, they always got stuck somewhere. No amount of research gave them everything they needed. It could only tell them what happened in the past and from a certain person's point of view. At this point, they only had one option which was their last resort and that was to hear directly from the people involved. Everyone that witnessed the silent killer's first murder. It was difficult trying to find people that didn't want to be found. Everyone ran for their dear life when the silent killer went rogue coupled with the fact that they had no home to live in after the fire. People left the town and never looked back. And now decades later, the people are haunted by a deed they know nothing about.

"We can't give up now. We'll find them." Tyler assured.

"How?"

"I don't know but we will."

CHAPTER EIGHTEEN

Imitators are
the End of the Trail

It was easy for humans to turn something sickening into a cult following, as was the case with the Silent Killer. The murders that happened in the small town of Riverwood eventually became worldwide, with many people obsessing over the details of the crimes. But as the investigation continued, it became clear that the Silent Killer's influence extended far beyond the initial murders.

Copycat killers began to emerge, mimicking the Silent Killer's methods and claiming their own victims. The police were faced with a serious task of separating the real killer's crimes from those of the copycats. It was a challenging and complex process, made even more difficult by the fact that the copycats seemed to be intentionally leaving behind false clues and misleading evidence.

As the body count continued to rise, the police found themselves struggling to keep up with the sheer scale of the problem. Maybe it would have been easy if it just happened in the same country but from the time the original killer emerged and was tagged, there have been reports of similar murders in France and the UK, and at least three copycats had emerged in Riverwood alone. The international authorities were working together to share information and coordinate their efforts, but the investigation was becoming more complicated.

The police were working around the clock to follow up on leads and track down suspects, but the copycats seemed to always be one step ahead. They were leaving behind a trail of cryptic messages and gruesome crime scenes, each one carefully crafted to throw the police off their trail. The investigation was becoming a deadly game of cat and mouse, with the police racing against time to catch the killer before another victim fell prey.

In all of this, the victim's bodies were never found. They never showed up, not then, not 20 years after.

A year after the Riverwood murders and the silent killer tag was becoming popular, a series of gruesome discoveries were made in Paris, France. Body parts were found scattered throughout the city, with no signs of the victims' bodies. The French police unit had their hands full with the murders. They didn't know what to make of it because there seemed to be no motive and there was no body there either. As they investigated further, they realized that they were probably dealing with a copycat killer.

The police found that the body parts were carefully arranged, with clothes and personal belongings left behind. But it was what was found with the clothes that caught their attention. Instead of flowers, like the original Silent Killer had left behind, the copycat had left small, intricately carved wooden figurines. The figurines were of various animals, and they seemed to be carefully selected to match the location where the body part was found.

The police were interested in the difference in the copycat's methods. While the original Silent Killer had left flowers, which seemed to be a symbol of respect or admiration, the copycat's use of wooden figurines seemed to be more sinister. It was as if the copycat was trying to send a message, but the police couldn't quite decipher what it meant.

As the investigation continued, the police found more body parts, each with a wooden figurine left behind. They were able to reconstruct some of the victims' identities, but the lack of bodies made it difficult to determine the cause of death or the exact circumstances of the murders.

The police were frustrated by the lack of leads and the copycat's seeming ability to always stay one step ahead.

As they dug deeper into the case, the police realized that the copycat was not only imitating the original Silent Killer's methods but also seemed to be trying to outdo them. The wooden figurines were just one example of how the copycat was putting their own twist on the original's methods.

They started to work closely with the police department in Riverwood to help them make more sense of what was going on and to see if they would be able to catch the perpetrator before a next strike, but it was futile.

Their hard work soon paid off as they were able to identify the person who was perpetrating these crimes in France. On the day of the burst, however, the copycat was found dead. This time a body was found. The chest was bare and cleanly cut from top to the navel. The legs were bashed and twisted at an off angle with the feet touching a side of the stomach on the left and the right. The hands were raised above the head and the fingers were touching at the tips. It gave the name to every copycat body found ever since, "the budding flower".

It was very clear the Silent killer did not appreciate the worship.

The police were left with more questions than answers as they searched the copycat's residence. What they found was a treasure trove of disturbing evidence that solidified their suspicions. The room was filled with printed copies of details about the Riverwood killings, including newspaper articles, police reports, and even handwritten notes.

There were also pictures of the scenes of the body parts and items found, both from Riverwood and France, plastered on the walls. The police found a large map of France with locations marked, corresponding to where the body parts were found. It was clear that the copycat had been meticulously planning and executing their crimes.

They discovered a collection of wooden figurines, identical to the ones found at the crime scenes in France. There were also tools and materials that matched the ones used to carve the figurines.

They also found a journal belonging to the copycat, containing disturbing details of their obsession with the Silent Killer and their desire to outdo them. The entries were chilling, providing a glimpse into the mind of a disturbed individual who had been driven to commit heinous crimes.

The copycat's death closed the cases of murder in France.

It was not long before the United States got a feel of what it was like. The city of London was gripped by fear as the police announced the discovery of a series of body parts.

This time, it was not difficult to identify this as another prototype of the silent killer. After the uproar in France, police units in different countries had gotten a full paper work detailing the silent killer and the first international copycat that was identified.

The copycat in London tried to be more original in duplication. The police discovered that the body parts had been carefully arranged, with clothes and personal belongings left behind with flowers in it. The only difference was in the kind of flower as this copycat went with dandelions. Also, it was a messier scene than usual.

The dandelion copycat didn't last long before he turned up another budding flower.

Another copycat started in London a few months after and the methods were so identical to the Silent Killer that the police had initially believed it was the real killer. But as they dug deeper, they found evidence that pointed to a copycat.

The police were able to track down the London copycat's identity and raided their residence. But when they entered the apartment, they were met with a gruesome sight. The copycat was dead, killed in a manner that was identical to the other two copycats.

Detective Rodriguez knew nothing about the case from 20 years ago. In fact he never knew how big of a thing it was until he joined the police department in Sunset Ridge. He was not fully invested in the case then because the killings were just stories.

He was a little unprepared for the scenes when they started unfolding in this town. Working closely with Dona was also a little consuming because she started to bring up the similarities to a certain killer from years ago. It made him go and carry out his research on it. He still had a vivid mental picture of what those bodies were like when they were found. He had never found a way to understand the kind of thinking that can make someone come up with the budding flower or anyone of the killings at all.

Ben Reed was the only missing person who was never found. The other people who went missing turned up, in a way, as victims.

What bugged him the most of these tragic events he read about was that they never went that they never went through with the case. He wondered if the boy lived or was rotten somewhere in that burnt down town.

The silent killer case was declared a cold case when all three copycats turned out dead too. Whoever the silent killer was, he clearly did not like to share and he was really good at keeping his tracks.

Riverwood was never really the same, it had not been since the killings started. It was very clear that people trusted each other less. They all believed the killer could be any one of them since it was a small town where everyone knew everybody. The laughter and warmth that once characterised the small town was lost and permanently when the fire came.

The silent killer destroyed what the town stood for and it's sense of community. The copycats emerging cemented the destruction. It became a stone in the gut that just anyone had the ability to kill.

Margret was in her couch, as she stared into space. It had been a very long twenty years and would have been a lot better without all of those killings. Maybe Riverwood had paid its dues and it was now Sunset Ridge's turn. But why wait till after so long? She let out a bitter chuckle into the dark she was sitting in. It was never a good story to hear. She felt a kind of pity for the children. She hoped they didn't have to get into trouble with their daring approach.

Their research had shown that Emma was killled and butchered exactly like the copycat killers in the other places. It was not a drill, it was still a whole messy road ahead.

CHAPTER NINETEEN

The Visitor

Margaret Ortiz had lived a thousand lives before she finally became the woman being sought out by many reporters and now curious kids. Maybe she would become a legend, that wouldn't be so bad after all.

Before she was Margaret of Riverwood, she had been a wanderer, a free spirit with flowers in her hair and the wind at her back. She had been a hippie once, roaming from city to city, dancing barefoot in the grass at festivals and living on nothing but music, the sun and moonlight, and whatever odd jobs kept her pockets just full enough for the next adventure. But at some point, the endless movement lost its magic. She craved something else. Something steady and quiet that held the balance of stillness and unpredictability.

Riverwood had felt like that place. It was small but not suffocating. Many would beg to differ but to her, Riverwood had life but not chaos. It was a town with secrets but not too many prying eyes. The kind of place where she could have roots but still feel like she had room to breathe. So she stayed.

At first, she found work as a nanny. The wealthy families of Riverwood were eager to have a woman like her, someone with experience, patience, and who wasn't one of those stuck-up perfectionist types that made kids feel like they were being raised in a museum. Margaret was none of those things.

She let kids stomp through puddles and climb trees at least to the extent that was tolerated in Riverwood. She told them stories about places they would never see, things they would never learn in their cold little classrooms. She was a favorite among the children. Less so among the parents.

Her mouth had always been her greatest weapon. She spoke her mind, whether people wanted to hear it or not. She told the rich mothers of Riverwood exactly what she thought of their husbands. She told the town's businessmen how ridiculous their uptight traditions were. She was both beloved and feared.

Margaret had saved many with her words, she had given advice that stopped one woman from marrying the wrong man, and warned another about a deal that would have ruined her family.

But she had also caused trouble for many. She had called out men who thought no one was paying attention to their affairs. She had exposed lies that people would have preferred to stay buried.

She was the town's mouthpiece, whether Riverwood wanted her to be or not. And when she grew tired of hearing babies wail and teenagers whine, she left the world of nannying behind and took a job at the diner.

She liked it there. It gave her a new audience, from strangers passing through, to locals who thought she was just another waitress but soon realized she was so much more. Margaret never just served food. She served stories. Some were true. Some were exaggerated. Some were a perfect blend of half-truths and rumors she had carried like currency, what did it matter anyway?

She could sit there and simply watch. From her usual spot, she saw everything that happened in town. She saw businessmen discussing deals over pancakes, tired mothers stealing a moment to themselves, teenagers sneaking in past curfew, hoping no one they knew would see them.

In that diner, she had learned the rhythms of the town. She knew which couples were having affairs just by the way they leaned too close over their meals. She knew which workers hated their jobs by the way they stirred their coffee.

The owner of the diner back then was a known man in Riverwood, with a belly full of stories and a laugh that could shake the windows. He had taken a liking to Margaret almost immediately. "You got the kind of mouth that keeps a place interesting," he'd told her one night as she lounged at the counter, watching the late-night crowd filter out. "Ever thought about working here?"

She had laughed at first. But then she thought about it. She had been a nanny, a wanderer, a woman with too many stories and nowhere to put them.

But here, she would have a stage. She started working at the diner not long after that. And for the first time in her life, she had a place that felt like home.

The man saw how much she loved the place, never wanting to leave. On nights when she had nowhere else to go, she would rest her head in one of the booths, staring at the lights outside until sleep took her. Maybe that was why, when he had passed away, she felt like her world was crumbling.

This diner has given her everything, from being even a home to allowing her to save enough money to finally have her own home. It was a modest house with creaky floorboards and windows that let in the morning sun. To Margaret, they were everything. When her boss's wife couldn't keep running the diner, she had to sell it.

Margaret thought that would be the end, she had assumed she would never step foot inside it. Until, to her surprise, the new owner had retained her services.

When the diner burned, it was like a piece of her had gone up in flames with it. She could still remember the thick smoke curling into the night sky. People had gathered, whispering, murmuring and wondering if it was an accident or something more sinister. Maybe that was why they didn't work together quickly enough to stop the fire from spreading and taking the town with it. Margaret hadn't spoken that night. She had lost everything.

Margaret never entertained those stories the townsfolk paddled. She knew what the diner had been. It had been her home. Losing it broke her heart in a way she never truly recovered from.

It took her a long time to rebuild herself. For a while, she kept to herself, licking her wounds and trying to pretend the loss didn't eat at her. But Margaret had always been Margaret. She was stubborn and strong. She moved on.

No one ever blamed her for what happened to the diner. And she never blamed herself either. She had accepted it as nature's cruelty to her. Another thing the world had taken from her.

The reporters had come, of course. The diner fire had been just another dark mark on Riverwood's history, and Margaret had become a permanent figure in the town's legend. They came with their notebooks, microphones, and eager questions.

"What do you think happened?"

"What do you think started the fire?"

Margaret had told them all sorts of stories. Some had been true. Others had been truths bent at the edges, softened to fit the audience that needed them. And some had been lies so good that even she had started to believe them.

Sometimes, she said it had been an accident, an old gas leak, a careless mistake. Other times, she spun tales of something more. A curse, perhaps. An act of revenge by someone or force. Maybe a restless spirit finally having its say. She never told the same story twice. And the best part was that everyone went with it, because Margaret Ortiz was the kind of woman you either thought was the wisest soul you'd ever met or just a woman completely out of her mind.

So when those kids walked into the diner that day, claiming they were there for a school project, she knew they were lying. They weren't reporters neither were they students. And if they were students, they were not there for a school project. They were just curious. And curiosity was the most dangerous thing to have in a place like Riverwood.

Margaret could have called them out, told them to leave while they still had the chance. But she was tired.

She was tired of the scrutiny and the endless cycle of reporters and strangers who came poking around, looking for answers she no longer cared to give.

So she played along. They wanted a story, and she gave them a story. Maybe this one would be the truth. Or maybe it wouldn't. Maybe it was a memory buried so deep that she no longer knew if it was real or just another story she had fabricated through those years. But it didn't matter. They wouldn't question her. No one ever did.

Later that evening, by the time the kids were gone, Margaret sat inside her home, alone as always. She felt satisfied and she hadn't felt that way in a long time.

It had been a while since she had spoken to outsiders. It reminded her of the old days. She sipped her tea and allowed herself a small smile.

Yes. It had been a good day. Margaret stood up and stretched her stiff legs before moving toward the kitchen. She reached for the cupboard, intending to grab a jar of honey for her nightly indulgence.

Then she heard something move, a creak. The kind that froze her at a spot. Sure, her house was very old. The wooden floors groaned under her weight on cold mornings, and the wind sometimes made the walls sigh.

But this creak was different. It was deliberate. It was the sound of a footstep. She turned her head slightly as her heart began to thump. And when she looked at her door, she could have sworn she saw the door handle turn. Maybe her eyes were deceiving her. That's why she looked closely and she was right.

Slowly, the door eased open and the hinges whispered against the silence. A man stepped inside.

Margaret couldn't see his face. All she could see was his domineering broad trunk. The way his shoulders moved with quiet control as he took another step into her home made her feel fear. And she knew she hadn't felt that in many years.

But besides that fear, she also felt something else. Something like acceptance. Maybe this was it. Could it be he had come to punish her for entertaining outsiders. Or he had come to kill her for the stories she had told, the truths she had hidden, and the lies she had spread.

She exhaled slowly, as a smile curled at the crinkled edges of her lips. Either way, she had lived a good life. The kind she could not regret in the face of danger.

CHAPTER TWENTY

Flower in Riverwood

Sara Lee had always been driven by a desire to uncover the truth. She was always the curious child that wore her teachers and parents out with questions. She wanted to know why a particular thing was the way it was and she persisted until she got an explanation that sat well with her. Being a journalist was the only way she figured would allow her to engage in her favourite thing on a full scale and get paid while doing so.

As a journalist, she had spent years honing her skills, chasing down leads, and asking tough questions. But one story had captivated her like no other: the Silent Killer case.

She had moved to Sunset Ridge on her own when she turned nineteen and had since heard about the boy who went missing in the burnt down town of Riverwood and the case was closed. Then, she believed it was the reason her heart chose Sunset Ridge, the closest town to Riverwood. She wanted to know more about this missing boy who was either dead or alive but people were not opening up. It seemed everyone was in a silent agreement not to say anything about the case.

That did not dampen her spirit anyway. Sara poured through every paper she could find trying to understand what had happened. It wasn't a lot and seeing as she needed to get an actual job too. Few years down the line and she was back at digging.

It was no wonder she was able to immediately identify a pattern when the killings in Sunset Ridge started. That was when she decided to make it a documentary. Something big she was going to be known for.

For months, Sara had been pouring over every detail of the case, from the initial murders in Riverwood to the copycat killings that had followed. She had read every article, every police report, and every interview. She had even managed to track down some of the original investigators, who had shared their memories with her.

Sara had always been passionate about storytelling, believing that every person had a story worth telling. This particular story, however, was different. It was filled with tragedy and pain, and she felt a responsibility to honor the victims by shedding light on their stories.

Sara's obsession with the case took a toll on her personal life. Her friends and family had grown tired of hearing about the Silent Killer, and her editor was starting to wonder if she would ever finish the documentary she had been working on. But Sara couldn't help herself. She was convinced that there was more to the story than met the eye, and she was determined to uncover it.

As she sat at her desk, the soft glow of her laptop reflected her focused expression. She was surrounded by stacks of papers and books, the walls of her office were filled with news articles, mostly cut out and each one was evidence of her dedication as a journalist.

This story did not jump into the tragedy that it is now known for. The newspaper heading was "Ben Reed is missing". Apparently, the child of a somewhat popular couple had gone missing. This was twenty years ago. Her digging deeper into the story began to bring forth all the horrors that connected to this one case. She went over every piece of evidence she could access, talked to people and kept going at it like a starved animal. It was like she dropped a load on herself but she did not stop. She could not keep away.

She found out recently that there was a living first hand witness. She had been trying to get in touch with Margaret, the elderly woman who was one of the last livings set of people from Riverwood to still be identified. She believed that by the time she had asked Margret questions, connecting the pieces of the puzzle that remained unsolved was going to be easy. But reaching her had proven difficult. Margaret was known to be reclusive, avoiding the media and only speaking to those she trusted.

As Sara stared at her computer screen, her phone buzzed, pulling her from her thoughts. It was a text from a friend and officer at the police department. Her heart raced as she read his message: "Sara, you need to get to the station. Margaret is dead."

The news hit her like a punch to the gut. Sara's breath caught in her throat, and her hands trembled slightly. Margaret had been a key to revealing the mystery, and now she was gone. It was clear that there was something serious going on and she was infuriated each time she was close to a breakthrough, she was sent five steps back. But as a journalist, Sara couldn't ignore the opportunity this presented. Margaret's death could provide new angles for her documentary, a tragic twist that would resonate with the audience and highlight the lives affected by the murders.

She quickly gathered her things, shoving her notepad and camera into her bag. As she drove to the police station, her mind spun with questions. How had Margaret died? Was it an accident? Or was someone trying to make her stay silent forever. She needed answers, and she needed them fast.

Upon arriving at the station, Sara pushed through the double doors and made her way to the front desk. The atmosphere was tense, with officers moving about, their expressions serious. The officer that had called her spotted her and waved her over.

"Sara," he said, his voice low. "You should have called so I can meet you outside."

"What happened?" she asked, not listening to what he was saying.

"Margaret was found in her home. I thought you might want to try and get some information."

"Of course I do," she replied, determination flooding her voice. "I need to know everything."

He led her back to the front door and followed her to her car. They got in and sat down as he filled her in on what he knew, the group of friends and officers visiting Margret and then the police department at Riverwood calling in to let them know she was found dead.

"She stayed in Riverwood?" Sara turned to the officer and the wheels in her head were already working.

"There's no convincing you to wait till tomorrow." The officer sighed.

"It's about a 45 minute drive, I can make it." Sara's curiosity juice was already overflowing. This is the kind of thing that kept her going. She was not going to let this run cold before she pounced on it.

Sara drove from the station in Sunset Ridge to Riverwood, her mind cooking up every questions and possible scenarios. She got to Riverwood in no time and she located Margaret's house in minutes.

As she approached the house, she saw a man standing outside, talking to an officer. He was a tall, imposing figure with a rugged face and a stern expression. Sara felt a flutter of nervousness as she approached him, but she pushed it aside. She was a journalist, and she had a job to do.

She went under the crime scene tape and walked towards them, extending her hand. "I'm Sara Lee, a journalist from Sunset Ridge. I'm here to cover the story of Margaret's death."

Jack looked at her warily, his eyes narrowing slightly. "Why are you talking to me then?" he asked gruffly.

"I want to know what happened to Margaret," Sara replied, her pen poised over her notebook. "Was it an accident?"

"I am not an officer; I am just a concerned neighbour." She looked at the man, unsure of the answer he just gave. Why did they allow a random person who's not an officer under the tape. She turned to ask why he was allowed but the man was no longer standing there. She quickly looked around but did not get any trace of him.

She walked back out to the police cars, which were parked outside Margaret's house. The officers were standing nearby, discussing the case in hushed tones. Sara approached them, her notebook and pen at the ready.

"What's the latest?" she asked one of the officers leaning against the hood of one of the cars.

The officer hesitated, clearly unsure how much to reveal. "We're still processing the scene," he said finally.

Sara nodded, taking mental notes. She asked a few more questions, but the officer was tight-lipped, refusing to reveal any more details. Sara thanked him and headed back to the house to take some photos. She knew she had to come back here alone if she was going to search this house. She walked towards her car and drove away from Margaret's house. She found a spot to park just down the street and she slouched behind the wheels, so her face was not so visible.

She just needed the police out of the way so she could do her thing without interruption. From her side mirror, she could see the police vehicles parked in front of Margaret's house.

At about thirty minutes past 8pm, she was certain there will be no one left at the house as the police vehicles had left a while ago. She came down from her car, locked it and walked back towards the house. Her camera was around her neck, and she had a little notepad attached to her hip. She took calculated strides and when she got to the house, she stood by the police tape and just took in the building from the outside. It was a portable building with an open porch. There was a flower bed just underneath the window facing out front. Typical older woman feels. The house was dark, and Sara wondered what Margaret's last living moments in that place were like.

She ducked under the tape and approached the front door. She turned to look around if anyone was around the area. Satisfied, she turned and continued towards the door that she found was left cracked open. She scrunched her brows at the door and quickly brought out her phone. She turned on the flashlight and slowly pushed the door open. She stepped in and slowly pushed the door back to the position it was.

She put her torch forward and scanned the house. It was just like it was in the afternoon. The curtains were drawn and were static, meaning the windows were shut.

She heard a creak coming from the house and she froze, lowering her torch to her side. After some seconds, she relaxed, she figured it was probably her mind playing tricks on her. She raised her torch and moved deeper into the house. She rounded a corner and came face to face with someone.

It seemed like her body system shut down at that point. She froze with her mouth open in silent scream, she wanted to run but her legs seemed to have a mind of their own as they decided to stay put.

The man before her quickly put his hand over her mouth and dragged her into the kitchen which was what was just by the corner. In her head, she was already apologizing to all her family and colleagues, she figured this was the end.

She realised that the man had put her in a chair, and he stood before her as if looking for answers. She could suddenly breathe again, and she took a proper look at this person who was probably going to be the last human she saw before she crossed over.

"Wait, it's you?" her eyes widened as she realised it was the same man who said he was a neighbour earlier. So, killers now mingled as regular people to revel in their kill?

She shuddered but she resolved that if she was going down, she could just do it bravely.

"Are you the killer?" she asked suddenly.

The man was taken aback but he quickly composed his demeanour, folding his arms.

"You wouldn't be asking me that If I was."

"So, who are you?"

Jack could almost guess who this woman was and what she does. He watched her in the afternoon as she tried to get answers from every corner, the annoying little box that flashes at everything.

Jack has always been wearied of journalists. They are the one entity he cannot stand. He looked down at the smallish woman sitting in the chair. He had caught her before her body system resumed function. That scream would have brought everyone within hearing distance there and that will be a lot of explaining to do. She had the same fire the journalist does, notes on her hips and camera around her neck.

"You are not an officer, which means you're tampering with evidence?" Sara accessed the man who towered over her and does not look so scary anymore. There was still an air around him she could not place yet but she didn't care. Her journalistic side kicked in. She just wanted answers.

"I am a private investigator." Jack said in defeat. He didn't have time to do any back and forth with this fiery small woman, so he had better get it over with.

The man said he was not an officer, but a private investigator and she almost jumped in joy. This person was a golden ticket to her documentary. A private investigator was more detailed and thorough in their search and since he was here, it meant he was also involved in the case.

"So what have you found so far?" she asked again, as her heartbeat slowly regulated. She stood up for the first time since he put her in the seat and she realised just how small she looked standing before him. She had to tip her head up to even look at his face and her head was barely reaching his chest. He turned and started looking at the walls and she stuck close to him.

Jack did not respond to her question, he just kept on checking for clues.

"If you are here, it means you believe there's something more to Margaret's death, what are your thoughts ?"

"Talk to one of the officers, they will fill you in." Jack just wanted her off his back. But he realised that she would not let him be if he didn't give her something.

Jack hesitated, clearly unsure of how much to reveal. "They are still investigating," he said finally. "They think Margaret's death was not an accident. They are looking at it as a possible homicide."

Sara's eyes widened in surprise. "A homicide?" she repeated. "But you know there is more and that's why you're here right?" she tapped her palm on her thighs.

Jack sighed, rubbing his temples. "Look, Ms. Lee, I don't have time to answer all your questions right now. They still processing the scene, and I need to focus on my investigation."

"Will you agree to help my documentary ?" Sara asked him. He looked at her and just walked further into the house.

She followed him closely as she had put off her touch and the only source of light was from him.

"I don't know how yet but I know this is very much connected to the silent killer case, we just need to find where the tracks are leading don't you think?" she continued to say other things that was getting on Jack's nerves.

Sara felt a surge of frustration. She knew that Jack was trying to brush her off, but she was determined to get the story. "I understand that you're busy, sir," she said, "but I need to get some information for my readers. Can you at least tell me if there are any suspects?"

Jack's expression turned cold and he tuned to her. "I'm not going to speculate about suspects or motives," he said. "You'll just have to wait for the official statement."

Sara nodded, making a note in her book. She knew that she would have to be patient, but she was determined to get to the bottom of the story.

As Sara continued to ask questions, Jack's expression grew increasingly irritated. She knew this man would be instrumental and so she decided to let him off the hook for a while.

At this point they had gotten to a room. It was clearly Margret's room. Jack pointed his torch at various corners of the room as if he was expecting something to jump out at him.

Sara was at the door, her phone torch on and she took in the room. It was a typical old lady room, with a spring bed and white sheets. The bed was laid, which meant Margret did not get to sleep in her bed for the last time. Shame.

There was a cupboard by the side of the bed and and old lamp was on the top of the cupboard. She pointed her torch at the walls, they were a boring cream colour that looked like it was fading. As she made to step further into the room, she saw Jack crouched at a corner of the room and she moved closer and saw that he was looking at something, his torch was focused on it. She went around him and stood before him. He was staring at the floor intently, his eyes narrowed in concentration.

She saw that he was examining a small, withered flower. It was , with petals that seemed to be barely clinging to the stem.

Sara's heart skipped a beat as she recognized the flower. She had seen it so many times before, in the photos and reports of the Silent Killer's victims. It was the same type of flower that was always found in the clothing of the victims.

Sara felt a chill run down her spine, not fear but from budding excitement. This could only mean one thing, the silent killer is back and this just took a whole new turn.

Jack stood up and stared at her with a brow raised. He saw the glint in her eye cursed under his breath. He reached into his pocket and pulled out a glove and bent to pick the withered flower.

He had more serious things to deal with. Why was the flower there? If it was the silent killer, it was to be fresh but this was withered.

Did Margret possess information that could have revealed who the silent killer really was?

He didn't know where to start thinking from, but he had to get the flower into an evidence bag. Thankfully, be brought a few with. He planned to 'borrow' evidence from the scene and return them later.

"You think the Silent Killer did this?" she asked with a tired voice. Jack paused for a moment and closed his eyes.

"Investigations will tell," he muttered.

He suddenly turned and grabbed her by the shoulders, firm but not hurting her. "you cannot tell anyone you saw me or that you even came here, you are going to get into trouble if you do and you will never find me. Are we clear?"

She was in shock for a moment and quickly shook it off as she slowly smiled, "then you should be ready to give me whatever I want, tit for tat."

Jack groaned and lifted his palms off her shoulder. He knew he had just gotten himself into a deal with a chatterbox.

CHAPTER TWENTY-ONE

Unseen

Yet another death, this time it's not some random guy no one knows, it's not just a familiar face you might have bumped into. This one's deeper, this one had the heart and soul of Riverwood growing within her. And might have been the solution to the silent killer's case. It looked like it. She was for a fact one of the main characters of the silent killer's original case. She could have easily put the puzzles together, filled in the gaps, and gave answers to the thousands of questions people had. She might have been the superhero in the story, the saviour everyone hoped for. So much for never giving up, because even if the kids had little hope left, they would definitely be pushed to the verge of giving up.

It's a whole different pain to have had something within grasp and then lose it. Sometimes it's better not to have had it at all. That is what Margaret's death felt like. Every death felt different, a different kind of hurt but this one, it left the night a bit darker than it already was.

Jack looked rougher than usual, not the hot looking bad guy kind of rough. The type that is exhausted, stressed out with bags under his eyes. He had not shaved in weeks and he looked like he would smell horrible too. From random deaths to more targeted victims. Shit just got real. Not like it wasn't real before but it seemed the silent killer's feathers had been ruffled and he wanted to make a statement, a loud one. It could only mean one thing though, they got close to the truth.

Against the light music and loud chit chats at the bar, Jack clanged his glass on the counter and caught the attention of the bartender who gave him a 'break that glass and I'll fuck you up' look. Their eyes crossed for a second just before Jack looked away, his mind too preoccupied to read his expression. "Aaah." He let out a quiet cry from the sting of the neat martini which burned down his throat. He loved the burn, it made him feel better, gave him a sense of satisfaction at least for the moment.

A Jasmine scent filled the air around him and someone pulled a stool closer to him. "I'll have what he's having." The soft voice said. Jack tried to ignore at first but his curiosity won't let him. He turned to his left, his expression mixed with confusion. "Martha."

"Try again."

"Maya?" Maya gave him a soft smile in approval. "What are you doing here?"

"Same as you, grieving."

"I'm not grieve… what the… you can't drink that, are you even eighteen?" Jack stuttered as he watched the bartender serve Maya. She took a sip and let out a long loud cry.

"Yuck." She said with her face squeezed and her tongue out. "That's disgusting. How do you guys drink this?"

"Stick to cocktails and soda, kid." Jack replied with a frown on his face.

"I definitely will. I'm twenty by the way, not a kid." Maya rolled her eyes. She stared at Jack who barely noticed her reaction with his face in his hands. "Hey…" she poked him softly on his shoulder. "…you ok?"

"I will be when that sucker's six feet deep." Jack rubbed his eyes, the wrinkled lines strained on his face.

"You look terrible." Maya blurted out.

"Thanks." Jack replied with a sudden expression, his hands out in the air like obviously, tell me something I don't already know. Jack was always the kind thrilled and excited by complicated cases like this, he never liked his cases simple, more of the ones that gave him a good adrenaline rush and spiked his blood pressure, bad for his health but good for his zeal. This case however, this one took a toll on him and it's admittedly written all over him.

"Hey," Maya whispered and leaned over him. "Why don't we go back to the crime scene, see what we can find."

Jack turned to Maya. Her eyes desperate, filled with curiosity and begged for a yes.

"It's a closed crime scene." Jack dismissed her.

"Oh come on, when has that ever stopped you. Do you really want to play good cop?"

Jack sipped his drink and then turned to her, he rubbed his eyes again and tried to decide if he should go or not. He already knew what he wanted to do. He just didn't want to go there with Maya. He never liked it when someone tagged along with him on a case, especially one that involved a serial killer. He had lost a good number of partners in his days as a cop and that had taught him the hard way to always stick alone. And the worse part of it, the damned do's and don'ts never allowed him to properly avenge them. He had gotten in trouble more than a few times for breaking and bending the rules. The police can only do much to cover for their own. When they had enough of his solo Rambo havocs, they were forced to let him go. Jack hated not having the badge on him. Being a cop was the only thing he knew so he didn't stop. He decided to be the one thing good hated more than criminals, a private investigator. No guiding policies, no rules, no boss to answer to and most importantly, no partner to risk, it was just perfect, everything he wanted.

"Come on…" Maya said in a singing tone. "…you know you want to." Her face beamed and Jack couldn't help but smile. He gulped down his drink and grabbed his keys.

"Let's go."

"You know the good thing about living in an old suburban house?" Jack asked as he picked open the window lock with a little metal tool.

"It's easy to break and enter." Maya blurted out.

"Don't say it like that, you make it look like we're doing something illegal."

"Isn't that what we're doing?"

Jack rolled his eyes as he climbed in and held up the window for Maya to climb in too. "We're trying to speed up the investigation, help catch a serial killer, that's what we're doing." Maya leaned on the window rail and struggled to get in. "For Christ's sake." Jack cussed as he grabbed her legs and pulled her in. She thumped on the floor and whispered in pain. "Shhh, keep your voice down." Jack ignored her.

They both walked around the house which pretty much looked the same except the bright white mark that was left where Margaret's body was found. It was dark but the moonlight was bright enough to light up the room. There was no sign of struggle. Why would there be? She was an elderly lady. It must have been very easy for the killer. Maya lifted an almost dead flower from a vase.

"Don't touch anything." Jack scolded. Just then, they heard a light ruffle but loud enough to echo in the dead silent of the night. Their eyes in synch darted towards the kitchen and in a split second, footsteps were heard running off. Jack in a swift move sprinted towards the sound and headed to the kitchen in pursuit. Maya just stood there, unsure of what to do. She stood on guard, flashed her eyes across the room and looked outside.

A few minutes later Jack rushed back in.

"Who was that?"

"No idea, he ran off. Come on, we gotta go." Jack pulled open the window and they climbed out.

It looked like Jack and Maya wasn't the only ones curious enough to go back to the crime scene. Either that or it could have been the killer which was unlikely. Killers usually returned to the crime scene but on many cases, it turned out not to be killer lurking. But would a serial killer return to the crime scene? It just increased their chances of getting caught. Jack hoped with everything in him that whoever it was did not see their faces. He hated entanglements with cops and most especially for the sake of Maya, he feared the killer might come after her.

"Hey guys." Alex greeted as he strode towards his friends. The gang had gathered at the river banks. Emily and Maya sat on Tyler's car trunk engaged in an endless conversation while Tyler was at the river shore, he threw stones in them and strived to see how far it would go before it sank. Ethan just sat under the tree and ignored the world around him with his headphones.

"Hey man." Tyler replied Alex, he panted a bit from the little activity he engaged himself in. They exchanged handshakes and nudged their shoulders. "You've been MIA man, didn't even reply my texts."

"Sorry bro. I've just been in my head…"

"Hey take it easy, we're in this together, if you need anything…"

"Sure man, of course." Alex replied.

"Hey Al!" Maya and Emily chorus as soon as they sighted Alex. Tyler threw a stone at Ethan who jolted up and tried to throw it back. The two ended up in a rough play, they pursued each other and threw themselves down.

"Hey, how have you guys been holding up?" Alex asked the girls.

"I've been pretty good. I don't think I'm shocked anymore."

"Not me." Emily cut in. "I can't even sleep with the lights off anymore."

"This is all our fault." Maya said sadly.

"Hey, don't do that. We can't blame ourselves, we didn't know."

"Yeah but if we hadn't gone to see her. She managed to stay alive for over twenty years and now she's…"

"Hey, Em's right." Alex added. "There's no way we would have known plus that was the best decision we could make at the time. We can't keep living in the shadows. We need the killer to know we're coming for him."

"At what cost?"

"Whatever it cost." Tyler joined in with Ethan. They both looked messed up from the play .

"Yeah, Al's right. We need the killer to know we're coming for him. I don't know about y'all but I'm done being scared. No more sitting ducks." Ethan added.

The rev of a car engine shut down caught their attention and they all turned towards the sound.

"Great, here comes the kill joy." Alex sighed.

Jack stepped out of his car, he looked tattered as usual, worse actually.

"Why is he here?" Emily whispered.

"Guys be nice, we're all on the same page." Maya said.

"I like how you guys are always together, nice tactics. Makes it hard for the killer to target any of you." Jack yelled from a distance as he approached them.

"It's not just about that, we're friends." Emily replied him.

"Hmmm, friends, can't recall the meaning of that. Must be nice anyway."

"What are you doing here?" Ethan asked.

"Oh the town was a bit too quiet so I thought to myself, what are those meddling kids up to?"

"We're just here minding our business." Tyler replied

Jack scoffed. "You guys have been doing everything but minding your business. Hey, relax.." Jack continued after he saw the look on their faces. "You don't need to be all defensive, you're not in any kind of trouble. However, I do need you guys to tell me if you know anything about… you know, everything."

"Why would we do that?" Tyler huffed.

"Listen big guy, I think we're way past all these." Jack calmly said with a smirk on his face. He gently paced around. "I need you guys to be careful. I know this is impossible to ask but you guys have to stop digging into the silent killer's case."

"And let you have all the fun? No way." Tyler responded.

"This is a joke." Emily said nonchalantly and walked away.

"I'm serious guys. We might be dealing with the original killer. Margaret's death wasn't a mistake. We might have poked the hornet's nest."

"Great, we'll do it again." Ethan retorted.

"Next time, it could be any of you!" Jack roared. "Don't you get it, we can't keep putting ourselves in his radar, it's risky."

"Oh please Jack, if you thought about the risk, you wouldn't have let me tag along last night." Maya responded.

The whole gang turned to her surprised. Tyler especially. His eyes widened. "Wait, that was you guys last night?"

Maya and Jack turned to him. "Was... was that you?" Maya questioned, just as surprised as he was.

"What the hell were you thinking going back to a crime scene?" Jack fumed.

"Same thing you were thinking." Tyler retorted.

"Unbelievable." Jack hissed. He brushed his fingers through his hair, disturbed at the fact that these kids were deep into the case and might just end up dead. He hated the thought of it, not after Dona, he just might never forgive himself.

***

Jack had left them alone finally and they were sitting in silence for the first time since that day. Maybe Jack was right after all, they were getting more and more involved, they could draw the attention or whoever harmed Margaret. Tyler drummed his fingers against the table, staring down at the half-empty glass of water in front of him. Maya had her arms crossed, her nails digging into the sleeves of her jacket. Emily stared blankly at the wall in front of her, Ethan leaned back, glancing at the doorway where Jack had disappeared, while Alex simply sat there, with his mind turning over everything they had just heard.

Something about this case wasn't adding up. At first, they had been so focused on Ben's case and the many other victims. But now, they wondered about the ones who could get away from Riverwood. Alex was the first to speak.

"Why did Lucy buy that diner?"

She had never been in the restaurant business. She had no reason to invest in a failing diner in a dying town. She had another life and fortune.

"You know, when rich people do weird things, it's usually because they feel guilty about something." Maya replied.

Alex glanced at her. "You think she felt guilty?"

Maya shrugged. "People don't just walk away from good lives unless they're running from something... or trying to make up for something."

"She never sold the diner either."

They all turned their gaze at him as if throwing him a big question mark.

"I mean, she left. She left, but she never sold the diner. She never passed it down to someone else. No one ever put up a 'For Sale' sign. Her staff was just left to manage it until the fire accident."

Ethan shrugged. "Her staff? You mean Margaret? And?"

Alex continued. "And she was never declared missing."

Tyler sat up straighter. "Well yeah, she left. That's what people do when they get bored of a place. That's what I'd do."

"She did lose her child and the town blamed her, her ex-husband and new wife for it. So maybe she got bored of the town." Emily added.

"Margaret," he said finally. "Why didn't she leave? Everyone else did. Everyone else who survived either moved away or shut up about what happened. But Margaret stayed."

Maya agreed. "She loved that diner."

"Yeah," Tyler added. "She called it home."

"And she worked there before Lucy ever showed up and continued working there after Lucy disappeared. She worked there when people started disappearing. She saw the fire and the aftermath, and she stayed even when she had nothing left."

"Until she died," Ethan muttered.

"Okay, but what?" Maya asked.

Margaret had been one of the only people left who still talked about the past. She had been the town's memory, a woman who never told the same story twice.

"Margaret must have had something on Lucy that made her buy the diner" he said. "And Lucy may have left town for the same reason. Lucy may have silenced Margaret."

No one spoke for a while as they exchanged glances, half-figuring if it made sense, because suddenly, the question of Lucy's disappearance was just as important as the question of Margaret's death.

CHAPTER TWENTY TWO

Reed Legacy

It was beginning to look like a constant field trip for them now. They had decided that since it would always be a hassle back at their town, they could as well continue to check around River wood for more clues to get to the root of this case. They had set out in the afternoon with Tyler driving them there.

They have been trying to avoid Jack since he was now bent more than ever to stop them from going on with the case. But they have gone too far now to back down from this case.

They were now in what used to be one of the living areas of the Reeds castle.

"Even with it being burnt down, you can just feel the grandeur that this place used to be" Emily said in awe as she turned around, trying to take it all in at once.

It was clear that the things they have read about the Reeds castle were true as it still stood strong and captivating despite the fact that it is now covered in black sooth and dust and fire marks.

When James decided to build his dream house, he spared no expense in ensuring it was a masterpiece. The house was designed in the classic Victorian style, with details and ornate features that showcased the era. The exterior was covered in sturdy stone, with tall spires that gave it a sophisticated look.

The house was covered with large windows, each framed in woodwork and stained glass. The front door, a grand entrance, was made of solid oak and it was lacquered.

Inside, the house was a breath taking work of interior design. The walls were painted in rich colours and accompanied with wallpaper to complement. The floors were made of polished hardwood, reflecting the light from the large chandeliers that hung from the ceilings. Each room was carefully furnished with pieces that reflected James' expensive taste from the plush sofas and armchairs to the finely crafted dining tables and chairs.

The house also known for its a grand ballroom, perfect for the lavish parties that the Reeds were known to host sometimes. The ballroom had a high ceiling, with a chandelier that sparkled like diamonds under the light. The walls were lined with sturdy wood on one side and the other side had mirrors fitted. The floor was made of polished oak, ideal for dancing.

Now this was about twenty years after the fire, and the house being abandoned, yet, the house retained much of its original charm. The pillars and the crafts on it, though weathered, still stood strong, The windows, mostly broken with the shards everywhere on the floor, still reflected the sunlight and casted a kaleidoscope of colours on the ground. The walls were mostly covered in black but there were still streaks of colour that used to provide the warmth for the castle. They went up the stairs, still sturdy under their feet but worn and filled with soot.

They went to the ballroom and looked around. It looked like a train wreck, a sharp contrast to the beauty it was.

The chandelier had somehow stood strong, hanging dangerously above, horrifying as against the beauty it used to be. The mirrors on the side of the wall were mostly shattered while some still stood strong with cracks in them.

The floor had thick dirt covering it but as they moved around, they still felt the solid oak floor.

There was still an air around the room, a reminder of what it used to be .

It was a quiet examination as everyone was wrapped in their own thoughts. Maya walked towards the side of the room with mirrors and stood in front of one that managed to stick together albeit cracked. She looked at herself in the mirror but all she could see was Donna's parts on the floor. She quickly shut her eyes and shuddered. It has haunted her everyday since then, in fact the whole thing was doing the same. Tyler almost dying, the deaths and Emma.

From what they know, after James brought Racheal in, they sold the house as they had planned to leave Riverwood even before the fire happened.

They got a buyer who paid and got documents but he never moved in. After they sold, the buyer realised there was a litigation case and he did not want to risk his new purchase being taken away from him at the end of the day. Well, the whole thing was abandoned in the end after the fire took the town. It has not been returned to since.

As the sun began to set, Maya, Tyler, Alex, Ethan, and Emily, made their way back to the car to gather their supplies. They had decided to stay the night at the castle so they came packed with their makeshift beds, overnight bags and torches. The darkness was starting to creep in, and they had found a room that they could stay in in the castle. It was a dusty room that still had some of the furniture like the side table and bed frame. It was in a slightly better condition compared to the other areas of the house. They turned on two of the torches they had with them and pointed it at the ceilings to serve the whole room with light.

The room was not entirely spared from the fire, but it was clear that it had been less affected than the other areas of the house they had seen. Streaks of burn marked the walls, and the air was still somehow thick with the smell of smoke and decay despite it being many years after. The windows of this particular room were not entirely intact but it was not as bad as the other room, and it allowed a faint glow of moonlight to filter in.

As they set up their makeshift beds, they couldn't help but notice the faded paintings that adorned the walls. They were old and worn, but they still managed to carry that aura of elegance and regal. The paintings depicted scenes of rolling hills, majestic mountains, and serene lakes, showing that whoever owned that room probably had a thing for nature.

"This place is actually kind of cool," Tyler said, his voice filled with excitement, as he set up his sleeping bag.

"I wonder if this was Ben's room," Maya said, looking intently at faded paintings.

"Yeah, it's like we're in a real-life horror movie," Alex replied, his eyes scanning the room with a mixture of fascination and fear.

"Shut up, Alex," Maya said, playfully rolling her eyes. "We're not going to let some creepy old castle scare us."

Emily was quietly unpacking their dinner and watched as the others bantered and laughed. She knew they were just trying to keep each others' spirits high and away from fear. She noticed that Ethan was quiet as she could not hear his voice amidst the chatter. She knew he was naturally quiet but he was not even responding to the jabs as usual.

She looked up and saw him at one side of the wall. He had a torch in his hand and it was pointed at the wall that he seemed to be carried away by. He is probably cooking up another theory in that nerdy head of his again.

She turned to continue unpacking. Maya, even if she was not saying, has been pretty unstable since the night of discovering Donna's body and she was really worried for her.

The night was getting colder and she was thankful she had her thick sweater on.

She turned to look at Alex as he kept talking and laughing. She felt the tiniest bit of anger rising in her gut. The audacity he had. She just wanted to match up to him and hit him in the face for what he did at the club. She just said the things she said that day to get out of the drama but she knew she had not forgiven him yet deep down. He apologized but she was not ready to forgive.

Just as she was about to call everyone to come pick up plates , Ethan, who had been quiet until now, spoke up, his voice filled with curiosity. "Hey, guys, look at this," he said, pointing the torch in his hand on a particular spot on the wall, it was one of the paintings on the wall. They turned to look but they didn't know what they were supposed to be looking at. They turned to look at Ethan, who nudged his head and pointed again. He turned his fingers in circles around what he was pointing at but still, nothing.

"You know you can just save us the time by saying exactly what we should be looking at" Tyler said and rolled his eyes.

"Look, it's really just tiny and a bunch of colours from our viewpoint here," Maya said slowly as she started to get up.

Ethan sighed and asked them to come closer. They all got up and walked towards him, huddling around as they got close.

They examined the spot Ethan was pointing his torch at. It was a painting, like what the walls were covered with but this was different. It was small, so small a palm would cover it up. It was a painting The first thing they noted was the image painted, it was a man and a woman with a little boy in front of them. The boy was not fully painted like the man and the woman as they could only make out the head, facial structure, shoulders and collar bone of the boy. The painting was so small but detailed that one palm could cover the whole thing.

They still were not sure what exact thing Ethan wanted them to see.

Just before anyone could say what was on all their minds, Alex suddenly gasped.

"This painting was made after the fire" Alex said like someone who just found a treasure.

The others huddled even closer at this revelation, Tyler took the torch out Ethan's hand and stood right in front of the painting, and almost put his forehead on the wall with how close he was standing.

He turned to Alex, who was still excited at his find and asked, " and how did you figure that out Einstein?"

Alex quickly shuffled to his side and took the torch. He pointed it at the painting and used his palm to wipe the surface of the painting.

"Look, it was just covered in dust, no soot or burn, this was definitely painted after the fire." He continued with determination.

Ethan spoke up after Alex landed, he added that the painting was most likely not done by a professional like the ones covering the room and the strokes of brush looked weird.

"Who do you think they are?" Emily asked, her voice coming out in breaths.

"I don't know," Tyler replied, "but they look like they were pretty important." He pointed at the details in the outfit on the man and woman. It was almost royal, pearls were depicted on the woman's slender neck, and she had a flowy ball gown. The man had a gold glint on his arm depicting a watch.

"What if the silent killer did this?" Maya asked quietly.

They all turned to look at her, an air of brood setting in.

Tyler noticed this and determined to not stay in fear decided to lighten the mood.

"Our first clue for the night, not a bad start? Can we go ear now?"

They all released breathes they did not realise they were holding and went back to the dinner Emily was laying out for them.

In no time they all got back to their pumped selves, the ones who will be having a slumber party in an abandoned castle.

They all released breaths they did not realise they were holding and went back to the dinner Emily was laying out for them.

In no time they all got back to their pumped selves, the ones who will be having a slumber party in an abandoned castle.

As they sat down to eat, Emily handed out plates to everyone and proceeded to fill each plate with meat balls. When Alex put his plate forward, she stared at it and then slowly up to him and dropped the bowl of meatball before him so he could serve himself. This did not go unnoticed but they all decided not to say anything about it. If they had issues with each other, they were grown to settle it.

Alex scoffed and served himself. He was not ready to pick the bait

As they began to eat, Alex made it his point of duty to lighten the mood once more. He cracked jokes and while the others seemed to enjoy it, Emily was always waiting with a tackle.

As the night went on, it was becoming evident that Emily was brewing for a fight with Alex.

Ethan was eating quietly, the fight between Emily and Alex worsened his grieving state. He had tried all he could to get over Becky's death but no luck. He had wondered time and again how things would have played differently. Maybe she would be there if he had manned up earlier and said something.

He sighed and dropped his plate, and looked from one person to the next. Tyler had just lived everyday like he was not just at the verge of death, and he knew they were all a ticking time bomb.

Soon enough, it erupted as he thought. Emily had decided to pick on something Alex had said. Her eyes narrowed and her voice became edgy. "You think that's funny, Alex? You think it's okay to just bring that up like it's no big deal?"

Alex's smile faltered, and he looked taken aback. "I was just trying to make a joke, Emily. I didn't mean and have not said anything to hurt your feelings."

The others shifted at the tension that was quickly building up. Emily was at that brink and she wasn't going to listen to anyone.

"You never mean to hurt my feelings, Alex, but you always seem to find a way. You're so insensitive, it's like you don't even care about how I feel."

They looked on uncomfortably as the argument escalated. Ethan, sighed, struggling really hard to push down on his own feelings and intervene, but Maya spoke up first.

"Hey, guys, can we just drop it? We're all trying to eat here."

But Emily was having none of it. "No, Maya, we can't just drop it. Alex needs to understand that what he did was not okay, and he needs to apologize for it."

Alex sighed, his eyes flashing with frustration. "Emily, I've apologized a million times. What more do you want from me?"

But Emily was not having it. She stood up, and glared at Alex. "I want you to understand that what you did was hurtful, and I want you to acknowledge it. But I guess that's too much to ask from someone as insensitive as you."

With that, she turned and stalked away, leaving the others in an uncomfortable silence.

Tyler, who had been watching the exchange with a mixture of fascination and concern, spoke up. "Well, I guess that's one way to clear the air."

But Maya shot him a look, her eyes welling up with tears. "That's not funny, Tyler. You have no idea what it's like."

Tyler's smile faltered, and he looked taken aback. "Hey, I was just trying to lighten the mood. We have a case to deal with here, remember?."

Maya bursted out at this and raised her voice "What the hell happened to you Mr? You're so caught up in this case, you've forgotten what it's like to be human. You're insensitive, just like Alex." She turned and glared at Alex.

Her eyes were shining with tears she was struggling to hold back.

Ethan spoke up, his voice soft and gentle. "Hey, guys, let's just take a deep breath and calm down. We're all stressed out, and we need to support each other."

But the damage was done. The tension was still high and Emily was not coming back in. They could hear her footsteps echoing somewhere close like a soldier.

The food was looking uninteresting at this point and they were all in their own thoughts.

Maya stood up after what seemed like minutes and walked away in the direction Emily went.

"Well, that's one way to ruin something important," Tyler said and picked up his plate.

The others looked at him like he had grown another head, each wondering what exactly was going through his head to keep behaving this way. Was he just trying to hide his fear behind nonchalance or he really had lost touch with reality?

CHAPTER TWENTY-THREE

Love and Chaos

Tyler stood at the door of the room they were camped in, an unreadable expression on his face. He didn't understand why Maya was suddenly acting up. Was there something they should do that he forgot about? Or was she just overreacting? Ladies could be a handful sometimes. He sighed, running a hand through his hair as he looked from left to right. Where was he supposed to look for her? The castle was massive, its dark hallways twisting and turning like a maze.

He groaned and went to the left, poking his head into each room as he moved. The air was heavy, the silence broken only by the sound of his footsteps echoing off the stone walls. He called her name softly, his voice barely carrying through the empty space. "Maya? You in here?"

No answer. He moved to the next room, then the next, his frustration growing with each step. Finally, he reached the staircase. He paused, looking up at the shadowy steps that led to the upper floors. Maybe she went up there. He climbed the stairs slowly, his boots scraping against the worn stone.

At the top, he found her. Maya was sitting on the edge of the staircase, her knees pulled up to her chest, her arms wrapped tightly around them. She was staring off into the distance, her face pale and her eyes red-rimmed. Tyler hesitated for a moment, watching her from a distance. She looked so small, so fragile, like a gust of wind could blow her away.

He walked over quietly, his footsteps careful so as not to startle her. When he reached her, he sat down beside her, leaving a small space between them. For a while, neither of them spoke. The silence stretched, heavy and uncomfortable.

"Maya," Tyler said finally, his voice soft. "What's going on? Why did you leave??"

Maya didn't look at him. Her gaze stayed fixed on some point in the distance, her expression unreadable. "I just needed some space," she said, her voice barely above a whisper.

Tyler frowned. "Space? From what? From me?"

Maya didn't answer right away. When she finally spoke, her voice was tight, like she was holding back tears. "You don't get it, Tyler. You don't get any of it."

Tyler's frown deepened. "What don't I get? Tell me. I'm trying to understand."

Maya turned to look at him then, her eyes blazing with anger and hurt. "You don't get how hard this is for me. For all of us. You're so caught up in this case, in finding answers, that you've forgotten what it's like to just... feel. To care." Tyler blinked, taken aback.

At that moment, Ethan passed by them on the stairs and they went quiet as they watched him go down the stairs and disappeared under it.

Tyler turned back to Maya, "That's not true. I care. I care about you, about all of us. But we have to focus on the case. We have to find out who's behind all of this."

Maya shook her head, her voice rising. "No, Tyler. You don't get it. This isn't just about the case. This is about us. About what we've been through. About what we're still going through. And you... you're just ignoring it. Pretending like everything's fine when it's not."

Tyler opened his mouth to respond, but Maya was already standing up, her movements sharp and angry. "I can't do this right now," she said, her voice trembling. "I can't be around you when you're like this."

Before Tyler could say anything else, she turned and stormed off, her footsteps echoing down the staircase. Tyler sat there for a moment, stunned, before letting out a frustrated sigh. He didn't understand what he'd done wrong, but one thing was clear, Maya was hurting, and he had no idea how to fix it.

Maya stormed down the staircase, her chest heaving with anger and frustration. She didn't know where she was going, only that she needed to get away from Tyler, from the tension, from everything. The castle felt like a maze, she didn't concentrate to know where she wanted to go. . She turned a corner, her footsteps echoing off the stone walls, and found herself in a dimly lit room.

Ethan was there, sitting on the edge of a dusty and sparily burnt iron bed frame. His head was bowed, his hands resting on his knees, his shoulders slumped like he was being pressed down . He looked up as Maya entered, his eyes hollow and tired, but he didn't say anything. He just watched her, his expression unreadable.

Maya hesitated in the doorway, her anger momentarily forgotten. She hadn't expected to find anyone here. There was something about the way he looked, so broken, so lost, that drew her in. She stepped into the room, her voice soft. "Ethan? Are you okay?"

Ethan shook his head, his gaze dropping to the floor. "No," he said quietly. "Not really."

Maya walked over and sat down beside him, leaving a small space between them. The room was silent except for the sound of their breathing. For a while, neither of them spoke. Maya didn't know what to say. She was still angry, still hurt, but seeing Ethan like this made her own problems feel small in comparison.

"I'm sorry," Ethan said finally, his voice barely above a whisper. "About everything. About Dona. About… all of this."

Maya's chest tightened at the mention of Dona. She hadn't talked about it much, not with anyone. The memory of seeing body parts was still fresh, still raw. She swallowed hard, her voice trembling. "It's not your fault, Ethan. None of this is your fault."

Ethan didn't respond right away. When he finally spoke, his voice was thick with emotion. "Maybe if we didn't go digging, maybe none of this…" he didn't seem to find the right words to complete his statement so he just made gestures with his hands.

Maya reached out, placing a hand on his arm. "You can't blame yourself. You're not the one who did this."

Ethan looked at her then, his eyes searching hers. "But what if I could've stopped it? What if I could've saved her?" Maya immediately knew he was not talking about just Donna anymore or Emma, but he was still hurting from Becky.

"You okay?" Ethan asked finally, his voice gentle.

Maya shook her head, her eyes filling with tears. "No," she whispered. "I'm not."

Ethan didn't say anything. He just sat there, his presence steady and comforting. Maya leaned into him, her head resting on his shoulder. She didn't know why, but being near him made her feel safe, like she could finally let her guard down.

"I don't know what to do," she said, her voice breaking. "Everything feels so... broken. Tyler doesn't get it. He's so focused on the case, on finding answers, that he doesn't see how much we're all falling apart."

Ethan sighed, his arm wrapping around her shoulders. "I get it," he said quietly. "I feel it too. But we'll get through this. We have to."

Maya looked up at him, her eyes searching his. "How? How do we get through this when it feels like everything's falling apart?"

Maya didn't have an answer. She didn't know what to say, how to make him feel better. So instead, she leaned into him, her head resting on his shoulder. It was a small gesture, but it was enough.

Ethan hesitated for a moment before wrapping an arm around her, pulling her closer.

The room was quiet, the tension slowly easing as they sat there, leaning on each other. For the first time in what felt like forever, Maya felt a sense of calm. But then, without warning, the moment shifted. Ethan turned to look at her, his eyes filled with something she couldn't quite place. Before she could think, before she could stop herself, she leaned in and kissed him.

It wasn't romantic, it was desperate, an attempt to feel something other than pain. Ethan froze for a moment, his body tense, before kissing her back. The kiss was brief, but it was enough to make Maya's heart race. She pulled away, her face flushed with guilt and confusion.

"I'm sorry," she said quickly, her voice trembling. "I shouldn't have—"

But before she could finish, she felt the stare before she even saw the person. Alex stood there, his expression a mix of surprise and discomfort. He didn't say anything, just stared at them for a moment until cleared his throat awkwardly. "Uh, sorry. I was looking for Emily."

Maya stood up quickly, her face burning. "It's not what it looks like," she said, her voice was shaky.

Alex held up his hands, taking a step back. "Hey, it's none of my business. I'll just… leave you to it."

He turned and walked out, leaving Maya and Ethan alone in the room. Maya sat back down, her head in her hands. "This is such a mess," she muttered.

Ethan didn't say anything. He just sat there, a blank expression on his face. The uncomfortable feeling was almost like a duvet wrapped around them. She shifted some metres away from him but it was no different.

Tyler was still seated at the top of the stairs moments after Maya left. He had his head in his hands. He was becoming frustrated with Maya not helping in the bud to solve this argument. Was he really that insensitive? He thought he was doing the right thing by focusing on the case, but maybe he'd been wrong. He stood up and sauntered down the stairs and headed for the front door. He pulled one of the door and stepped out into the night. It was a little chilly and he rubbed his arms. The shuffling sound of feet scared him for a split second before Emily stepped into his eyes view. He took a breath of relief. " You kind of scared me." He said with a small laugh.

"Sorry, I heard someone come out and wanted to see who it was." Emily replied as she folded her arms.

"Mind if I join you?" Tyler said out of the corner of his mouth but Emily heard him.

Emily shrugged, as she walked back to the railing. "Sure."

Tyler walked over and stood beside her on the railing, the floorboard making a little creak sound underneath his weight. The silence was hanging like a bloated Ballon waiting to be popped, but it wasn't uncomfortable. It was the kind of quiet that only exists between people who've known each other for a long time.

"You okay?" Emily asked finally, breaking the silence.

Tyler sighed, running a hand through his hair. "Not really. I don't get it, Em. Why is Maya so mad at me? I'm just trying to figure this out, you know."

Emily shrugged and didn't say anything. " You are also angry, is it like a time of the month thing or what?" Emily was getting annoyed and Tyler noticed so he quickly raised his hands in surrender. "Hey hey, I didn't mean that in the wrong way, I'm sorry if that was insensitive."

Emily nodded, her gaze fixed on the floor. "I get that. But you have to understand, Tyler, this isn't just about the case. It's about us. About what we've been through. And you… you've been so focused on finding answers that you've forgotten to check in with the people around you."

Tyler frowned, his chest tightening. "I haven't forgotten. I just... I thought I was doing the right thing."

Emily turned to look at him, her expression softening. "I know you did. But sometimes, the right thing isn't just about solving the case. It's about being there for the people you care about. Maya's hurting, Tyler. And we need you to see that."

Tyler was silent for a long moment, his mind racing. He thought about everything that had happened—Dona's death, Emma's betrayal, the constant fear that the killer was still out there. He'd been so focused on finding answers that he hadn't stopped to think about how it was affecting the people around him.

"I didn't realize," he said finally, his voice quiet. "I didn't mean to hurt her."

Emily placed a hand on his shoulder, her touch reassuring. "I know you didn't. But you need to fix this, Tyler. Before it's too late."

Tyler nodded, his gaze dropping to the floor. "You're right. I'll talk to her. I'll make it right."

Emily smiled, though it didn't quite reach her eyes. "Good."

The conversation shifted then, the tension easing as they started reminiscing about the past. They talked about simpler times, before the silent killer saga had turned their lives upside down. "Things used to be simpler before we decided to get involved you know," Emily allowed a sad smile linger on her face.

Tyler sighed and looked out into the darkness.

"Remember that time we all went camping?" Emily asked, a small smile tugging at her lips. "And Alex tried to cook dinner but ended up burning everything?"

Tyler chuckled, the sound low and warm. "Yeah. And Ethan spent the whole night complaining about how hungry he was. Good times." They laughed.

The conversation eventually circled back to the case like a loop.

"Do you think we'll ever figure it out?" Emily asked, her voice quiet. "Who the original killer is, I mean."

Tyler sighed, his expression grim. "I don't know. But we have to keep trying. "

Emily nodded, though her eyes were distant. "Yeah. We do."

Tyler felt a little clearer, the cold night air was acting like a relief.

"We should head back," Emily said, her voice breaking the silence. "It's not safe to be out here."

Tyler nodded, his gaze lingering on the castle's dark windows. "Yeah. Let's go."

They made their way back inside. As they climbed the stairs, they ran into Alex, who was coming down. He stopped when he saw them, his expression a mix of relief and annoyance.

"Where have you two been?" he asked, his voice low but sharp. "Do you have any idea how dangerous it is to wander around this place alone?"

Emily held up her hands, her tone calm but firm an hint of anger rising. "We were just talking. We're fine, Alex."

Alex sighed, running a hand through his hair. "Yeah, well, next time let someone know. We're supposed to be sticking together, remember?"

Tyler nodded, though he didn't say anything. The tension between them was still there, simmering just below the surface, but they didn't have time to address it now.

They continued up the stairs to the room they were camping in. Maya and Ethan were there, clearing up the remnants of their unfinished dinner.

Alex looked around, his expression grim. "Was this even a good idea in the first place? Staying here, I mean."

Maya glanced up, her eyes tired but defiant. "It's too late to leave now. We're here. We might as well make the best of it."

No one argued. They all knew she was right. There was a killer out there anyways and it was enough wake up call that leaving in the middle of the night wasn't an option. They needed to stick it out until morning.

They managed to create makeshift sleeping spots close to each other, the proximity offering a small sense of security. But sleep didn't come easily. The castle's silence was unnerving, broken only by the occasional creak of old wood or the distant sound of wind whistling through the cracks in the walls.

Tyler, surprisingly, was the first to fall asleep. The exhaustion of the day finally caught up with him, and he drifted off, his breathing deep and even. The others weren't so lucky. They lay awake,all in their small thoughts.

Early the next morning, the group began to stir. The pale light of dawn filtered through the castle's dusty windows, casting long shadows across the room. Emily was the first to get up, her movements quiet as she started packing her things. The others followed suit, their movements with low sense of urgency.

Tyler was the last to wake, his sleep having been deeper than the others'. He sat up, rubbing his eyes as he took in the scene around him. "What's going on?" he asked, his voice groggy.

"We're leaving," Emily said, her tone firm. "We need to get out of here before anyone realizes we were here."

Tyler nodded, quickly gathering his things. The group worked together to clear all traces of their presence, removing their food packs and packing up their belongings. The tension from the night before was still there, but it was muted now, overshadowed by the urgency of their situation.

When they were done, they stepped out of the castle, the cool morning air a reassurance that they made it through the night. They moved quickly, their footsteps quiet as they made their way to the car.

As they drove away, the castle grew smaller in the side mirrors. No one said anything to the other as Tyler drove all in their own thoughts and their unspoken arguments the icing on the cake.

CHAPTER TWENTY FOUR

Stranger Loom

_____

Sara stepped out of her car, her boots crushing gravel was the only sound she could hear. She shut the door of her car and looked around. The remnants of Riverwood lay before Sara like a ghost town, swallowed by time and tragedy. But that's what it was, right? A skeleton of what it was.

The burnt buildings stood quiet and still, their dark, crumbling shapes cutting into the pale sky. Empty window frames, where life and laughter once filled the air, now looked like hollow eyes. They were either shattered or boarded up, and the few remaining signs swung creakily in the breeze. The faint smell of smoke hung in the breeze, a glaring reminder of the fire that had destroyed this town twenty years before. Weeds and vines pushed through the broken pavement, slowly taking over what was left. There was this slight cold that she could tell was not from the weather.

This part of the town had not been reinhabited since.

She would have done this when she came days ago, but she was so tired by the morning after her little break- in episode. Besides, she was needed at work back in Sunset Ridge. So she decided to use her off day to come back to Riverwood for more digging.

Sara had been going over the things she saw since she left. She felt like she was close to unravelling the mystery. Margret's death felt like the final thread she needed to pull.

She tucked her hands in her jacket pocket and turned to the diner, well, what was left of it. She decided to start there and move to the castle later. Her footsteps echoed in the empty street. The building was like charred wood, what was left of the door was hanging by the hinges. She stepped inside, her boots kicking up ash that still clung to the floor.

Here she was at the scene zero of the fire. Where it all started. It never ceased to amaze her, the disastrous monster fire was if it was untamed. She wasn't expecting to see anything here, everything was burnt beyond recognition and the police then had checked the ace several times 20 years ago when it happened. She just wanted to take pictures, and maybe, see something that meant something. She walked towards what must have been the counter, it was all coal and burnt through, and it was going to be difficult for a neutral person to decipher what it was. She poked at the counter and it broke off.

The only light was from the gaps in the roof, and a bit from the window and door. She pulled out her camera and began taking pictures, the click of the shutter breaking the silence. She tried to step past the rubbles behind the counter to get to the door behind it but it was impossible without getting injured or covered in dirt.

As she stood, she realised there was not much lighting as before she turned. She slowly turned towards the diner door and was shocked for a split second before she recovered herself. There was a shadow standing there, fitted into the door frame with wide shoulders covered in a jacket. She sighed and muttered under her breath. Escaping through the door was out of it, her eyes darted to the windows, as plotted a backup.

The shadow stepped into the shop and stood where the light streaking in could properly show his face. He raised his hands in a peace gesture, still saying nothing as he stared at her.

Finally he dropped his hands. "Sorry, didn't mean to scare you," he said and flashed a grin. Sara observed him. He was tall, with dark hair and a sharp jawline. She then noticed the camera dangling by his elbow with the strap slung over his shoulders. He took a step towards her and she unconsciously took one step backwards and held on to her camera. They both stared at each other, waiting for the person who would go first.

The man suddenly spoke up, breaking the silence. "I saw you entering the shop" he took a step closer and put out his hand. "I'm Ronald."

She sized the man up and then took his hand. "Sara." There was a few seconds of awkward silence. "What are you doing here?" she asked.

"Same as you, I imagine," he replied, his tone casual. "Looking for answers. This place has a lot of secrets, don't you think?"

Sara rolled her eyes in her head. "Too forward," she thought. She had only wanted a straightforward answer. Besides, why did she not see him when she was coming into the shop?

Before she could say anything further, Ronald started talking. " I am a journalist, freelancing though but one of the best around." She could almost taste the pride in his tone. She knew she was not as annoying as this person. He could even be a fake. Everyone seemed to be claiming their prestigious job these days.

" I see, so what have you covered so far?" Sara asked to let him know she was not rude. He explained that he had been putting a story together about the Ben Reed case, and asked her how much she knew about it. She scoffed at the audacity and said, " a lot".

He went on to let her know that she would not be finding anything in the diner as over the years, various people had come to check from clues and besides, the police report after the fire made it clear that the diner was burnt to ashes.

As they discussed the case and compared notes, Sara got a shocker. "Well with my research so far, I believe Rachel is the silent killer we need to find." She laughed and asked him what made him come to that conclusion. " Well, walk with me. Ben Reed was the first victim and Rachel took the place of Lucy in that family. She killed Ben to get him out of her way of comfort." He paused here and popped a gum in his mouth. Sara folded her arms, waiting for where this would end.

"She was able to convince her husband to join in and so they carried out the other killings together. The death couple." Ronald seemed pretty convinced with his submission. She shook her head and let out a little laugh.

"Did I say something funny?" He asked, a little frown crossing his face.

"No, not at all. The thing is, Lucy had to be the silent killer." She submitted. Ronald squeezed his brows, an immediate silent protest.

"No, she can not be." He said. She asked him to learn to listen to other perspectives so he would not have to repeat what he just said.

His face hardened and he fixed it. He did not like it when people, especially women talked to him like that.

He listened as she broke down in detail why she thought Lucy could be the silent killer. He could not lie, she was good at details, but he was not about to tell her that. So he just nodded and hummed to what she was saying.

She said that it could be a psychological problem as some women are capable of harming their children out of action for them.

"Lucy may have not liked that Ben was with the new family that her husband was building with another woman and her own son. She probably started building up resentment for her son for staying and then when she got the chance, she ended his life." She had a look of satisfaction on her face like she just delivered the killing blow in a rap battle.

Ronald was not bought by Sara's submission as he pointed that the stories did not say if Lucy got Ben to herself. Sara laughed and told him he had not been reading the right submissions and if he really was into the case, he would have known.

"What are you anyway?" Ronald threw at her. He wasn't sure if she was a police officer or something else.

"I'm a journalist from Sunset Ridge," she said with a hint of pride she felt every time she had to identify as one. She saw Ronald's face brighten for a moment and then he shut it down.

"Oh." He let out. Of course, that explains the annoying attitude. He registered the camera she was holding at that moment and mentally face palmed himself. That was enough give away, but he was too engrossed in winning an argument to notice.

They continued to discuss why their pick could be the killer and about two minutes later, Ronald said, " what if none of them were the killers?" Sara paused and asked him to explain.

"Well, from what we know, Ben's body or belonging were never found right?" Sara nodded. "What if he was kidnapped and maybe, the killings started after, he disappeared."

"Hmm." Sara took some time to digest the new piece of information.

"Ah ha, I was still right then. You just corroborated MY point. Lucy may have kidnapped her own child! Thank you for bringing that up." She brought her pad out of her pocket and penned something down.

Ronald rolled his eyes. The clichés about journalist never moving without a pad is being proven, he had his too. She tucked the small pad back in jacket pocket and turned to Ronald.

"But we could just take a look around, you never know what can turn up." Sara said slowly as she looked around.

The diner yielded no clues, so she decided to head to Reed Castle. It was a long shot, but she had to try. The castle had always been a place of rumours and speculation, and if there were answers to be found, they might be there.

Ronald was about to start another line of thoughts when she cut in. "Look," she said, cutting him off mid-sentence, "I appreciate your input, and it sure has been a good morning but I've got other things to do. It was nice to meet you" she turned on her heels and walked towards the door.

"Going to the Reeds Castle?" Ronald threw from where he was standing, a faint smirk on his lips. Sara paused and face palmed herself in her head. She did not like people tagging along with her but it seemed she just got herself a sidekick for the day.

She drove as Ronald rode in the passenger seat beside her. It was a parade with burnt buildings as cheerleaders. Most of the parts from the diner to the Reeds mansion was still left as it was, uninhabited. She barely responded to Ronald as he kept talking.

She brought her car to a crawl as she got to what used to be the gate of the castle.

The gates were permanently opened and just hung there. The building was up ahead and she could not help but admire it despite the burn scars. It still managed to convey its elegance and sophistication.

Her tires made a crunch sound as she pulled the car to a stop. They got down and she locked the car and put the keys in her pocket. She waited for a moment to take it all in. It was like a gothic structure. There were weeds climbing the pillars and the surrounding grounds were overgrown with weed. She was one that barely got intimidated but for a moment, this building did.

She took the stairs leading to the front door. She heard Ronald coming behind her, but she had her own mission and she had done her good deed of the day, driving him there.

Sarah looked around the hall she stepped into, she could not tell what part of the house it was supposed to be but it was a hall. The floor as far as eyes could see was covered in broken furniture, shattered glass, and fragments of what might have been artwork. The hall was lit by the gaps in the tall windows on opposite ends of the wall.

Sara's footsteps echoed as she made her way deeper into the castle. She paused occasionally to take pictures, the click of the shutter breaking the silence. She got to the foot of the staircase and placed her hands on the railing. She ran her hands back and forth on it for some seconds which gave way to a dull burn streaked wood. Her attention was caught by something on the stairs.

She raised her head and simultaneously called Ronald. "Hey, there's something here." She listened to his footsteps as he marched quickly to where she was.

"I think someone was here before us." She pointed at the footprints that were in the dust on the stairs. It went all the way up as she looked at it. She was too caught in the prints that she did not look at Ronald's reaction. She started to wonder who had come to the castle and what they were looking for.

She made a mental note to trace the footprints later as she took pictures of the walls and windows in the hall. She paid attention to the details in the finishing of the house and it was quite fascinating how something so simple looking could carry such exquisite air. She moved to the stairs and started to trade the footsteps, she began to realise there was more than one of that. How many people were here exactly? At the top of the stairs, she turned to take in the hall at the elevated level and a small smile slipped through her lips. She was really intrigued by the sight in the castle, it was like she could see what it was before the fire came.

Ronald came up the stairs, watching Sara who was carried away. "You know you should check the rooms now and admire them later."

He wondered what could be fascinating about a burnt building. He got close and snapped his fingers twice. That got her back. " Oh, sorry," she let out. She moved towards the other rooms, Ronald following closely. They checked the rooms, some were really burnt, some were not so affected.

The ball room spoke of the elegance it used to be, the high ceiling, the dangerously hanging chandelier, the hard floor, it was all a lot to take in. She took pictures, more for personal perusal than documentation.

They left the ballroom and moved through the castle to check other rooms. Most of the rooms were in ruins, as expected. Charred walls, collapsed ceilings, and debris scattered everywhere. They soon came to the one where Tyler and the group had slept in the night before. Ronald was immediately drawn to the paintings on the wall while Sara observed the room. It wasn't as damaged as the others. The walls were blackened in places, but the structure was intact. The floor was covered in a thin layer of dirt. She couldn't place it but the room looked like it was cleaned or used recently. It seemed whoever did tried to throw dirt around to make it look like they had not been there but they did a poor job at it. This piqued her curiosity further. First the footprints and now a room that was occupied recently. She joined Ronald at the wall. There were interesting paintings that she took pictures of.

She wondered which member of the Reed family this belonged to. She could picture Lily standing and rubbing her son's shoulders and staring at the walls, a peek into the world in her son's head.

Or was it a passion room for Rachel, putting the things she destroyed into painting.

One painting in particular caught her eye. It was smaller than the others, and the colours were darker like it was more recent than the others. She had been here a few years ago and she was almost certain she did not see this there.

"This was done after the fire, don't you think?" She motioned to Ronald to come closer.

He turned and walked over, his eyes narrowing as he examined the painting. "Interesting," he said after a moment. "It's different from the others." An expression crossed Ronald's face but Sara did not see it. She was engrossed in the painting.

Sara nodded in response to Ronald's response. "It feels like it doesn't belong here. "

Ronald tilted his head, studying the painting with a critical eye. "Maybe it was. Or maybe it's a clue. Something the Reeds didn't want anyone to see."

Sara pondered on what Ronald said, she took her camera and took pictures of the small painting. It would all make sense Soon.

Sara and Ronald walked back to her car, she was a little downcast that she did not find any specific clues that could help. She wondered how long she'd have to dig to get to the bottom of it all.

"You know you could stop by Margret's house, see what you can find." Ronald said and broke the silence. Sara looked at him, she was just there the night before but she definitely was not about to tell him that and so she nodded. "Yeah, thanks, I'd do that."

Ronald stepped back from the car as Sara got in and wound down the car glass on the passenger side. "It was nice to meet you." She said as she started her car. Ronald threw a small salute and Sara chuckled as she revved the car as she reversed to the street looking at Ronald as he grew smaller in her side mirror.

CHAPTER TWENTY FIVE

Hide and Seek

Sara pulled her car to a stop at the same spot she was parked the last time she snuck into Margret's house. This part of town, though not fully restored, had a few people who still stayed there. She did not want anyone who would register her face in their subconscious, anything could happen and she did not want to be identified.

She looked out the street, she was not really paying attention the last time she was here, besides, things did look different at night.

The houses and street were an uneven blend of new and rust. A few places had been retouched to liveable situations and most of it still had evidence of the fire. The neighbourhood was quiet. Maybe Margret's death had worsened the fear in the hearts of the people. She could see Margret's house at the end of the block, still and looking like the aura of light had been dimmed.

She did not expect any more drama today, considering the last time she was there, it was Jack who almost made her paralyzed with fear. She chuckled a little as she remembered that night. This was her last stop for the day, and she planned to make it back to Sunset Ridge in good time, so she checked to confirm her pad was still in her jacket pocket and the camera over her neck.

Sara stepped out of the car, the slam of her car door interrupting the eerie silence.

She always tried to tag what the air in Riverwood smelled like. It was like a mix of smoke and muddy water. There was something in the mix she could not place too.

She walked up to Margret's front porch and the floor board gave a little creak. Maybe it cooperated with her the last time. She held the handle and pushed the door in slowly, stepped in and pushed it closed behind her. She did not know what exactly she was expecting to find or what made Ronald particular about it but she was just doing this for the fulfilment of righteousness.

It all looked the same to her, the living room. It didn't look like anyone else had been there after her and Jack. The silence in the house was different though. She could not explain it, but it was like a coup silence planning to jump at her.

● ●

All five of them had been searching the house for what felt like hours. Alex, Tyler, Maya, and Ethan moved quietly through the rooms, their footsteps soft on the floor. They were all really just doing their own thing since there was this tension between them.

They were looking for something, anything, that could help them make sense of what had happened to Margaret. It was the little they could do considering they were probably the last person to see her alive. Luckily, they didn't have to worry about who's dying next yet since they didn't discover the body.

Alex was in the kitchen, as he rummaged through drawers filled with old utensils and faded receipts. Tyler was in the living room, flipping through a stack of yellowed newspapers. Emily was in the bedroom sitting on the edge of the bed looking around. Maya was standing by the window looking to the street. She imagined how many times Margret had probably stayed there and tried to entertain herself with the empty street, maybe played a game of how many people passed on her watch . Ethan was still interested in walls and was in the passageway looking at the painting and a few pictures on the wall.

Alex leaned out the kitchen door after a while, his eyes asking a question. Ethan turned towards the living room too and saw Maya stepping away from the window. They just heard a car engine dying down not too far away. Emily came out of the bedroom too in a rush. " You all heard that right? What if someone was coming?" She asked, her voice already shaky.

"Could be the police." Alex said in a low tone.

Ethan sighed and rubbed his forehead. "If it's the police, we're screwed. We shouldn't even be here."

"We're not doing anything wrong," Tyler said, though he didn't sound convinced. "We're just… looking around."

"Yeah, looking around in a dead woman's house," Ethan shot back. "That's not suspicious at all."

"Shut up," Alex hissed, holding up a hand. "We don't know who it is yet. Let's just stay quiet and see what happens."

They all nodded, nervous but trying to put up a brave face. They crouched low, their breaths shallow as they listened for any sign of movement outside. The house was silent except for the faint creak of the floorboards under their weight.

Minutes passed, and nothing happened. Alex started to relax, thinking maybe they'd overreacted. Maybe the car had just been passing by. But then Maya, who was closest to the window, suddenly stiffened.

"Someone's coming," she whispered, her voice barely audible. "I can see someone from here. They're walking toward the house."

Alex's heart skipped a beat. "Are you sure?"

Maya nodded, her eyes wide with panic. "What do we do?"

"We hide," Alex said quickly, his mind racing. "Now. Everyone, move!"

They scrambled to their feet, their movements frantic but quiet. Tyler and Ethan darted toward the back of the house, disappearing into a small pantry. Maya followed, her hands shaking as she pulled the door shut behind her. Alex stayed in the kitchen, his eyes scanning the room for a place to hide. He grabbed a frying pan from the counter, holding it like a weapon, and ducked behind the island. Emily went back to the bedroom and ducked under the bed flat on her back as she shut her eyes.

The front door creaked open, the sound echoing through the house. Alex held his breath, his grip tightening on the pan. He could hear footsteps. Slow, deliberate, and getting closer. His mind raced with possibilities. Was it the police? Someone else investigating the case? Or something worse?

Sara was looking at the walls and the ground. She looked at the window and then at the stack of papers on the table. She furrowed her brows, trying to remember if she saw anything like it the night before but it was blank. She shrugged and moved towards it. She suddenly froze as she heard a shuffle from the house. She wanted to be sure it was not her mind playing tricks on her. Was Jack back? It couldn't be, he had found something earlier. She waited for a moment and continued towards the papers.

She reached for the papers, but a noise stopped her in her tracks. It was faint, but it was there, a soft shuffling sound, like someone moving in the next room. Sara froze, her hand instinctively reaching for her bag. She wasn't armed, but the weight of her camera felt like a weapon at that moment.

She slowly turned to the passageway tiptoeing towards the kitchen. Her heart was in her throat. This could be the actual killer. She swallowed, took a breath and slowly advanced. She could hear it better now. There was whispering and more shuffling. She swallowed again. Two killers? Where were they hiding?

The footsteps stopped in the living room, and for a moment, there was silence. Then they started again, moving toward the kitchen. Alex's heart pounded in his chest, his knuckles white as he gripped the pan.

Then, suddenly, the footsteps stopped again. Alex waited, his breath caught in his throat. The silence was unbearable. He could hear his own heartbeat, loud and fast, in his ears. He heard shuffling and he wondered if it was from the intruder or the others. He quickly stood up from behind the island and plastered himself on the wall beside the door leading out of the kitchen. At least if anyone was going down, it should be him.

And then, without warning, the person stepped into the kitchen.

She rounded the corner and found herself face-to-face with Alex. He was just as startled as she was, his eyes wide and his hands raised in defence with a pan in it. For a moment, neither of them moved, the tension thick in the air.

"Who are you?" Alex demanded, his voice low and wary.

Sara held up her hands, her heart still racing. "I'm Sara. I'm not here to hurt you."

Alex didn't lower his hands, his eyes narrowing as he studied her. "What are you doing here?"

"I could ask you the same thing," Sara shot back, her voice steady despite the adrenaline rushing through her veins. "This is Margaret's house. What are you doing here?"

Alex hesitated, his gaze flickering to the door behind her. "We thought you were the police," he finally admitted. "We were hiding."

Sara lowered her hands slowly, her mind racing. "We?" she asked, her tone softer now. "Who's we?"

Alex finally lowered the pan, as he sized Sara up and was alert in case she made any move. He gestured and Sara walked out the kitchen door, pausing in the passageway for Alex to step out.

"Guys, you can come out now." Alex said loudly. Sara watched as a door opened at the far end of the passageway and a young lady stepped out closely followed by two guys. At the door of the bedroom, another young lady was there fidgeting. She was amused and suddenly burst into a fit of laughter.

They have all walked up to her at this point and looked at each other, unsure of what to do as Sara could not hold her laughter. After a moment, she took a deep breath as the laugh reduced to chuckles and she looked at them all one after the other.

"You guys just gave me a stupid death scare. I thought I was going to die or kill someone." She said amidst chuckles. She noticed they all looked at her with straight faces so she sat up and stopped with the laughter.

She could feel the tension rising, they didn't know her and there was a killer roaming, it was understandable. She inhaled, let out a small smile and her voice came out calm and steady.

She introduced herself properly this time, her hands raised slightly to show she meant no harm. "I'm Sara," she said, her tone firm but not threatening. "I'm a journalist. I've been working on the Ben Reed case for a while now."

They exchanged glances, their expressions a mix of suspicion and curiosity. They were seated in Margaret's living room, the furniture worn but still functional. Sara sat across from them, her bag at her feet and her camera resting on her lap. She kept her posture open, her hands visible, trying to put them at ease.

"A journalist?" Tyler repeated, his brow furrowed. "What are you doing here?"

Sara leaned forward slightly, her gaze steady. "I'm trying to find out what happened to Ben Reed. The killings and now, with Margaret gone, I think there's more to this story than anyone realizes."

The room fell silent for a moment, the weight of her words hanging in the air. Alex was the first to speak. "We've been looking into it too," he admitted, his voice cautious. "Not like, officially or anything. But we've been... curious."

Sara nodded, her expression softening. "I get that. This case has a lot of layers. It's not easy to walk away from."

Maya shifted in her seat, her arms crossed tightly over her chest. "Why do you care so much?" she asked, her tone sharper than the others. "It's been twenty years. Why now?"

Sara hesitated, choosing her words carefully. "Because I think there are people who deserve answers. Besides, I did not just start like I said. I've been on it for years. She cleared her throat and continued, "also the killings that have been happening, it's all interwoven somehow."

Ethan, who had been quiet until now, spoke up. "We've been here to talk to Margaret before she died," he said, his voice low. " We were probably the last ones who saw her alive."

Sara's interest was piqued. "Oh wow. What were the things she told you?"

The group exchanged another glance, this time more hesitant. Tyler was the one who broke the silence. "We can't just start to pour out everything to you. We also have to be careful."

Sara's eyes widened, but she kept her expression neutral. "Well, you can ask me anything too, you guys have to trust me. "

For the half hour, they all exchanged information and asked questions. It was a rollercoaster of emotions from annoyance to pity, and all that was in between. They soon got to their involvement with

Emma and Jack, but Tyler was quick to notice the shift in Sara's composure at the mention of Jack.

"Do you know Jack?" Tyler suddenly interjected. Sara was taken off guard and she blinked and it took her a second to ask "what?"

"You surely do. How do you know him?" Tyler followed up, not letting her settle.

"I know Jack," she said finally, her voice measured. "Or at least, I've met him. He's... I don't know much about him. All I know is he's a private investigator."

They seemed to relax a little with this, if she knew Jack, then they were assured of safety at least.

The room fell silent again, everyone trying to digest all that has just been said.

Sara leaned forward again, her expression earnest. "We can work together, you know. I've been working on this for a while, and I've got resources you don't. Together, we might be able to piece this thing together."

The group exchanged another glance, this time less guarded. Maya was the first to nod. "Okay," she said, her voice firm. "But if you're lying to us, or if you're just using us for your story, we're out. Got it?"

"Look," she said, her tone calm but firm, "I get that this is a lot. You don't know me, and you've got every reason to be cautious. But I think we're on the same side here. We all want answers, right?"

They looked at each other, their expressions a mix of uncertainty and curiosity. Alex was the first to nod. "Yeah," he said slowly. "We do."

Sara met their gazes, her expression serious. "I'm not here to use anyone. I want the truth, same as you."

For the first time since she'd arrived, the tension in the room eased. The group seemed to relax, Sara knew it was a small victory, but it was a start. She had their trust, or at least, the beginnings of it. Now, she just had to figure out how much they really knew, and how much they were willing to share.

Sara smiled, a small, reassuring gesture. "Good. Then let's keep talking. But not here. We must not be caught here, it's going to be trouble." She glanced around the room. "How about we grab some lunch sometime? My treat. We can sit down somewhere… normal, and share notes."

The suggestion caught them off guard. Maya raised an eyebrow, her arms still crossed tightly over her chest. "Lunch?" she repeated, her tone skeptical. "You think that's a good idea?"

"Why not?" Sara shrugged. "We are now associates right?." She chuckled. " Besides I need to get to work, so not necessarily today." She waited, saw them look at each other, probably agreeing on something silently. After a few seconds, Alex spoke up. " Sure, we'll take your number and let you know when we are free to meet up." The others nodded at this. Sara nodded and removed her phone from her breast pocket, she stretched it towards Alex who took it and punched in his phone number, he dialled it and returned Sara's phone.

Sara got up promptly as she returned her phone into her pocket. She tapped her thighs, "it was nice to meet you all, be safe." With that, she walked towards the front door. She could feel their eyes boring holes in the back of her head but she didn't mind. At least that was progress.

As she shut the door and made her way slowly to her car, she felt a kind of progress, she doesn't know how but she knew that day was profitable. With Jack, Ronald and now the friends, things should be okay.

CHAPTER TWENTY SIX

Shadows and Warnings

I t'd been a few days since the little drama at Margret's house with Sara. They had left some twenty minutes after Sara did, her car disappearing down the street, mostly because they wanted to be sure she was not coming back. They found a back door and left quietly, retracing their steps to the end of the street where they had parked the car. They didn't want to risk being seen, so they'd chosen a spot away from the main road, tucked behind an overgrown hedge.

There was not much conversation on the drive back as they were all in their own thoughts. They had agreed and reached out to Sara a few days later to take her up on her lunch offer.

The group stood outside the diner, the faint smell of coffee and baked pastries drifting through the air. Sara had suggested the place, and it looked cozy enough, a small, brick-walled diner with a neon sign that flickered slightly in the afternoon light. Maya checked her phone, frowning. "Where's Tyler? He said he was on his way."

Alex shrugged, leaning against the wall. "Knowing him, he probably got distracted. Or lost. Or both."

Ethan chuckled, scrolling through his own phone. "Should we call him? He's gonna miss out on the free lunch."

Maya rolled her eyes but dialled Tyler's number anyway. The phone rang a few times before he picked up. "Hey," his voice came through, slightly muffled.

"Hey," Maya said, putting the call on speaker. "Where are you? We're outside the diner."

There was a pause on the other end. "Oh, uh… I'm not coming."

Maya's brow furrowed. "What do you mean you're not coming? Sara's already on her way here. We're about to go in."

"I've got classes," Tyler said, his tone defensive. "I can't just skip them."

Ethan snorted, leaning closer to the phone. "Since when do you care about classes? You've skipped for way less."

"Yeah," Alex chimed in, smirking. "that is a very lame excuse."

Tyler groaned. "I am behind on a lot of classes so I want to make up for that. Is that very difficult to understand?"

Maya shook her head, cutting in before the conversation could derail further. "Tyler, this is important. Sara might have more information. Don't you want to hear what she has to say?"

There was another pause, longer this time. "I do," Tyler said finally. "But I can't. Not today. You guys can fill me in later, right?"

Maya sighed, glancing at the others. Alex mimed zipping his lips and throwing away the key, while Ethan pretended to toss something over his shoulder. She rolled her eyes again. "Yeah, we'll fill you in. But don't blame us if we forget something important."

"Or if we just don't tell you at all," Alex added, grinning.

"Yeah, good luck with that," Tyler shot back, though there was a hint of a laugh in his voice. "I'll catch up with you guys later."

"Alright," Maya said, her tone softening. "Do not get in trouble."

"I won't," Tyler replied. "See you."

The call ended, and Maya slipped her phone back into her pocket. Alex and Ethan were already fuming their voices carrying down the quiet street. "He's making that class up," Alex said, shaking his head. "Classes, my ass. He's probably not interested in what we're doing anymore."

"He can do whatever he wants though," Ethan added dismissively.

Emily spoke up for the first time, "let's just go in and wait for her there." They all moved towards the door of the diner.

* *

The walk to class was quiet, the streets mostly empty. Tyler kept his head down, his hands still in his pockets. His mind was all over the place, thinking about everything and nothing at once. Tyler shook his head, trying to clear his thoughts. He needed to focus. Classes had been piling up, and he couldn't afford to fall behind. They have been too involved in all that has been going on and it has started to tell on their personal lives.

By the time he made it to the lecture hall, he realised he was a bit late as the lecturer was already in. He took a deep breath, and he slipped into a seat at the back, hoping to avoid drawing attention. The professor had filled the board with things he was not even ready to start comprehending. It was worse because he could not even concentrate. His mind kept drifting, wandering like a lost dog in the forest.

Five minutes later, he was pulling all the forces to stay awake. He kept nodding off, the lecture sounding like a lullaby.

He didn't know when he got back to this particular house that was strange but so familiar. He just knew he was looking for something. He seemed to know his way around and he decided to go to the room. There were shuffling noises and it got louder as he got closer. He saw the face first before he could process what was going on before him. Maya was locked in a kiss with someone whose back was to him. He could feel his chest tighten as he got closer, in a bid to see who this person was. His hands were suddenly sweaty and a little cold, he slowly moved his hands to touch the person's shoulder and it was like the whole image before him dissolved into thin air. He looked around, taken aback . Was he imagining things now? He wiped his forehead with the back of his palm as he could feel sweat breaking out. It seemed like the air was still and the silence was gnawing at him. At that moment, he felt something else. A faint shuffle, like footsteps but he wasn't sure. His heart was racing in his chest now and his chest had started to tighten. The shuffle came again, this time he was sure he heard it, it was coming from outside, somewhere near the house.

Tyler stood in the empty room, his breath coming in short, uneven gasps. The image of Maya and the shadowy figure had vanished, leaving him alone in the dimly lit space. The air felt heavier now, the silence pressing in on him. He wiped his forehead with the back of his hand, his skin damp with sweat. His heart was still racing, the tightness in his chest refusing to ease. Tyler froze, his head snapping toward the window. The curtains were drawn, but he could see a sliver of light filtering through the gap. Someone was out there.

He could feel the blood rush in his veins as he moved towards the window cautiously.

Tyler reached the window and pulled the curtain aside just enough to peer out. The yard was dark, the moon casting shadows over the garden. At first, he saw nothing. Then, movement, there was a figure, barely visible, slipping around the corner of the house.

His breath became shallow. Who was that? He couldn't make out any details, just a silhouette, tall and lean, moving with purpose. Tyler's mind raced. The only thing he could think about was getting outside the house. He had to find out.

He turned away from the window and headed for the door, his movements quick but silent. He reached the front door and hesitated, his hand hovering over the handle. The air felt colder now, a chill creeping up his spine. But he couldn't stop. He had to know.

He pushed the door open and stepped outside. The night air was almost freezing, biting at his skin. The yard stretched out before him, the shadows shifting as the wind rustled through the trees. Tyler scanned the area, his eyes straining to see through the darkness. The figure was gone.

He heard it again, the shuffling sound, this time coming from the side of the house. Tyler moved toward it, his steps careful, his senses on high alert. His steps were crunching dry leaves, the noise too loud in the quiet night. He rounded the corner, his heart pounding.

The figure was there, standing in the shadows. Tyler squinted, trying to make out their face, but it was too dark. He took a step closer, then another, his pulse racing. The figure didn't move, didn't speak. They just stood there and watched him. Somehow it felt like he knew this person but he just could not make it out

The figure turned and disappeared into the darkness. Tyler hesitated for a moment, then followed. He had to know. He had to see.

He trailed the figure through the yard, his breath coming in short, shallow gasps. The shadows seemed to close in around him, the air growing colder with every step. The figure moved quickly, always just out of reach, always just out of sight. Tyler's chest burned, his legs aching, but he couldn't stop. He had to keep going.

Then, suddenly, the figure stopped. Tyler froze, his heart slamming against his ribs. The figure turned and without any notice, lunged at him, their movements fast and effortless. Tyler barely had time to react before hands closed around his throat, cutting off his air. He stumbled back, his vision blurring, his hands clawing at the figure's grip.

And then he saw it, the face. It was Jack, his eyes cold and empty, his expression was unreadable. Tyler's breath caught in his throat, his struggles growing weaker. Jack's grip tightened, his lips curling into a faint, cruel smile.

"You shouldn't have come here," Jack whispered, his voice low and menacing.

Tyler's vision darkened, the edges closing in. He tried to scream, but no sound came out. Everything was in twos, the shadows swallowing him whole.

Tyler woke with a start, his heart pounding. The lecture hall was quiet, the professor still talking and he seemed to be the only one who was lost. He ran a hand over his face, trying to calm his breathing. The dream had felt so real, so vivid. He could still feel Jack's hands on his throat and how difficult it was to breathe. He was not getting anything in this class so he decided to trace his next class and get in early and calm himself before it started.

As he gathered his things, from the corner of his eye, he noticed someone standing at the back of the room. It was Jack, watching him intently. Tyler's stomach dropped. For a moment, he thought he was still dreaming. But then Jack motioned for him to follow, and Tyler knew this was real.

He hesitated, his mind racing. What did Jack want? Why was he here? And how did he even know where he was? Was his dream a sign? But before he could decide what to do, Jack turned and walked out of the room. He had no choice but to follow.

Tyler stepped out of the lecture hall, his bag slung over one shoulder, his heart still racing from the dream. The hallway was empty. At the far end of the corridor, Jack stood waiting, his hands in his pockets and his expression unreadable. He didn't say a word, just turned and started walking, expecting Tyler to follow.

Tyler hesitated, his mind racing. The dream flashed in his mind again. Jack's hands around his throat, the cold, empty look in his eyes. Tyler shook his head, trying to push the image away. This was real. He had to keep it together.

He followed Jack down the hallway, his footsteps echoing in the silence. Jack led him outside, the cool afternoon air hitting Tyler's face like a slap. Jack's car was parked a few feet away, in the campus lot. Jack unlocked the doors with a click of his key and slid into the driver's seat without a word. Tyler hesitated again, then got in on the passenger side.

The interior of the car was spotless, the leather seats were smooth under Tyler's hands. The smell of air freshener and something metallic filled the air. Jack started the engine, the low rumble vibrating through the car, but he didn't pull out of the lot. Instead, he turned to Tyler, his eyes sharp and calculating.

"Your statement on Emma, I need you to do it again, right now " Jack said, his voice low and flat.

Tyler was unprepared for the question so for a moment, he was blank and confused. Then he chuckled, an uncertain one. "I don't understand, you were there through the whole thing, where is this coming from?"

Jack's expression didn't change. "You don't respond to my questions with another question, answer me, young man." He gripped the wheels so hard his knuckles were becoming white. Tyler was unsettled for a moment, as he stared at Jack. He didn't know where he was going with this but it started to piss him off.

Tyler clenched his fists, his nails digging into his palms. "You know what? I don't understand what you're playing at, but you have to ease that tone. How did you find out about my campus in the first place? Nothing better to do with your time? Were you tracking me?"

Jack leaned back in his seat, his gaze never leaving Tyler's face. "You and your little group have been poking around where you don't belong. You went to Reed Castle, I specifically told you guys to steer clear of this case! You are going to answer my question now, else…" He drifted off as he released heavy breaths.

Tyler's chest tightened, but he held Jack's gaze. "We're just trying to figure out what happened. To Ben, to Margaret, to Emma. You know this."

Jack's lips curled into a faint, humorless smile. " You think you're some kind of hero? This isn't a game, kid. People are dying. And if you're not careful, you're next."

Tyler's jaw tightened. He was tired of being talked down to, tired of the threats. "I'm not a kid," he said, his voice sharp. "And I'm not scared of you. If you know something, why don't you just tell me? Or are you too busy playing the mysterious tough guy?"

Jack's smile faded, his eyes narrowing. For a moment, Tyler thought he might hit him. But then Jack leaned forward, his voice dropping to a whisper. "You think you're brave, standing up to me? You have no idea what you're dealing with. The killer's still out there. And they're not going to stop just because you're playing detective."

Tyler didn't back down. "Then help me stop them. If you know something, tell me. Or are you just here to scare me?"

Jack studied him for a long moment, his expression unreadable. Then he leaned back again, his hands gripping the steering wheel. "You've got guts, I'll give you that. But guts won't save you. Be careful, Tyler. The killer's closer than you think."

Jack tapped a button and a clock came, signalling the car doors unlocking. He didn't say anything but Tyler got the message and got down.

With that, Jack started the car and pulled out of the lot, leaving Tyler standing on the curb, his heart pounding and his mind racing. He watched the car disappear down the street, the sound of the engine fading into the distance.

CHAPTER TWENTY-SEVEN

The Past, The Strings and the Pact

T he diner was extra busy, filled with loud chatter and the constant flow of people coming in and out. It was one of those days when life in Riverwood seemed to move on as if the Silent Killer didn't exist.

They had waited an extra thirty minutes after going into the diner before Sara finally showed up. They were seated in a booth by the corner of the diner, the kind with chairs built into the table. Ethan had already ordered a soda, sipping it slowly as he stared out the window, his foot tapping impatiently under the table. Alex was scrolling through his phone, his annoyance growing more evident by the minute. Emily and Maya sat across from them, quietly discussing whether they should just leave.

"Tyler was probably right for not coming," Alex muttered, not looking up from his phone. "This is a waste of time."

"We've already waited this long," Emily said. "What's another ten minutes?"

"Ten minutes?" Ethan scoffed, setting his glass down a little too hard. "She's already half an hour late. If she's not here in the next five, I'm out."

Maya didn't say anything, but her face said it all. She was just as frustrated as the others, but she wasn't ready to give up yet.

Just as Ethan was about to slide out of the booth, the door to the diner opened, and Sara walked in. She looked a little flustered, her hair slightly disheveled and her coat half-buttoned, but she smiled when she saw them.

"Sorry I'm late," she said, sliding into the booth beside Maya. "Traffic was a nightmare."

"Traffic?" Alex raised an eyebrow. "In Riverwood?"

Sara waved him off, already flagging down a waitress. "You know what I mean. Anyway, what did I miss?"

The kids exchanged glances, but no one said anything. They were still annoyed, but Sara had a way of diffusing tension without even trying.

The waitress came over, and Sara ordered a coffee before turning her attention back to the group. "So, what's the plan? Have you made any progress?"

The waitress returned with Sara's order in a small tray and set it on the table. Sara looked up and noticed only Ethan had an almost-finished cup in front of him. She asked if the others wanted anything, and after a moment of hesitation, they placed their orders one after the other. The waitress returned with their snacks in minutes, and they thanked her as she left.

They attended to their snacks in awkward silence for a few minutes before Sara cleared her throat and shifted in her seat. "So... where do we start?"

Alex responded immediately, like he had been waiting for her to say something. "What do you have for us?"

"Well, you share what you've found so far, and we'll figure out where to go from there," Sara said, pushing the ball back to their court.

There was a moment of hesitation before Maya spoke up. "We can start by sharing what Margaret told us when we visited her." She looked around for silent approval, and the others nodded quietly.

Sara observed them and then said, "That will be great. I suppose this is something new compared to what's been known about her before now."

"Yeah," Maya agreed.

In the minutes that followed, they filled Sara in on the details of their visit to Margaret's. They recounted everything she had told them, their observations, and the questions that had arisen. "Tyler thinks there's something she wasn't telling," Emily added.

Sara suddenly looked around and slapped her forehead. "I totally forgot about him. Why isn't Tyler here?"

Maya responded, explaining that Tyler had to meet up with his classes. Sara shrugged and asked them to continue. Alex also mentioned how Tyler had noted that the sprinkler was supposed to have gone off when the fire started, but Margaret hadn't been able to provide details.

Sara nodded. "Margaret's been around for a long time. If anyone knows what happened back then, it's her. But it's also been twenty years, and she's old. It's understandable that she's forgotten some details."

The conversation naturally shifted to Lucy, Ben, James, and Rachel. Sara stirred her coffee thoughtfully, her expression serious as she listened to the kids recount their visit to Margaret's.

"So, Margaret thinks Lucy was unfairly blamed for everything," Maya said. "She said Lucy was a strong woman who built her own empire even after the divorce, but the town turned on her."

"And Ben?" Sara asked, her brow furrowing. "What did she say about him?"

Emily leaned forward; her hands wrapped around her mug. "Margaret said Ben's disappearance was the final straw for Lucy. She thinks Lucy left Riverwood because she couldn't take the hate anymore. But she also said Lucy should have fought more for Ben, that maybe things would've been different if she'd taken him with her."

Sara nodded slowly. "What about James and Rachel?" Alex interjected, his tone sharp. "Margaret said Rachel hated Ben because she thought he was the reason her relationship with James was rocky. Do you think she could've had something to do with his disappearance?"

Sara hesitated, her fingers tapping lightly against the edge of her coffee cup. "It's possible. But we can't jump to conclusions without evidence."

"Tyler thinks the fire at the diner wasn't an accident," Ethan added, his voice quieter than the others. "He thinks someone set it to hurt Lucy, to take away everything she'd built."

Sara's eyes narrowed. "That's a bold theory. Did Margaret say anything about the fire?"

Maya shook her head. "Well, she was traumatized by it. But Tyler's convinced it wasn't her fault."

"It's not a bad theory," Sara admitted. "If someone wanted to hurt Lucy, destroying her businesses would be one way to do it. But connecting that to Ben's disappearance... that's a stretch."

"What if it's not a stretch?" Alex pressed, his voice rising slightly. "What if the fire and Ben's disappearance are connected? What if someone wanted to destroy Lucy's life completely?"

Sara sighed, leaning back in her seat. "It's possible. But we need more than theories. We need proof."

They all fell silent. They had pieces of the puzzle, but they didn't know how they fit together. Sara could see the determination in their eyes, the refusal to give up, and it both worried and impressed her.

******

The kids were a good catch; no one was as committed or invested as they were.

Sara was surprised they were all still alive. From what they had gathered, the killer was consistent with his M.O. He only deviated when he felt threatened, when someone got too close to the truth. Maybe the kids were still safe because the killer hadn't felt threatened by them enough. It couldn't just be luck. They hadn't gotten close enough to discover who the killer was—except for Margaret. Their visit to Margaret had spooked him.

"Do you guys ever wonder what Riverwood would be like when the Silent Killer is finally found?" Alex asked, his mouth stuffed with chips.

"Pretty much the same," Sara replied. "If there's one thing I've learned over the years as a crime reporter, it's that grief is momentary. Take Ethan, for example. I heard your girlfriend was a victim…"

"She's not my girlfriend," Ethan cut her off, annoyed that she had brought it up.

"Yeah, but you had a thing for her, right? You might miss her, but look at you, moving on with your life."

"Don't say that, Sara. I bet you've never lost someone close to you," Maya hissed, equally annoyed by Sara's insensitive comments.

Sara let out a chill laugh. "I know grief. I've experienced it firsthand, and it does nothing but take from you—but only when you feed it." Her eyes stared into the distance; her voice cold. It was clear from her expression that she was reliving a painful past. But her eyes looked cold. Everyone really does have a skeleton in their closet.

"Hey," Maya reached out for her hand, but Sara quickly withdrew and forced a wide grin on her face.

"Everyone moves on, eventually," Sara said, her tone final.

"I, for one, know I'll sleep better at night knowing he's gone," Emily added.

"I just want to see his face, look into his eyes, and ask him why," Alex said quietly. "Who could he be?"

"It's always the person you least expect," Sara said.

"It could be one of us," Alex joked.

"Not funny, Alex," Emily hit him on the shoulder.

"Come on, bro, you seriously don't mean that," Ethan snapped.

Alex laughed at their reactions. He was always one to make jokes out of serious matters. "Kidding, I'm just kidding. Chill out, guys."

"Maya's right, though," Sara said. "It's always the person you least expect. I mean, he doesn't come from another town to commit a murder and travel back. No, he knows too much—when to strike without being noticed. He walks amongst us."

The air grew heavy, and the diner seemed to quiet down. Sara's words were chilling. It was obvious the killer knew his way around town to escape unnoticed, but hearing someone say it out loud sent shivers down their spines. It really could be anyone. Everyone was a suspect.

"Whatever," Emily broke the silence. "It can't be any of us. The Silent Killer is probably old—well, not too old, but he's been around for the past twenty years. He should be, what, forty?"

"Oh my God, you're right, Em. Why didn't I think of that?" Sara said, gently smacking her head. "We need to start looking at the possible age of the killer. That way, we can narrow it down to a certain group of people."

"Yeah, we also have to check anyone who might have had a grudge against the Reeds. It has to be someone on the inside, very close to them," Ethan added.

"How do we check if people who existed then are still around?" Maya asked.

"History, my dear Maya. We check Sunset Ridge's history," Ethan replied.

"Or we could do it the old-fashioned way and ask around. Nothing's better than hearing stories directly from people's mouths. That way, they tell you more," Sara added, her voice laced with determination.

She wouldn't be the first to try to save Riverwood, and she certainly wouldn't be the last if she wasn't careful enough. The killer knew how to dim any flicker of hope the people of Riverwood might have. He targeted the overly invested, the ones who were eager and gave their all to finding out who he was. Just when they discovered a breaking point, he hunted them down and got rid of them. It had happened before, and it was very likely to happen again.

Ethan looked at Sara and scoffed. His expression was stuck between being impressed and pitying. "She reminds me of Dona. I just hope she doesn't end up like her," he said quietly.

"I actually started to like Dona. She really did care about us and finding the killer," Emily admitted.

The gang agreed, and the air grew still once more—a moment of silence for the dead. The realization hit them again that the Silent

Killer was still out there, and it could be anyone at any time. Margaret would have been the answer to all their questions. She might not have known who the Silent Killer was, but she definitely would have pointed them in the right direction.

The gang pondered a lot of "whys," and every answer they had led to more questions. No matter how much they dug, they couldn't seem to get to the bottom of the pit. And while they tried to solve one murder, the killer would strike again.

"I think we should go with Sara's idea—do this the old-fashioned way. Find people from back then and ask them what they know," Alex said.

"That's risky," Alex replied. "Have we all forgotten Margaret? If we hadn't paid her a visit, she'd still be alive. We can't do that to someone else."

"That's a small price to pay. It'll be worth it when we catch him," Sara objected.

"Someone's life is not a small price to pay. How can you even say such a thing?" Emily retorted.

"Sara's right, though. We can't just sit back. The killer will kill more people if we don't do anything," Alex argued.

"Sorry, guys, but I'm gonna have to go with Alex on this. I couldn't sleep for days after Margaret. I don't want to be the cause of someone's death," Maya added.

"Come on, guys, we've come this far. We can't give up now," Alex urged.

"No one's giving up, Alex. We just need to find another way," Emily argued.

"There is no other way. We've tried everything. We just need to be careful," Alex insisted.

"Okay, guys, enough!" Sara roared. "I'll do it. Since you guys are too scared to…"

"We're not scared," Alex objected.

"Yes, you are! All of you. You're scared the killer might come after you or someone else because of you. But let me tell you something— if you want to get this done, you have to think like him. He's not afraid to get his hands dirty, so you have to be willing to play his game."

"Unbelievable," Maya slammed the table and got up to leave.

"Where are you going?" Sara asked.

"I need to use the restroom," Maya said as she walked away.

"Don't go alone. I'm coming with you," Emily yelled as she got up and followed her.

"Do you know what happened to the last investigator who tried to go after him?" Alex asked Sara.

"Yes, Dona. I know all about her. I did my homework. She may be dead, but at least she didn't chicken out," Sara replied.

"Come on, guys. A lot more people are gonna die if we don't try. For Dona, Becky, for Margaret—their deaths have to be worth something," Ethan urged, trying to make them see why it was the best time to go harder. "Jack can help too. I don't even like the guy, but we're all on the same side here."

"Jack, the investigator? I don't think a cop would be willing to help, plus he's very uptight," Emily said.

"He's not a cop; he's a private investigator," Alex clarified.

"Yeah, and Dona's death hit him hard, so he'd be willing to help," Ethan added.

"Wait. Private? Do you think someone hired him?" Sara asked.

The guys turned and stared at each other, intrigued by the idea of someone hiring Jack. That was something they had never thought about. If someone had hired Jack privately to find out who the Silent Killer was, that person must be connected to the murders. Jack was too invested in the case, and he wasn't like Sara or Dona, who were doing it because it was their job. He was everywhere the Silent Killer was mentioned and knew much more than the actual investigators.

"If someone hired him, we need to find out who it is," Emily said as she slid back into the chair with Maya.

"Did you guys give yourselves a pep talk in there? I thought you weren't in support of finding people anymore," Alex jeered.

"Jack knows too many people. He knows his way around town too…" Maya began.

"And he isn't very likable. No one really knows anything about him," Emily added.

"Yeah, Dona tried hard to get rid of him. She never wanted him around the case," Ethan continued.

"The guy seems shady. I have to find out what he's really up to, who he is, and if someone hired him," Sara said.

"You won't get a thing from him," Alex warned.

"Yeah, we'll see about that," Sara replied confidently.

"We'll go with you, see if we can lure him to talk," Maya suggested.

"No! I'll do this one myself. I don't want you guys meddling in it," Sara insisted.

Ethan chuckled. "You've got to be kidding. You really think we'd just sit by and let you handle the case alone?"

"Jack knows you guys. You're just a bunch of kids. He won't tell you anything. Let me handle this one," Sara said firmly.

"No way, lady. We're all in this together," Emily said adamantly.

"Yeah, you don't know this town like we do. You don't know the case like we do, so you actually need our help," Alex added.

Maybe the kids were right. Sara might know how to get information from anyone, but she still needed help from people who knew their way around. She was just a visitor, after all, and wouldn't know a thing if people didn't talk to her. And although the kids had their hands full—finding people from twenty years ago, chasing leads on Ben and Rachel—they still wanted to be involved.

"I can make Jack talk more than any of you could," Sara bragged. "Why don't you guys chase your hints and clues, and let me do the drilling?"

"Not going to happen, lady," Alex said firmly.

"Yeah, not gonna happen. The girls can go with you, see what you can get from Jack, while we try to find Ben and his parents," Ethan added.

"Okay, here's what's gonna happen. Why don't you leave Jack to me and go find Ben? It'll be a lot faster when you guys work together. And if I find anything on Jack before you guys find Ben, you'll drop the case," Sara proposed.

The kids stared at each other, confused. They probably wondered why she would come up with such a deal. They could do whatever they wanted. What was she trying to prove?

And just as if Alex could hear what everyone was thinking, he asked, "Why the hell would we do that?"

"You don't have to. But it'll save us a lot of time, plus you'll get to see how persuasive I can be," Sara said with a smirk.

"Fine," Alex scoffed.

"What?" the gang chorused, shocked at his reply.

"Come on, guys. What have we got to lose? She'd be helping us anyway, and we're gonna find Ben," Alex reasoned.

"So, do we have a deal?" Sara extended her hand, and Alex took it. "Deal."

CHAPTER TWENTY-EIGHT

Forgotten Truths
and the Tattletale

Alex sat at his desk, the sunlight streaming through the raised curtains and spilling across the room. His desk was cluttered with papers, old photographs, and a bottle of water was on the edge of the desk. The room was warm, the afternoon light softening the edges of the clutter and casting long shadows on the walls. He had been at it for hours, digging through digital archives, old newspaper articles, and public records. There were some loose ends that needed to be tied.

He was checking everything available on the Diner where Margret worked to see if he missed anything. He made sure his research was broader and he was simultaneously checking on Jack too.

It was probably the conversation they'd had with Sara that had pushed him to look into it again. He wanted to see just how much he could get on Jack and what his life was like.

He clicked through another article, his eyes scanning the text quickly. The diner had been owned by a man named Harrison, He was known in Riverwood at the time. He could not get a last name for the man but according to the article, Harrison had died in a hit-and-run accident before the fire happened. He leaned back in his chair, running a hand through his hair as he stared at the screen. The article included a photo of Harrison, a middle-aged man with a kind smile and firm eyes. There was something familiar about him, something Alex couldn't quite place.

Alex opened another tab and began searching for Harrison's burial records. It took a few minutes, but he eventually found what he was looking for—a series of photos from the funeral. The images were grainy, the colors faded with time, but they were clear enough to make out the faces of the attendees.

His eyes scanned the crowd, looking for anyone he might recognize. And then he saw them, the Reeds. Lucy and James were there, standing near the back of the crowd. Lucy's face was somber, her eyes downcast, while James stood stiffly beside her, his hands on the shoulder of a boy who he assumed was Ben. Alex's heart skipped a beat. He hadn't expected to see them there.

But it wasn't the Reeds that caught his attention the most. It was the small boy standing at the front of the funeral. It was like he was leading the funeral with the position he was standing but the priest was close to the casket so he knew the boy was not leading the funeral procession. He had to be a member of the deceased family. He was lean, with dark hair and sharp features. Alex squinted at the screen, zooming in on the photo. The young man's face was partially obscured, but there was no mistaking who it was.

Jack.

Alex chuckled. They had never really tried to look into Jack and where he was from. They just went with whatever he told them. The child in the photo had an oversized suit on. His facial features did not change much, just became firmer. He tried to place that picture and one of the deceased man side by side and the resemblance was striking. Ho was he related to this man? Why had Jack never mentioned it to them? He quickly pulled up another search, this time typing in "Jack Harris Harrison." The results were vague, but one article caught his eye—a brief mention of a Jack Harrison, the son of Harrison. Alex's heart pounded as he read the article. It was short, just a few lines, but it confirmed what he had suspected.

Jack Harris wasn't just Jack Harris. He was Jack Harrison, the son of the man who had owned the diner.

Alex sat back in his chair, placing a palm over his face. If Jack was Thomas Harrison's son, then his connection to the case went much deeper than anyone had realized. He grabbed his phone and quickly typed out a message to Ethan: *"We need to talk. Now."* he hit send and got up. As he moved towards his wardrobe, there was a knock. . Alex frowned, glancing at his door. The knock was coming from the main entrance. He opened his room door and walked down the hall to the living room and then to the main door. He opened it to find Emily standing there.

She was dressed in jeans and a plain tee, her hair loose and slightly messy. She gave him a small smile when she saw him.

"Hey," she said softly.

"Emily," Alex replied, his voice hinted at his surprise. "What are you doing here?"

She did not give a response immediately as she raised her brows.

Alex sighed, he thought she was back with arguments. "Em, I am deeply sorry for whatever I do not have time for fights right now, we can talk and settle later, okay?"

Emily's face was expressionless, but she didn't argue. Instead, she stepped closer, her eyes locking with his. Before Alex could react, she leaned in and kissed him.

For a moment, Alex froze, caught off guard by the suddenness of it. But then he gave in, his hands moving to her waist as he kissed her back. When they finally pulled apart, Emily looked up at him, her eyes searching his. "Can I come in?" she asked softly. Alex stepped to the side of the door and gestured for her to come in.

• •

Tyler had been pissed since he got back from classes. He was sure he wanted to do more than he did when Jack showed up like that. He hated it when someone had the thought that they could intimidate or scare him. At the same time, he did not know what to make of the threats and warnings Jack gave. They were not going to get themselves killed. Tyler was beginning to get tired of Jack's sassiness and at the same time suspicious of his activities.

He was in his room laying on the bare floor. The curtains were closed and it kind of blocked out the light from outside. He sat up and reached for his phone he had earlier placed on the bed. He laid back down on the floor, opened FaceTime and tapped Ethan's name. The call connected after a few rings, and Ethan's face appeared on the screen. He was sitting at his desk, his back to his bed.

"Hey," Ethan said, his voice filled the room. Ethan looked up and tried to figure out Tyler's expression. "What's up?" Ethan squinted and let a small chuckle escape. "Why are you sprawled on the floor? You got hit or something?" he noticed Tyler was not getting caught in his effort to lighten the mood so he sat up and waited for Tyler to speak.

Tyler hesitated, "I don't know, man. We need to look into Jack. I can't explain it, but I feel like he's hiding something big. We need to figure out what his deal is."

Tyler leaned forward, his voice urgent. "I need you to do some digging on Jack. Something's not right with that guy. He showed up at my class today, threatened me. Said we're going to get ourselves killed if we keep looking into this."

Ethan's brow furrowed. "What? Jack threatened you? What did he say exactly?"

As Tyler made to respond, his eyes caught something in the background of Ethan's room. On the bed, just behind Ethan, was a handbag. A familiar one. Tyler's stomach dropped. He sat upright and held his phone tightly.

"Ethan," Tyler said, his voice sharp. "What's Maya's handbag doing on your bed?"

Ethan turned slightly, to see what Tyler was talking about. For a moment, he just stared at it and then he turned back to his laptop where Tyler was still on.

"I... I don't know," Ethan stammered, and raised his brows. "She definitely dropped it there and I didn't even notice it was there."

Tyler's jaw tightened. "You didn't notice? Seriously?"

Ethan opened his mouth to respond, but no words came out. He looked genuinely confused, but Tyler wasn't buying it. Without another word, Tyler ended the call and immediately dialled Maya's number.

The phone rang once, twice, and then Maya picked up. Her face appeared on the screen, her expression calm, almost indifferent.

"Hey," she said, her tone casual, like nothing was wrong.

"Where are you?" Tyler demanded, his voice tight.

Maya hesitated for a split second before answering. "I'm at Ethan's."

Tyler's chest tightened. "Why?"

Maya didn't flinch. "We were talking about the case. That's all."

Tyler's mind raced, but before he could say anything else, Maya turned the camera around, revealing Ethan's room. Ethan was still sitting at his desk, his face a mixture of guilt and confusion. Maya walked over and stood beside him, her handbag now clearly visible on the bed behind them.

"See?" Maya said, her voice steady. "Nothing to freak out about."

But Tyler wasn't convinced. The way she stood there, so calm, so unbothered, made his skin crawl. It wasn't just the handbag. It was the way she looked at him, like she didn't care what he thought, like none of this mattered.

"Maya," Tyler said, his voice low. "What's really going on?"

Maya shrugged, her expression unchanging. "Nothing. We're just trying to figure things out, same as you."

Tyler stared at her, his mind spinning. He wanted to believe her, but something felt off. The way Ethan just stared, the way Maya seemed so detached, it all added up to something he didn't know yet.

"Okay," Tyler said finally, though the word felt heavy on his tongue. "Just… be careful."

Maya nodded, her face still unreadable. "We will."

That was the height for Tyler, he is dealing with too much already for this to add to it. How dare Ethan? Why did he not find someone else? They would have to meet and talk it out.

CHAPTER TWENTY- NINE

It's Him

The late afternoon sun streamed through the half-drawn curtains, and the ripple effect was obvious on the floor of the room. Alex was shirtless on one end of the bed, his back propped against the headboard, while Emily stretched out on the opposite end, as she scrolled through her phone. Alex, not lost in thought but he was focused on the wall. It was quiet as they were both in their little bubble and unwound in ways they deemed fit.

Alex reached over to the stand beside the bed and grabbed the glass of water. As he took a sip, his eyes moved to the desk to his far left filled with papers and his laptop that seemed to be sinking under the papers. He'd been meaning to bring it up earlier, but the day had slipped away from them, filled with other things fuelled by emotions. Well, he was back to the thing at hand.

"Hey," he said, breaking the silence. His voice was casual, but there was an edge to it that made Emily look up from her phone.

"Hey," she replied, setting her phone down on the bed. "What's up?"

Alex swung his legs over the side of the bed and stood, walking over to the desk. He picked up the stack of papers and his laptop, then returned to the bed, sitting cross-legged in the middle. Emily shifted, sitting up straighter.

"I've been looking into Jack, obviously" Alex said with a little snort, opening the laptop and pulling up a folder filled with documents and images. "And I think I found something... interesting."

Emily raised an eyebrow. "Interesting how?"

Alex clicked on a photo, enlarging it so it filled the screen. It was an old picture, slightly grainy, of a group of people standing outside a diner. The sign above the door read *Harrison's Diner*, and in the foreground was a young boy, no older than ten, with a full head of hair that was hard to decipher its colour and a shy smile.

"That's Jack," Alex said, pointing to the boy. "I found this online. It's from Sunset Ridge, years ago."

Emily leaned closer, studying the photo. "Yeah, that's definitely him. But what's the big deal? He could've just visited Riverwood as a kid."

"That's what I thought at first," Alex said, scrolling through more documents. "But look at this." He pulled up another photo, this one of a newspaper clipping. The headline read, *Local Diner Owners Celebrate opening*. The article was accompanied by a picture of a young Jack, who was holding a cap in his hands and an older version of him holding him by the shoulders.

"Wait," Emily said, her eyes narrowing as she read the caption. "Jack Harrison? That's his full name?"

Alex nodded. "Yeah. And get this—the diner in the first photo? That's his family's place. They ran it for years in Sunset Ridge."

Emily sat back, processing the information. "So Jack didn't just visit Riverwood. He grew up there."

"Exactly," Alex said, his voice entering that mode that gave away his interest in the case. "And that's not all. Look at this." He opened another document, this one a timeline he'd put together. "Jack left Riverwood after high school and moved to France."

Emily leaned back and rested her weight on her arms. She let out a small chuckle.

"There is so much about this man we had not known." she asked if Alex remembered where and how they got to know him.

"Exactly," Alex said, tapping the screen. "And it gets weirder. Look at this." He pulled up another photo, this one was taken at a burial procession. The crowd was small, and they could not make out the colours of their outfits but their faces were enough to tell of the sadness. Emily moved closer, squinting like she knew what to find and when she was not getting anything, she looked up at Alex and raised a brow, a silent "what am I looking at."

Alex pointed at a middle-aged woman who was standing just a few steps behind a younger boy.

Emily's eyes widened. "Is that…?"

"Margaret," Alex said. "She worked at the Harrisons' diner. And look who else is there." He zoomed in and it was the younger Jack. to the far end of the picture, there was a family of three, the parents and a young boy child who looked sophisticated. Alex was pointing at them when he said, "and those are most likely the Reeds."

Emily shook her head, trying to piece it all together. "Okay, so Jack grew up in Riverwood, his family ran a diner, and he was there when… whatever this is, happened." She gestured to the photo.

"'Whatever it is', was the burial of his father that was killed by a runaway driver."

Emily rubbed her forehead and removed her hands and fell on the bed. "I get it, there is more he had not told us about himself, but how does this help the case?"

"That's what I'm trying to figure out," Alex said, closing the laptop and setting it aside. "Why is Jack so invested in this case? Is it just because he's from Riverwood or is there something more to it?"

Emily was quiet for a moment, her gaze fixed on the stack of papers. "You think he's hiding something else aside from his identity?"

"I don't know," Alex admitted. "But it feels like there's a piece of the puzzle we're missing. Something that ties Jack to all of this."

Emily nodded slowly, her mind racing. "We need to dig deeper."

Alex agreed, his expression serious. "Yeah. And if we're going to figure out what's really going on, we need to find out what Jack's not telling us."

Outside, the sun was beginning to set, and it was casting shadows in the room already. Alex set the laptop down by his side on the bed and started to pack the papers together.

****

"Ashes to ashes, dust to dust," the priest said in a deep baritone voice that rang deep in the air. "We commit this body to the ground, in the sure and certain hope of the resurrection."

The cemetery was quiet, not the regular kind, it was surreal, like the place was alive and aware of what it exists for. It was at the edge of the town just a few metres off the road. The perimeter was fenced, and trees were sparsely scattered. The headstones were different shapes, sizes and designs.

The grave had been dug earlier that morning, the earth piled neatly to one side, dark and damp. A simple wooden casket rested beside it, its surface polished but plain. There were no grand decorations, no flowers and no music.

The crowd was small, no more than twenty people standing in a loose semicircle around the grave. At the front stood Jack, just twelve years old, his hands clenched at his sides. He was dressed in a suit that was too big for him, the sleeves hanging past his wrists. His face was pale, his eyes fixed on the casket, but he didn't cry. He just stood there, his jaw tight, like he was trying to hold everything together.

Behind him stood Margaret, her hands clasped in front of her. She was in her late thirties and her face hadn't yet been worn away by life. She worked at the Harrisons' diner, and though she wasn't family, she had come to pay her respects. Her eyes were red, but she didn't make a sound, just stood there quietly, her gaze fixed on the ground.

A few steps away were the Reeds, Lucy and James, with little Ben between them. Ben was too young to understand what was happening, his small hand clutching his mother's as he looked around with wide eyes. Lucy's face was solemn, her lips pressed into a thin line, while James stood stiffly, his arms crossed over his chest. They weren't close to the Harrisons, not really, but in a town like Riverwood, you showed up for things like this.

The priest stood at the head of the grave, his Bible open in his hands. He was an older man, his hair grey and thinning, his voice steady as he read the verses. The words were familiar, the kind of thing you heard at every funeral. "The Lord is my shepherd; I shall not want," the priest continued, his voice carrying over the quiet crowd. "He maketh me lie down in green pastures: he leadeth me beside the still waters."

Jack didn't look at the priest, didn't look at anyone. His eyes stayed on the casket, like if he looked away, it might disappear.

The priest closed his Bible and stepped back, nodding to the men standing by the casket. They moved forward, took their positions on the sides of it and began to lower the casket into the grave. The ropes creaked as they unwound, cutting into the silence.

Jack's sharp intake of breath cut into the air too and Margaret reached out and put her hand on his shoulder. He wanted to look away, wanted to close his eyes, but he couldn't. He just stood there, frozen, as the casket settled at the bottom of the grave.

Margaret looked down at him for a moment, her eyes filled with tears she was trying hard to fight. She slowly withdrew her hands from his shoulders and took a few steps back.

Lucy's hands were on Ben, and she slowly leaned and whispered something to James. He nodded, stretched his hands to Ben and walked away with him while Lucy stayed back.

People started to disperse as the men who lowered the casket started to fill the hole with their shovels.

Jack watched as the first shovelful of dirt hit the casket, it was no longer a bad joke.

He was little but somehow, he understood what was going on and it made his heart hurt. He wanted to cry but his tear glands seemed not to work, they were not cooperating. He could hear as people silently left but his gaze was fixed on the men covering his father up with sand. He was there until it was all covered up. The only thing he could hear now was the sound of leaves being blown by the air.

He stood there for what seemed like a long time, he was not looking around, but he knew someone was at the far end, but he did not look up to see who the person was. He only did when he caught the person from the corner of his eye leaving. It was a woman; she had on a knee length black dress that flattered her curves. His eyes got blurry as he continued to stare at her and his blink confirmed that the tears were running down his face. He closed his eyes and did not see the woman turn at the gate to look at him before finally leaving.

Jack was the only child of his parents. His mother died a few months before he clocked one year. All the memories he had of her were the pictures his father kept and decorated the sitting room walls with. His father did not get married to anyone else and focused of raising Jack on his own. He was still very little when his dad moved them to Riverwood so he didn't have much memories from then. But if there was anything Jack could not forget, it was that his father loved him, he was stern and disciplined but it never made Jack doubt his love for him and so for years after his death, he was not able to mourn because he was numb. He just existed.

***

The years after the burial were a blur. Jack was left alone by his own parents to figure out life with no manual or guide. He never forgot about them, especially his dad. Somehow, he was able to go through school and college without much stress. He was told there had been plans to sell the diner anyway, but he didn't know how that had played out. Riverwood was a small town, the kind where everyone knew your name and your story. For Jack, that story was one of loss, it followed him wherever he went. He hated the pitying looks, the whispered conversations that stopped when he walked by. He hated the way people treated him like he was fragile, like he might break if they said the wrong thing. He wasn't fragile; he just needed the right time and resources, and he was going to find out who took his father from him. That was enough motivation to join the police department, and he did so a few months after he turned nineteen.

The job gave him a sense of purpose, a way to channel all that anger into something productive. He was angry, he had been angry for years. But he was good at the work, too. He was a detailed and thorough officer, the kind who noticed things others missed. Riverwood, though, was a quiet town. Most of his work involved breaking up fights, catching petty thieves, and handling other routine crimes. There was always the lingering case of the Reed boy, the one they believed had been kidnapped, but even that had gone cold.

Then came the first Silent Killer case.

It was new, and for Jack, it was intriguing. A killer in their quaint old town? It didn't make sense. The first victim was found through the usual ways, someone who was missing and then their parts found. The town was in shock.

A few months later, another victim was found. The details were the same. By then, Jack's application to the police department in France had come back positive. He didn't have a particular reason for choosing France. Maybe it was the hope that a bigger city, a bigger department, might give him the resources he needed to thrive. Whatever the reason, he got the job and moved.

France was different. The cases were bigger, more complex, and Jack found himself drowning himself in the work. And then, not long after he arrived, the Silent Killer cases began in France. The victim was like the ones back in Riverwood and Jack couldn't shake the feeling that it was connected. He tried to convince his superiors, but they dismissed it as a coincidence.

There was more and no matter how hard they tried, they got no leads. The perpetrator was a ghost. It was even worse that copycats started springing up too.

Then, during a short break in the United Kingdom, the first Silent Killer case happened there. Jack was on leave, visiting, when the news broke. Jack's thoughts took a new turn. He now believed it wasn't a coincidence. The killer was following him, or he was following the killer. He wasn't sure which.

He returned to France, and they were getting more copycat cases there too. By this time, police officers across the countries were communicating. They were not quite sure what pandemic was breaking out.

Eventually, he decided to retire from the police force. He couldn't do it anymore, he had his personal plans, and he wasn't getting to them. He moved to the United Kingdom and became a private investigator. The work was different, but it gave him the freedom to pursue the cases that mattered to him. He built a reputation for himself, taking on cold cases and unsolved mysteries that no one else wanted to touch. But no matter how many cases he solved, the Silent Killer case stayed with him.

Years passed, and Jack continued to work as a private investigator, moving from one case to the next. But the Silent Killer case was always there, lurking in the back of his mind. He couldn't let it go, not completely.

And then, he moved to Sunset Ridge.

***

His car was parked away from sight around Margret's house. He was standing at the edge of the green outside Margaret's house. It was sundown and there were shadows that were quickly fading into the darkness. The light at the end of his cigar burned brightly as he took a slow drag and puffed out the smoke into the air. He had dark shades on, and his posture was like someone who had nothing else to do with his time.

The neighbourhood was quiet, and Margret's house was the only one that was not lit on the outside. The windows gave no hint of light either.

He had waited in his car for a while and could not say specifically how long he had waited before he stepped out to where he was waiting now. It didn't bother him; he was used to it. Patience was a virtue he has mastered in the years.

The cigar burned down to a stub, and he flicked it onto the pavement, grinding it under his heel. He reached into his pocket and pulled out another, lighting it with a match. The flame caught, and he took another slow drag, his eyes never leaving the house.

He allowed his mind to wander for a bit and he was ten again, watching the only person he knew being lowered to the ground. He held the cigar between his lips and rubbed his arms aggressively up and down his leathered arms.

The sound of a car engine broke the silence, and Jack's head turned slightly, his gaze shifting to the street. A Nissan breezed past, not slowing down, the windows were slightly tinted so he couldn't be sure the person saw him. His eyes followed the car till it disappeared down the street.

He took another drag from his cigar, as he turned back to the house. He wasn't worried. He had been in this game long enough to know when to move and when to stay still. Right now, he was exactly where he needed to be and what needed to be done.

CHAPTER THIRTY

The Confrontation

Jack waited until the night felt thick enough for him to waltz into Margaret's house without anyone seeing him. Once the dark settled, he returned to her house, the one place everyone avoided like a curse waiting to happen. The yellow tape was still there, flapping lazily in the cold night breeze, a useless warning to a man like Jack. He stood for a moment, staring at it, then tore it down without a second thought. He wasn't here to play by the rules.

Inside, the house smelled of death and secrets.. Jack moved slow, his boots thudding against the floorboards until he reached the spot that had been clawing at the back of his mind since that night.

It was subtle and so well-crafted that even the police, with their bright lights and forensic teams, had missed it. A section of the floor just a shade off. Not different enough to raise alarms, but enough for a man desperate for answers to notice. He dropped his bag with a dull thud and pulled out a small shovel. His hands trembled with rage as he forced the metal through the worn wood, tearing into the lies buried under this house.

It wasn't easy. The ground fought him, and every crack of the wood felt like it might collapse under him, but Jack didn't stop. He was a man possessed by the maddening need for the truth. And finally, the ground gave way.

Below, the dirt looked unnatural because it had been disturbed once, years ago, and forgotten. He dug deeper, pulling out boxes wrapped in moldy cloth, a decayed wooden chest, papers browned with time, photographs half-eaten by rats. The air smelled like rot. This was what the cops never found. Because they weren't looking for it.

Jack sat back, panting, staring at the haul of forgotten sins. This wasn't just about Margaret. This was everyone. Every single name tangled in the Riverwood nightmare.

He wiped his face with a dirt-covered hand. Margaret was the key. The old hag knew more than she ever let on. So he'd gone farther than anyone would've dared to know what she knew.

The body he left behind, the one the police thought was hers, wasn't Margaret at all. He set the scene perfectly, making sure when the fire took the place, no one would question it.

Now, the real Margaret sat in his basement, tied to a rusted chair, the ropes biting into her fragile skin. Jack poured the contents of the bag in front of her and tons of letters dropped with a loud slap, papers yellowed by age, names scribbled in trembling hands, they were all threats clear as day.

"Read them," Jack growled. Margaret's pale eyes lifted to meet his, a little bit of her fear in her battled with her defiance. She was old, but not stupid. She knew why she was there.

"You thought you could play this town forever, didn't you?" Jack sneered. "They paid you. You took their secrets and you sold them back. But not this time."

Margaret said nothing, as her eyes darted between the letters and the man before her. Jack leaned down to make sure she heard him. "I will burn this whole town down before I let you die with those secrets. You will talk about Riverwood. Ben. Everyone you had contact with and you will tell me everything."

Margaret gave a thin smile. "And what happens when you find the truth, boy? What will you do then?"

Jack stood, staring down at the woman who knew Riverwood better than it knew itself. "I don't care what happens to me. But someone's going to answer for all of this."

In the dark of his basement, surrounded by letters soaked in lies, Jack felt it, the war for Riverwood's soul had begun. And Margaret was just the first piece he needed to break.

Jack breathed heavily as Margaret's smile faded. She looked like a ghost of herself, weak, but still holding on to that sharp tongue she'd used as both weapon and shield all her life.

"Why did you burn the diner, Margaret?"

Margaret's lips trembled, and for the first time, Jack saw something raw in her eyes, regret, maybe. Or the recognition that there was nowhere left to run. She let out a long, shuddering breath before speaking with a hollow voice. "I didn't mean for it to go that far," she whispered. "I just… I needed the attention off me. The town was growing sick of me, my mouth and questions. People were starting to look at me too closely. I thought a fire… a small one… would buy me some breathing room. They'd blame the wiring, the damn age of the building. But the fire…" She shook her head slowly, "It got out of control. Much like everything else I ever touched."

It was almost pathetic hearing her like this about a diner that he was once connected to, spilling the truth now, when it was too late to fix anything. He crouched lower, his face just inches from hers. "And Ben? Why did you kill him?" His voice cracked at the name as he had hope he would be the final piece of the puzzle he hadn't wanted to face.

But Margaret looked at him sharply as her pale eyes narrowed. "I didn't kill Ben," she said as her voice gree stronger with that confession. "That boy... he's still alive. He always was."

Jack blinked with disbelief. "Don't lie to me."

"I'm not," she spat. "I never touched that boy... not like that. I... I took him, yes. Because it was the only way to keep Lucy tied to this cursed town. That girl wanted to run. She would've vanished the moment her conscience couldn't carry the weight of what she did. But with Ben? She couldn't leave without him. So, I took him."

Jack jerked. "You kidnapped a child... to keep a business?"

"No," Margaret snapped back, "To own everything. I wrote that blackmail letter to Lucy and James. I thought it would work... that they'd fall in line, keep the company afloat, and I'd finally have the leverage I needed. But Lucy... she wasn't as weak as everyone thought. She didn't care about the company. She wanted freedom. So, instead of covering for that bastard James, she chose to leave him. And that's where it all went to hell."

Jack felt his stomach twist as he listened. "What she had done? What do you mean what she had done?"

Margaret gave a bitter laugh as her head tilted back against the chair. "Oh poor boy. Didn't you know? I watched her do it. I watched as Lucy took that stick to finish him off when she accidentally ran over him. She couldn't have people saying all kinds of stuff after she had just divorced her husband. I watched her cover it up. That was my ticket. My way out. I could've turned her in… but no… I saw the bigger picture. If I kept her secrets, I owned her."

Jack exhaled slowly, piecing it all together. "And when that didn't work, you took Ben."

Margaret's nod was slow. "I took him because she had to stay. And when she finally bought the diner from your family, I found a family… some couple desperate for a child, too blind to ask questions. I gave him away. Paid enough to keep mouths shut."

"You… sold him?" Jack's voice broke into rage boiling over.

Margaret sneered. "I saved him. That's more than his own damn family was ever going to do. You think Lucy or James ever cared? They were too busy pointing fingers, drowning in guilt and greed. Ben was better off."

Jack paced around. The rage threatened to consume him, but deep down, he knew she wasn't lying. Even if she was lying, most of it were true. Her voice was too calm, she had nothing left to lose. That was the most dangerous kind of honesty.

"And Margaret," Jack turned slowly, "You really thought you could blackmail an entire town? That no one would come for you?"

Margaret laughed, and it was hollow. "They were too scared. Every single one of them. I had dirt on everyone, cheating husbands, gambling debts, stolen inheritances. I was Riverwood, Jack. That's what you don't get. I made the rules. I broke them. And when it was over… no one even had the guts to point fingers."

Jack shook his head, a lot of disgust curling in his gut. "That's why you're down here. Because the town's finally fighting back."

Margaret's smile suddenly began to fade away, and for the first time, she looked more afraid than she was defiant. "You… you're not like them."

"No," Jack agreed coldly. "I'm not. I'm worse."

Margaret coughed, her body quivered as the years crushed down on her. "So what now, Jack? You gonna kill me?"

Jack didn't answer. He stared down at the old woman, the frail body that had held Riverwood's sins in her fists for far too long. The truth wasn't enough anymore. But even he didn't know if revenge would make the past any less rotten.

Instead, he gathered the letters, stuffing them into a bag, but his eyes never left hers. "You're going to tell me everything, Margaret. Every single name. Every secret. And when I'm done with you…" He didn't finish because he didn't need to.

Inside the basement was becoming suffocating now. Jack knew he'd crossed the line. He wasn't here for justice anymore. He was here to burn Riverwood down, and Lucy for what she did to her father. That was the point of it all, finding out the truth about his father. But if Lucy killed his father in that manner, then she must have so much to do with the disappearance of all those people. As for Margaret, she was going to help him do it whether she wanted to or not. As for Ben, if he was truly alive, then Margaret's death would lure him out.

CHAPTER THIRTY-ONE

Full circle

They say the truth has a way of finding you, even when you're not looking for it. It hides in the quiet moments, in the spaces between words, waiting for the right time to surface. But when it does, it doesn't always bring clarity. Sometimes, it brings more questions than answers. And sometimes, it changes everything.

It had been a few weeks since Margaret's death, and thankfully, there had been no new drama, no more deaths, no more shocking revelations, at least. For Sara, it was a rare moment of calm in what had been a whirlwind of chaos. She was at home, sitting at her desk, surrounded by stacks of notes, photos, and newspaper clippings from the Reed case. The room was quiet, save for the occasional hum of her laptop fan and occasional noise.

Sara leaned back in her chair, rubbing her temples. She'd been going over the same details for hours, it was almost like a case of madness at this point. She does not know why but no matter the number of times she looked at the situation, it was always like a puzzle that was almost completed but the completing piece was missing. It infuriated her, but her journalistic side always prevailed, and she wasn't backing down.

And the journalist she'd met in Riverwood. She had not even thought about him in weeks. Ronald. She had her doubts about him being a journalist anyways. He looked like he was just there for the fun of it.

Her phone buzzed on the desk, startling her. She glanced at the screen. The number was unfamiliar, her brows arched. She picked up the phone, her voice cautious. "Hello?"

"Sara?" The voice on the other end was hesitant, almost nervous.

"Yes, who's this?"

"It's Ronald. We met in Riverwood."

Sara sat up straighter, her mind racing. Ronald. That was very coincidental, too coincidental even. She hadn't expected to hear from him again. "Oh, right. Hi. What's going on?"

There was a pause, like he was choosing his words carefully. "I'm coming into Sunset Ridge tomorrow. I was wondering if we could meet."

Sara frowned. "Meet? For what?"

Another pause. "There's something I need to tell you. Something important."

Sara's attention lit up at that but she kept her tone neutral. "Okay. When and where?"

"I don't know my way around Sunset Ridge, pick a place and we can we meet there around noon?"

"Sure," Sara said, though she wasn't entirely sure why she agreed. Something about his tone, hesitant, almost pleading, made it hard to say no.

"Thanks," Ronald said, his voice softening. "I'll see you tomorrow."

The call ended, and Sara set the phone down, staring at it for a moment. Why did Ronald want to meet? And why now? She tried to recall their last conversation in Riverwood. He'd been just another journalist chasing the same story.

She shook her head, trying to push the thoughts away. It didn't matter. She'd find out tomorrow. For now, she needed to focus on the case. Besides it was probably more information. She shrugged and went back to writing a story she had abandoned earlier when she got carried away with her thoughts.

• •

Sara sat in a corner booth at the Sunset Grill, a milkshake in front of her. She'd chosen the spot carefully, a seat by the window where she could see the parking lot clearly. The diner was quiet, the kind of place where the hum of the air conditioner and the occasional clink of silverware were the only sounds. She stirred her milkshake absently, her eyes scanning the lot for any sign of Ronald.

When his car pulled in, she noticed it immediately, a small, unassuming sedan that looked like it had seen better days. She could not tell how she knew that was his car, it just looked like him. Ronald stepped out, and Sara took a moment to study him. He was of average height, his hair cut short in a neat crew cut that caught the sunlight, giving it a faint golden glint. His face was lean, his eyes heavy, like they carried the weight of too many experiences. He wore a simple round-neck shirt and loose plaid trousers, the kind of outfit that blended into a crowd. She realized she didn't even observe him in detail the first time they met.

He walked into the diner, his eyes scanning the room until they landed on her. Sara raised a hand to catch his attention, and he nodded, making his way over. She stood up as he approached, offering an awkward smile. "Hi," she said, her voice a little too bright.

"Hi," Ronald replied, his tone quieter, more reserved. They shook hands briefly before sitting down across from each other.

For a moment, neither of them spoke. The silence stretched, heavy and uncomfortable. Sara broke it first. "So, what brings you to Sunset Ridge? You said you had something important to tell me."

Ronald hesitated, his fingers tapping lightly on the table. "Yeah," he said finally. "I did."

Sara waited, giving him space to continue. When he didn't, she prompted gently, "Is it about the case?"

He nodded, his eyes dropping to the table. Actually, yeah. It's about that."

Another pause. Sara was beginning to feel uncomfortable with the probing before getting responses. She took a sip of her milkshake, trying to stay patient. "Okay," she said slowly. "What about it?"

Ronald took a deep breath, his hands clasped tightly in front of him. "I… I need to tell you something. Something I haven't told anyone in a long time."

Sara's curiosity was triggered, but she kept her expression neutral. "Okay. I'm listening."

He looked up at her then, his eyes searching hers like he was trying to gauge her reaction before he even spoke. "I'm Ben," he said finally, his voice barely above a whisper. "Ben Reed."

The words hung in the air, heavy and surreal. Sara stared at him, her mind racing.

It did not register at first. It was like she was glitched, after a moment, she furrowed her brows fully comprehending what he just said. "What?" she asked, her voice sharper than she intended.

Ronald nodded, his expression serious. "I'm Ben Reed. The boy who went missing twenty years ago."

Sara leaned back in her seat, trying to process what he'd just said. Her first instinct was to doubt him, to question how this could even be possible. But something in his eyes, the plea, the pain, made her hesitate. "How?" she asked finally. "How is that even possible?"

Ben sighed, running a hand over his face. "It's a long story," he said. "But the short version is… I was taken. I didn't run away. I didn't get lost. Someone took me, and they kept me hidden for years."

Sara's mind was spinning. She'd spent weeks digging into the Reed case, trying to piece together what had happened to Ben. And now, here he was, sitting across from her, telling her the truth she'd been searching for. "Why are you telling me this now?" she asked, her voice softer now. "I need details if you want me believe."

Ben looked down at the table again, his hands clenched into fists. "Because Margaret's dead," he said, his voice breaking slightly. "She was the only one who knew. The only one who cared. And now... I don't know what to do."

Sara felt a pang of sympathy, but her journalist instincts kicked in. "What do you mean, she was the only one who knew? Did she... did she help you?"

Ben nodded, his eyes still downcast. "She found me, well kidnapped me years ago. For some, reasons I may not be able to fully tell you right now. When she was ready to release me, I did not leave." He paused and signalled for a waiter and ordered sparkly water. They waited for the waiter to return with it. He took a sip and then continued. "See, I had a thought that my parents didn't want me. Worse, they were now separated and I didn't want to be there anymore. So I begged to stay back with Margret. She kept my secret, protected me. But now that she's gone..." He broke down, and Sara reached out and took his hand, he took deep breath and looked up at sara. "I don't know who else to turn to."

Sara leaned forward, her elbows on the table. "Ben, this is... huge. If you're really Ben Reed, you need to come forward. You need to tell people the truth."

Ben shook his head, his eyes darting around the room like he was looking for an escape. "I can't," he said, his voice low and strained. "I've spent years hiding. If I come forward now… I don't even know what will happen."

"But you can't keep living like this," Sara said, her tone firm but gentle. "You deserve to have your life back. And the people who care about you, your family, your friends, they deserve to know the truth."

"They don't care about me, I don't have a family, the one I had is now dead." He said in a low tone. Sara became conscious at that point and withdrew her hands from his. She was taking time to digest this piece of information.

Sara kept her tone calm but firm. "I get it. This is terrifying. But think about it—you've been living in the shadows for twenty years. Don't you want your life back? Don't you want to stop running?"

Ben's hands clenched into fists on the table. "It's not that simple. What if no one believes me? What if they think I'm lying, or worse, that I had something to do with what happened?"

"They'll believe you," Sara said, her voice steady. "We'll make sure of it. I'll help you tell your story. We'll present the evidence, the timeline, everything. People will have to believe you." "I'll help you. We'll do this together." She added.

Ben was silent for a long moment, his breathing uneven. Sara could see the conflict in his eyes, the fear, the hope, the exhaustion. Finally, he looked up at her, his voice barely above a whisper. "What if I'm not ready?"

"You don't have to be," Sara said gently. "But you'll never be ready if you don't take the first step. And you don't have to do it alone. Like I said, I'll be there with you every step of the way."

He looked at her, his eyes searching hers for something—reassurance, maybe, or just a reason to believe. Finally, he nodded, his shoulders slumping like a weight had been lifted. "Okay," he said quietly. "Okay. I'll do it."

She threw him a small smile as she said it will be a great news and there was going to be a press conference and live transmissions as a lot of people have been caught up in the story for years and this will become something big for them.

Sara felt a surge of relief, but she kept her expression calm. "We'll take it slow," she said. "We'll plan everything out, make sure you're comfortable. But this is the right thing to do, Ben. For you, and for everyone who's been waiting for answers."

Ben nodded again, his gaze dropping to the table. "Just… promise me one thing," he said, his voice barely audible.

"What's that?" Sara asked.

"Don't let them twist this," he said, his tone firm now. "Don't let them turn it into something it's not. This is my story. I want to tell it my way."

Sara squeezed his hand. "I promise," she said. "This is your story, Ben. And I'll make sure it's told the right way."

The days leading up to the press conference were a blur of activities. Sara spent hours on the phone, reaching out to journalists, coordinating with the venue, and preparing Ben for what was to come. It wasn't easy. Ben had tried to back out more than once, his nerves getting the better of him. Each time, Sara talked him down, reminding him why this was important, not just for him, but for everyone who had been affected by his disappearance.

"This is your chance to take your life back," she told him during one of their calls. "You've been hiding for too long. It's time to step into the light."

Ben didn't respond right away. When he finally spoke, his voice was quiet but resolute. "Okay. I'll do it."

On the day of the press conference, Ben arrived in Sunset Ridge early. He had driven to Sara's office where she was waiting for him in her own car. He looked different. She noticed he was clean-shaven, his hair neatly trimmed, wearing a suit that hung a little loose on his frame. But his eyes were the same, heavy with the weight of everything he'd been through.

"You ready?" Sara asked as he slid into the passenger seat. They had agreed to leave his car at Sara's office parking lot and have him ride to the venue with Sara.

Ben nodded, though his hands were clenched tightly in his lap. "As ready as I'll ever be."

The venue was a small conference hall downtown, already buzzing with activity when they arrived. Journalists milled about, setting up cameras and microphones, their voices a low hum of anticipation. Sara led Ben to a back room, where they went over the plan one last time.

"I'll introduce you," Sara said, her tone calm but firm. "You just need to tell your story. Stick to what we practiced. And remember, you're in control. If it gets too much, we'll stop."

Ben nodded, though his face was pale. "What if they don't believe me?"

"They will," Sara said, placing a hand on his shoulder. "You've got this."

When it was time, Sara stepped out onto the stage, the room falling silent as the journalists turned their attention to her. She introduced herself briefly, her voice steady and confident. "Thank you all for coming today. What you're about to hear is a story that has been twenty years in the making. It's a story of survival and of truth. And it's a story that deserves to be told."

She paused, glancing toward the side of the stage. "I'd like to introduce someone very special. Someone who has been living in the shadows for far too long. Please welcome Ben Reed."

The room erupted in gasps and murmurs as Ben stepped onto the stage. Cameras flashed, the sound of shutters clicking filling the air. Ben hesitated for a moment, his eyes scanning the crowd, before walking to the podium. He adjusted the microphone, his hands trembling slightly.

"My name is Ben Reed," he began, his voice quiet but clear. "Twenty years ago, I disappeared from my home in Riverwood. I didn't run away. I didn't get lost. I was… taken."

The room was silent now, every eye fixed on him. Ben took a deep breath, his grip tightening on the podium. "I was kidnapped, yes, but someone found me. Someone who cared enough to help me, to protect me. Her name was Margaret. And without her, I wouldn't be here today."

The journalists were scribbling furiously, their cameras still flashing. Ben's voice grew stronger as he continued, his words spilling out like he'd been holding them in for years. "Margaret kept my secret. She kept me safe. But now she's gone, and I can't keep hiding anymore. I need to tell the truth. I need to live my life."

He paused, his chest rising and falling as he caught his breath. The room was still silent, the weight of his words hanging in the air. Then, the questions started.

"Mr. Reed, can you tell us who took you?" one journalist called out.

"Do you know why you were targeted?" another asked.

Ben shook his head, his expression pained. "I don't know. I don't remember much from that time. It's... it's all a blur."

The questions kept coming, faster and more aggressive. "Do you think Margaret was involved in your disappearance?" one reporter asked, their tone sharp.

Ben's eyes widened, his hands gripping the podium tighter. "No," he said firmly. "Margaret saved me. She was the only one who cared."

But the journalists weren't satisfied. "Are you sure? Could she have been working with the people who took you?"

"But how did she find you?" another voice pressed. "Was she involved in your disappearance?"

"If she wasn't involved, why did she keep you hidden for so long?"

"Did she ever tell you why she helped you?"

"Was she protecting someone else?"

Ben's answers were not forth coming. He could not keep up with the pace of the questions. He stuck with saying what he needed them to hear "I—I don't know. She never said. She just… she wanted to keep me safe."

"Safe from who?" a journalist near the front demanded. "If she wasn't involved, who was she protecting you from?"

Ben's mouth opened, but no words came out. He lifted his head and looked around the room, the flashing lights making it hard to focus.

"Did you remember seeing anything suspicious in the place she kept you?"

"Were there others?" Ben scrunched his face and tried to find who asked that. These people were being stupid and focusing on something else.

"There was..."

"Was Margaret connected to the people who took you?" another voice called out.

"Did she ever mention the Silent Killer?"

Ben's face paled, his hands trembling on the podium. "No, she—she wasn't like that. She was good. She was kind."

But the journalists were like blood sucking demons who just found a prey.

"Are you sure? Could she have been working with the Silent Killer?"

"Why would she keep you hidden unless she was involved?"

One of the journalists stood up and asked, "is Margret the silent killer?"

It was like someone cast a frozen spell in the room. You could hear a pin drop in the silence that followed this question.

Ben shook it off first and then shook his head, his voice rising. "No. She wasn't like that. She was good. She was kind."

The room erupted into chaos, the journalists shouting over each other, their questions growing more absurd. Sara stepped forward, placing a hand on Ben's arm. "That's enough for now," she said, her voice cutting through the noise. "Thank you all for coming. We'll have more information soon."

She guided Ben off the stage, his face pale and his hands shaking. As they stepped into the back room, he turned to her, his eyes wide with panic. "They think she was involved," he said, his voice breaking. "They think she was a killer."

Sara placed a hand on his shoulder, her tone firm but gentle. "They don't know the truth, Ben. They're just looking for a story. But we'll set the record straight. I promise."

Ben nodded, though his expression was still troubled. Sara hesitated, then asked the question that had been nagging at her since the conference began. "But what if they're right? What if the truth you believe isn't the truth?"

Ben stared at her, his face a mix of shock and confusion. "What are you saying?"

Sara shook her head quickly. "Nothing. Forget I said anything. Let's just focus on what's next."

Ben left the press conference feeling drained, his mind a rollercoaster of emotions. The questions from the journalists, the accusations about Margaret, Sara's unsettling comment, it was too much on him. He drove home in silence, the streets of Sunset Ridge passing by in a blur. When he finally pulled into the driveway of the hotel he was lodged, he sat in the car for a long moment, staring at the steering wheel.

The hotel room was quiet when he stepped inside. It was like the room was also mocking him. That was what that press thing was. A mockery. He dropped his keys on the table and sank into the couch, his head in his hands. The press conference replayed in his mind—the flashing cameras, the shouting voices, the way Sara had looked at him when she asked, *"What if the truth you believe isn't the truth?"*

He didn't want to think about it. He couldn't. He needed to clear his head, to focus on something else. He walked to the small fridge in the room. He opened and got a bottle of water, his hands shook a bit as he took it. He walked back to sit on the couch when the phone rang. The sound was sharp and sudden in the quiet. Ben froze, his heart skipping a beat. He hesitated before picking it up, his voice cautious. "Hello?"

He could hear steady breathing on the line but no voice. "Who is this?" he tried again.

"Ben? It is Lucy, your mum."

CHAPTER THIRTY-TWO

Clashes and Closure

W hen it comes to friendships, it is like the weather. There are the good times, the sunny times and there are the times where there is a lot or little thundering and lightning. The good part is it goes away and then the sun comes up again and in other times it leaves serious damages.

They were at Emily's house, in her room where they rendezvous briefly because they needed to update themselves on their findings so far. Tyler was slouched in a couch that was close to the door of Emily's room staring intently at Ethan who was on the other side of the room on the chair facing Emily's reading table. He was crouched over the system scrolling intently Alex was resting on the side of the cupboard and Emily was sitting on the floor with her leg pulled to her chest.

Emily's room was always neat. The bed was made neatly, her shelves looking neat and there was even the scent of fresh flowers and oranges in the air.

There was no one saying anything. The only sound was the faint click of the keyboard from Ethan's end. Tyler was on the edge of the chair now, shaking one of the legs.

"So," Tyler said suddenly, his voice sharp and edgy. Everyone looked towards his direction. He did not break eye contact with Ethan. "Ethan, how's your room looking these days? Still cozy with all the... extra stuff lying around?"

Alex shifted and looked from one person to the other, he glanced at Emily and they both shared a confused look.

Ethan looked up, raising an eyebrow. "What's that supposed to mean?"

Tyler leaned forward, his jaw tight. "You know exactly what I mean. Maya's bag on your bed. Care to explain?"

Maya walked in at that moment holding a jar of chips. She noticed immediately that there was tension in the room. " Uhmm, what's going on?"

No one answered her question.

Ethan shrugged, his tone casual but his eyes narrowing. "It's not what you think, man. She just left it there when we were…"

"When you were what?" Tyler interrupted, his voice rising. "Hanging out? In your room? With my girlfriend?"

Maya rolled her eyes as she heard this and was about to say something, but Tyler's tone was getting harsher, so she paused.

"You didn't think that might look bad?" Tyler snapped, ignoring every other person in the room. He stood, stepping closer to Ethan. "You think I'm stupid? You think I don't see what's going on?"

Ethan stood up at this point, his tone was losing the usual calmness. "Dude, you don't need any of this, you're being paranoid."

Alex stood, holding up his hands. "Guys, come on, let's not do this here."

Emily jumped to her feet, her voice trembling. "Yeah, this isn't the time…"

But it was too late. Tyler was standing in front of Ethan in a second and he swung his fist connecting with Ethan's jaw. Ethan stumbled back, crashing into the chair he was sitting on. Ethan held his mouth, blood already seeping through his fingers.

Maya screamed, rushing between them. "Tyler, stop! What the hell is wrong with you?!"

Tyler was breathing hard, his chest heaving as he glared at Ethan. "Stay away from her," he growled. "Or next time I won't miss."

Maya grabbed his arm, her nails digging into his skin. "We need to talk. Now."

Tyler hesitated, his eyes flicking to Ethan, who was still clutching his face, then to Maya. Finally, he let her drag him out of the room, the door slamming shut behind them.

The room was silent for a moment, the only sound Ethan's heavy breathing. Alex sighed, running a hand through his hair. "Well, that went great."

Emily hurried to the kitchen, returning with a damp cloth. She handed it to Ethan, who pressed it to his split lip. "Thanks," he muttered, his voice muffled.

Alex was bent next to him, inspecting the damage. "You're gonna have a killer bruise tomorrow. Maybe even a black eye."

Ethan winced as he placed the cloth over his jaw. "Great. Just what I needed."

Emily sat back on her heels, her hands twisting in her lap. She wondered aloud asking what was wrong with Tyler. She was sure something was wrong but Alex shrugged and told her it was just one of those things and he was probably jealous or needed to take out his frustration on something or someone.

Ethan groaned, leaning his head back against the wall. "Yeah, well, he needs to chill. I'm not trying to steal his girlfriend."

Alex smirked. "Could've fooled me."

Ethan shot him a glare, but there was no real heat behind it. "Shut up, Alex."

Emily sighed, standing and brushing off her jeans. "We need to figure out what to do next. This isn't helping anyone."

Alex nodded, his expression turning serious. "Yeah. We've got bigger problems than Tyler's jealousy. Like Jack Harris."

Ethan lowered the cloth, his brow furrowing. "What about him?"

Emma launched into detail of what they found on Jack with Alex supporting with interjections. They told him how they found out his name was actually Jack Harrison and his father was a victim of a hit and run years ago in Riverwood. She also mentioned the Reeds attending the burial with means they most likely knew each other.

"We know his dad owned the diner," Alex added once Emma landed.

Emily nodded. "And now Ronald or Ben, whatever we're calling him, is finally coming forward. Now we know this brother didn't die twenty years ago."

Ethan sighed, leaning his head back again. "Great. More mysteries."

Alex had a little smile starting in the corner of his corner of his mouth, the sound of mysteries amused him. He turned to Ethan to take a jab at him for getting a scar. Ethan jrolled his eyes and called him an idiot.

Outside, the sound of raised voices filtered through the window. Maya and Tyler were still arguing, they could not make out their words but they could hear the intensity in the voices as they were loud. Emily glanced at the door, her expression worried. She asked Alex and Ethan if they thought they would be okay. Alex shrugged and said they will. Ethan nodded in agreement which caused him to wince.

The three of them fell silent, as they went back to their positions, this time Emily sat on the edge of her bed. They could still hear the muffled argument but it was not their business. .

• •

The door slammed shut behind them, leaving the others in the room.

Maya dragged Tyler down the hallway, her grip tight on his arm. It was a cold evening so the cool evening air made them pause momentarily as they stepped out. Tyler yanked his arm free, running a hand through his hair as he paced the sidewalk.

"What the hell was that, Tyler?" Maya demanded, her voice sharp but trembling with emotion. She crossed her arms, her eyes blazing. "You can't just go around punching people because you're jealous!"

Tyler stopped pacing, his jaw tightening as he turned to face her. "Jealous? Maya, I saw your bag on his bed. What was I supposed to think?"

Maya let out a frustrated sigh, running a hand through her hair. "You were supposed to talk to me, not assume the worst! Ethan and I are friends. That's it. I left my bag there because we were checking something out. End of story."

Tyler's eyes searched hers, his expression a mix of anger and hurt. He asked her what she wanted him to think and make of what he saw then.

Maya let out a frustrated sigh and her time dropped a notch as she stepped closer to Tyler. She told him that if he trusted her, then he would not have thought there was something else going on. She added that he was being very distant and she didn't know if their relationship was a thing anymore.

Tyler's shoulders slumped, and he looked away, his gaze fixed on the ground. "I'm sorry, Maya. I've just been… stressed. With everything going on, I feel like I'm losing control. And seeing your bag there… it just set me off."

Maya reached out, her hand brushing his arm. "I get that, but you can't take it out on me or Ethan. If you're feeling this way, you need to talk to me. We're supposed to be a team, remember?"

Tyler nodded, his eyes filled with regret. "You're right. I'm sorry. I've been neglecting you, and that's on me. I'll do better, I promise."

Maya smiled faintly, the tension between them easing. "Good. And for the record, I would never do anything to hurt you. I love you, Tyler."

Tyler pulled her into a hug, his arms wrapping tightly around her. "I love you too. I'm sorry for being an idiot."

They stood there for a moment, letting it all soak in. For the first time in weeks, Maya felt like they were on solid ground again.

Back in Emily's room, the others waited. Ethan sat on the edge of the chair, the damp cloth had been replaced by an ice bag There was an evident swell on his jaw. Alex leaned against the wall, his arms crossed, while Emily was now seated at the edge of her bed.

"Well," Alex said, breaking the silence. "That looks better I think."

Ethan groaned, lowering the bag. "Yeah, just peachy. Thanks for the help, by the way."

Emily sighed, sitting down next to Ethan on the arm of the chair. "Are you okay? That looked like it hurt."

Ethan shrugged, wincing as he touched his lip. "I'll live. But if Tyler ever pulls that crap again, I'm not holding back."

Alex raised an eyebrow. "Oh, really? You're gonna take on Tyler? The guy who just knocked you on your ass?"

Ethan shot him a glare. "Shut up, Alex."

After a few seconds, Ethan put the bag back to his jaw. He told the others that he was somewhat sure that Sara put Ben up to revealing his identity to the press and there must be a reason why. Emily noted that Sara was not forthcoming as they wanted as she had listened to them more than given information so far. Ethan suggested they reached out to her.

Alex shrugged. "We won't know until we try. And if she doesn't cooperate, we'll just have to find another way."

Ethan smirked, despite the pain in his jaw. He made a joke that they could break into Sara's house to which Emily quickly said no but Alex got in on the joke and they taunted her with it.

Emily shot them a look of annoyance. "We're not breaking into anyone's house." She rolled her eyes but could not help the small smile that slipped out of her mouth. She dismissed the conversation when she said they could figure it all out later.

The three of them fell silent, Emily glanced at the door, her expression softening.

"Do you think they'll be okay?" she asked quietly.

Alex shrugged. "Who knows?"

The door creaked open, and Maya stepped back into Emily's room. Tyler followed closely behind her.

They all looked at the both of them, waiting to see if they had something to say.

Maya glanced at Ethan, who was still sitting on the edge of the chair holding the ice bag "Are you okay?" she asked, her voice soft.

Ethan shrugged, wincing as he touched his jaw. "I'll live. Thanks for asking."

Tyler stood awkwardly by the door, his hands shoved into his pockets. He looked at Ethan, then at the floor. "Look, man... I'm sorry. I shouldn't have hit you."

Ethan raised an eyebrow, his tone dry. "Yeah, no kidding."

Alex, leaning against the wall, smirked. "Wow, Tyler. An apology. Didn't think you had it in you."

Tyler shot him a glare, but there was no real heat behind it. "Shut up, Alex."

Emily stepped forward, her hands clasped in front of her. "Okay, let's just... move on, okay? We've got bigger things to worry about."

Maya nodded, sitting down on the arm of the couch. "She's right. We need to figure out what to do next."

Alex pushed off the wall, crossing his arms. "Yeah, against our wish, we still have a killer out there that we don't know how to find or stop."

Emily shared what they found out about Jack and they realised Jack was probably not being plain with them. "There is every reason to believe that Jack knew who Ben was all those years ago. Why didn't he mention that in all of the items we had discussions?" Emily looked around. Everyone were in their own thoughts.

She continued, " the pictures we found, the Reeds attended the burial, I am sure they didn't go about attending random burials in their day so yes, there was something that guy conveniently missed out or forgot to tell us."

Tyler said, "I've always been weary of that guy you know, always doing his things like a secret agent. At least now we know more about him. What do you say we also question him?" He saw everyone move with uneasy looks on their faces.

"Seriously? You all are now scared of that guy?" He huffed and walked to the bed. Emily was eyeing him already as he sat at the edge of the bed.

"But it's sad loosing a parent to a hit and run'" Maya said with a note of pity.

Alex suggested that he text Sara and see if they could set up a meeting with her and the others agreed. She now had a lot of information and they wanted to see if she would be willing to share in exchange with what they found.

The others nodded and they somehow fell into discussing what kind of childhood Jack must have had based off that experience. Their voices were overlapping as they continued. In the midst of it, Tyler was watching Maya with an unreadable expression. He knew they would still have to talk, really talk but everything was fine for now. They had more important things to deal with.

CHAPTER THIRTY-THREE

Final Goodbye

Jack's car hummed as the tires rolled slowly on the sparsely tarred road two streets away from Margret's. The car pulled to a stop and the engine idled softly before it cut out. The windows were up and the tinted. In the car, Jack looked straight ahead as he spoke to the person who was strapped in the passenger seat. "This is as far as I go. You can walk the rest." There was a click as the person unbuckled the seat belt and another indicating the car doors being unlocked. The passenger said nothing as they opened the car door and slowly pushed it shut behind them. Jack zoomed away immediately leaving a light pool of dust in his wake with the alighted passenger staring at the car as it moved further away.

It was very silent with the sun high and bright in the sky, the heat was a lot as the passenger walked slowly in the direction the car went. The only sound was the crunch of gravel under her shoes as she walked away. She didn't look back. She didn't need to. She kept walking, her back straight, her steps steady, with her hands in her pocket.

There was no one else as far as the eyes could see. Margaret's breath came in shallow puffs, the hot air caused her to be breathless. . She wrapped her arms around herself, her fingers digging into the fabric of her coat, not because she was cold but because she needed to feel like it was not a dream. It was the same coat she'd been wearing the night Jack took her.

As she walked, the memories came flooding back, unbidden and unwelcome. The days in captivity, the nights spent staring at the same four walls in the room, the sound of Jack's voice echoing in her mind. "There's nothing left for you out there," he'd said, his tone almost pitiful. "The world thinks you're a killer. Even Ben couldn't save you."

She'd seen the press conference, watched it on a small, grainy television in the room at Jack's house. She was not even sure if that was his house but it did not matter. Ben had tried to defend her, his voice shaking with emotion as he denied the accusations. But it hadn't been enough. The journalists had pounced, their questions sharp and relentless, their eyes gleaming with the thrill of the hunt. Margaret had turned off the TV after that, unable to bear the sight of Ben's face, the pain in his eyes.

Jack had made sure to rub it in. "See?" he'd said, his voice dripping with mock sympathy. "Even he can't save you. You're alone, Margaret. You always have been."

The words had cut deeper than she cared to admit, but she hadn't let him see it. She'd kept her face blank, her eyes empty, until he'd finally grown bored and left her alone. But now, as she walked down the empty road, it was like a cloud hung over her dropping those things afresh.

She was finally at the start of her own street and as she turned to walk the street down to her house, she kept her head down, her eyes fixed on the ground. It was not because she cared if anyone saw her, she just did not want to see the all familiar place again.

A few blocks away from hers, she could start to feel the unavoidable gaze. People behind their curtains peeping as she passed. She had gotten accustomed to it. Everyone clearly looked at her as the root cause of what Riverwood is now and she knew they probably saw the press conference too. Besides, was she not just pronounced dead a few weeks ago?

Margaret didn't stop. She kept walking, her steps steady. She didn't care. Let them talk. Let them stare. She had nothing left to lose.

Her house came into view, its familiar shape a welcome sight that should have brought a kind of relief she could feel was noticeably absent. There were still police tapes that sealed the house away and she could not help but let out a small chuckle. It was an irony, a comedic one. The one who was found dead is somehow resurrected. She cut the tapes and even if she did not glance back, she knew there were people coming out to look at the wonder going on. Margaret hesitated at the door, her hand hovering over the knob. For a moment, she thought about turning around, about walking away and never looking back. But where would she go? There was nowhere left for her. Jack had been right about that, at least.

She pushed the door open and stepped inside, the familiar scent of home hitting her. The air was stale, and smelt of intrusion. She moved through the rooms slowly, her fingers brushing against the furniture, the walls. Each touch brought a flood of memories, some sweet, some bitter, all tinged with regret.

She walked down to her bedroom and went straight to the bed and sat at the edge. She heaved and let her back slowly sink into the mattress. She closed her eyes and tears rushed from the sides. There were no sounds, just the tears. Another sigh and she sat up again. She reached into the pocket of her jacket, and brought out a tiny bottle. It looked like it was empty. When she had picked it from Jack's, the name on the pack she had slipped it from was cyanide. She had randomly remembered that she read about a very poisonous gas and that was why she picked it. She did not know what she would use it for at the time she picked it but she knew the perfect time would come.

She put the tiny bottle back and moved to the cupboard on the side of her bed. She opened the first and pulled out a sheet and a pen. She closed the drawer and knelt before it. Her hands trembled a little as she looked at the paper before her. She brought the pen close to it, took a deep breath and wrote the words: "It wasn't me."

She set the pen down and stared at the note, her vision suddenly blurred. She had endured enough, taken enough, and there was no use for more. She stood up and pulled the bottle out. She placed it on the top of the cupboard and carefully removed the jacket. She laid it at the end of the bed and climbed back into the bed, this time she drew the covers to her waist. She reached for the bottle and opened it. A pungent smell with traces of bitter almond filled the air as she brought the bottle close to her face. She dropped it beside her head and closed her eyes. In minutes, she started to feel weak and her head hurt. She turned on her side as she began to feel nauseous, in minutes, she began to grapple for consciousness and that was when the tears came. She anticipated it, but truly dying this time is something she was never going to be fully prepared for. Her body slowly stopped moving as she stopped all struggles with the effect of the poisonous gas.

****

"This is 911, what is your emergency?" The voice had come on frantically and the dispatcher had sat up. She could not believe what she was listening to. "She's back. Margaret's back. I saw her walking into her house. I don't know how, but she's alive."

The police arrived quickly, their sirens cutting through the quiet of the neighborhood. The patrol cars pulled up in front of Margaret's house, their lights flashing in the sun. Officers stepped out, some with guns, the others with protective jackets. The neighbor who had made the call stood outside his door, arms folded. Others in the street were out and slowly approached the house with murmurs and hushed tones. Bad

The officers approached the door, their footsteps rhythmic and almost in sync on the cracked pavement. They knocked once, twice, the lead officer's voice firm but polite. "Margret? This is the police. We need to speak with you."

There was no answer. The house remained silent. The officers exchanged a glance before one of them tried the knob. The door creaked open, revealing the dim interior.

The inside smelt funny as they stepped inside carefully. One officer covered his nose with his sleeve, his eyes narrowing as he stepped inside. The others followed, their eyes darting around. Meanwhile, outside, a media van had pulled up and a cameraman had placed his video recorder out while the reporter tried to gather details from the small crowd that had now gathered.

They found her in the bedroom, lying on the bed, her body still and her face pale. The tiny bottle lay on the bed beside her, its cap off and empty. The officers moved quickly, their training kicking in. One checked for a pulse, his fingers pressing against her cold wrist. He shook his head, his expression grim. "She's gone." The note on the cupboard caught their attention, "It wasn't me."

The house was sealed again, the yellow police tape crisscrossing the door and windows. The officers moved methodically, one radioed for an ambulance, the note was bagged, the bottle and the house was searched. Outside, the neighbors who had gathered, whispered as they watched things unfold.

"Did you see her? She was really alive?"

"I can't believe it. First she's dead, then she's back, and now… this."

"What kind of person does something like that?"

The sound of the ambulance cut through the air which caught unexpected gasps from the people gathered. It moved in reverse as the driver pulled closer to the house with the rear of the ambulance. The doors were thrown open and the examiners rushed in. Another news van pulled up, its antenna rising like a skeletal finger against the sky. The reporter came out, their cameras and microphones at the ready. The officers tried to keep them back, but the crowd was growing, their curiosity outweighing their fear.

Lucy sat in her living room, the TV's lights were illuminating her face with various colours. She'd been watching the news, half-heartedly flipping through channels, when the breaking news alert flashed across the screen. "Miracle or Tragedy? Margaret Found Alive—Then Dead Again."

She froze, the remote slipping from her hand and clattering to the floor. The screen showed Margaret's house, the police tape, the flashing lights. A reporter stood in front of the camera, her voice urgent as she recounted the strange sequence of events.

"Earlier today, neighbors reported seeing Margaret, the woman at the centre of the Riverwood silent killer case, walking into her home. This comes weeks after her supposed death, which was widely reported following the discovery of a body believed to be hers. However, moments ago, police confirmed that Margaret has been found dead in her home, apparently by suicide. A note left at the scene reads, 'It wasn't me.' Authorities are now investigating the possibility that the first body found was not Margaret's, raising new questions about this already complex case."

Lucy's heart pounded, her hands gripping the edge of the couch. She stared at the screen, her mind racing. Margaret had been alive. She'd been alive, and now she was gone again. Who was the first body? And why had Margaret come back only to end her life?

The questions swirled in her mind, what was going on? She thought of Ben, her son, he was coming to see her soon. How was he going to take this?

The TV cut to a live shot of the scene outside Margaret's house. The neighbours were still gathered, The reporter was interviewing one of them, a middle-aged woman who looked like she'd seen a ghost.

"I saw her," the woman said, her voice trembling. "She looked... different. Like she wasn't there, you know? And now this... I just can't believe it."

Lucy turned off the TV, the room plunging into silence. She sat there for a long time, her thoughts a tangled mess. Margaret was gone. Again.

****

Ben felt like the road was going in circles. It was like the longest journey he had to take but no end in sight. He occasionally gripped the steering so tight his knuckles paled. It was like a battle of water guns in his mind, chaotic and all over the place. He did not know what to expect. What would she look like now? Older or the same as all those years ago? He knew he was very angry with her for years but right now, he didn't even know what he felt towards her. He had so many questions, why was she here at this time? How did she know where to reach him? To be fair, everyone probably saw his coming out press conference. A part of him missed her, what could have been if things played out differently.

The car radio was on and turned down to the lowest volume that he could not make anything out of the sounds. He sighed as he thought back to the press conference. He should not have done it. He shouldn't have listened to Sara. he tried to defend Margret, show people she was not what they thought she was, but he failed at that. She would be remembered as that, a killer.

His phone's backlight came on a split second before it started to ring, he glanced at the screen. It was Sara. He hesitated, his finger hovering over the answer button. He had told her when Lucy reached out to him, and he had told her he was not sure what he wanted to do, and she had convinced him to go and see his mother. he was not here because he listened to her, he just wanted to see Lucy. But why was she calling? He was on the way already and he did not feel like it was something she should know.

The phone kept ringing. He sucked his teeth and slid the call icon up.

"Hello?"

"Ben," Sara's voice came through, void of emotions. "I'm so sorry… I just heard the news."

Ben frowned, slowing the car slightly. "What news? What are you talking about?"

There was a sharp intake of breath on the other end. "You haven't heard yet?"

"Heard what?" Ben asked, his mind went to his Lucy. Did something happen to her?

"Margaret… she's dead," Sara said.

The hiss came out before he could hold it back. "Did you wake up in a different universe? of course she is dead."

He heard Sara sigh on the line. "Turns out she was not dead the first time."

"What?"

"A neighbour called in that she was seen walking to her house. The police are there now."

Ben's foot instinctively pressed the brake, the car slowing to a crawl. "So, she is back and dead?"

"I don't know all the details," Sara said quickly.

His hands shook as he tried to process what he'd just heard.

"Where are you?" Sara asked when Ben said nothing still.

He looked up, his eyes falling on the house in front of him. The number on the house was the same as the address she sent to him. He hadn't even realized he'd arrived. The house was small, its paint peeling and its windows closed from the outside.

"I'm here," he said, his voice quiet. "I'm outside Lucy's house."

There was a pause on the other end. "You're there? Now?"

"Yeah," Ben said, his eyes fixed on the house. "But… I don't think I can do this."

"Ben, wait," Sara said, her tone softening. "You don't have to see her if you're not ready. But you're already there. Maybe it's worth hearing what she has to say."

Ben shook his head, even though Sara couldn't see him. "I can't… not now. Maybe not ever."

"Ben—"

He hung up before she could say more, his hands trembling as he set the phone down. He stared at the house for a long moment, his mind numb. She was just a few steps away. His past, the one he had questions for. When he left his place, he was so sure he wanted to do this, but now that he was here. He was beginning to think it was a mistake.

He started the car again, his hands steadying as he pulled away from the curb. He made a U-turn and started the journey back. He didn't look back. He couldn't. The house grew smaller in the rearview mirror, as did the memories that could have been unlocked. He stepped on the accelerator, in a bid to get out of there faster.

Maybe if he had stayed a minute longer, he would have seen the person who walked up to Lucy's front door and knocked before stepping inside.

****

Inside the house, Lucy sat in her wheelchair, her hands resting uneasily on the armrests. The faint sound of a car pulling away outside barely registered in her mind. She wasn't sure how Ben would arrive or if he would even come at all, but she clung to the hope that he would. She thought on how she would greet him, what she would say to comfort him after the news about Margaret, how she could begin to mend the years of separation between them. She had played the moment over and over in her mind, imagining his face, his voice, the chance to finally explain herself.

Then came the knock on the door.

Her heart leapt, a surge of joy flooding through her. It had to be him. It had to be Ben. Before she could even call out or reach the door, it creaked open.

Her breath caught in her throat as the door swung wider, revealing the figure stepping inside. For a split second, her face lit up with relief, her heart swelling with the belief that her son had finally come. The person didn't wait for an invitation. They stepped inside, closing the door behind them with a soft click.

But that relief was short-lived, dissolving into a cold, sinking dread as she realized who it was. Lucy's hands froze on the wheels of her chair, her body stiffening as fear crept into her chest. She opened her mouth to speak, but no words came out

It wasn't Ben.

CHAPTER THIRTY-FOUR

A Call from the Past

Lucy gripped the armrests of her wheelchair, motionless as the man walked into her home like he belonged there. She didn't know him. She was certain of that. But he moved through the space with the ease of someone who had walked the floors before, like he had seen the walls at their best and worst.

He was a young man, compared to her. Mid-forties, maybe late thirties. He had those unreadable eyes that made her uncertain of his motive. He wasn't bulky, but there was a quiet strength in the way he carried himself like he didn't need to make threats to be threatening.

And he wasn't her son. Lucy knew that much. Her son would be younger, her son would be younger and softer around the edges, with the kind of hesitant presence that came from being sheltered too long.

This man wasn't hesitant. He walked like a man who had already seen the worst of the world and learned to walk through it untouched. He wasn't searching for belonging nor was he waiting for approval.

There was something about the way he looked at her that terrified her. Like he expected her to remember him. But she didn't.

Her fingers twitched against the wheelchair's worn leather arms. "You should knock before walking into people's homes," she said, forcing her voice to stay steady.

The man, Jack - if she'd heard his name correctly before - didn't respond. Instead, he stepped further into the house, hands tucked into his pockets, and his eyes drifting over the framed pictures on the mantle. He studied them like he was trying to place himself in the memories. He didn't belong in them. But for some reason, he didn't look disappointed.

"Did my son send you?" Lucy asked, not liking how small her voice sounded in the empty house.

Jack let out a small hum, stopping in front of a bookshelf. He ran a finger along the dusted surface, then picked up a ceramic bird figurine and turned it over in his hands. "Nice place," he said finally. "Bit lonely, though."

Lucy's stomach twisted. People didn't talk like that unless they wanted something.

She kept her face neutral. "I like my peace."

Jack smirked like that answer amused him. "That so?"

He set the bird down, carefully, then turned toward her. His full attention was on her now, and Lucy felt it like a physical weight that pressed down on her chest.

She could feel it in her bones that this man was dangerous but it was in a way that she didn't fully understand yet. And that made him even more of a threat.

Lucy forced herself to meet his gaze. "What do you want?"

Jack tilted his head slightly. "That's the question, isn't it?"

She didn't like the way he said that. He walked past her now and paused just beside her chair. Too close. He was shadowed over her, but he never touched her nor did he lean into her. He didn't have to.

Lucy gripped the armrest of her wheelchair tighter. "If you're here to rob me, you'll be disappointed."

Jack let out a quiet chuckle. "Now why would I do that?"

Lucy's lips pressed into a thin line. He wasn't here for money. She knew that now. He was here for her.

Jack exhaled, almost like he was bored with the whole situation, then took a step back. "You don't remember me, do you?"

A sharp shiver ran down Lucy's spine. Something about him made her feel like she should remember him. "I think I'd remember someone like you."

Jack smirked again, but there was no humor in it. "Would you?" he asked.

Lucy said nothing.

"You were responsible for the kidnappings, weren't you?"

"What?" She gasped, lost for the brief second that was said. Who was this man questioning her in this manner? She inhaled deeply. "No," she said immediately, shaking her head. "No, I -" She continued knowing now they were talking of Riverwood and this man knew her from somewhere. But he cut her short.

"For the disappearances," Jack continued, stepping closer. "For the deaths. For Ben"

"I wasn't -"

"You were mad Rachel stole your husband, and you took it out on your son, the town…" he stopped and gazed down into her soul.

Lucy's breath hitched. The room felt smaller. Jack hadn't raised his voice, but she could feel the tension winding tighter with every second. "I never…I never took anyone. I never killed anyone," she insisted.

Jack tilted his head slightly. Then his voice dropped lower. "My father…" he said it like a statement, but it also felt like a question. And instantly, she knew who he was. Her lips parted, but no words came.

Jack didn't move. He waited like he already knew the answer but wanted to hear it from her. Lucy's hands trembled. She could feel her past crashing down on her, a memory she had spent years trying to bury. "I…" Her voice cracked.

She couldn't deny it, not this time. Her throat closed as guilt clawed its way up like bile. "Jack… I never wanted to hurt him. I never—"

"But you did. And you ran afterwards…did you think you were going to live happily ever after?"

Lucy broke down in tears as she buried her face in her hands. She had spent so long running, trying to forget and pretend that maybe if she left Riverwood behind, she could leave behind what happened too. But ghosts didn't stay buried. And neither did guilt.

"I'm sorry," she whispered. "I never meant for it to happen."

Jack didn't speak. Lucy lifted her head, her face streaked with tears. A choked sob escaped her lips. "Please," she begged. "I never wanted this. I never wanted to hurt anyone. I-"

A tear dropped from Jack's eyes. "I spent all these years believing you killed all those people. And I searched for you not just because of them, but because I needed to look you in the eye and ask you why you did it. What did my father, your son and all those people do to deserve this." He looked at her wheelchair. "You deserve this. Your son turning away from you. You, in this wheelchair. You will die alone."

She gasped and gripped her chest as if she could physically hold herself together. Jack took a step back, as if the sight of her disgusted him.

But before he could turn away completely, Lucy whispered something that made him stop and hesitate.

"I didn't leave Riverwood because of you, Jack."

Jack froze. "I left because of James."

Jack turned. "James?"

Lucy nodded slowly, wiping her face with the back of her sleeve. "You thought I was running from you," she said weakly. "But I was running from him."

"Why?"

Lucy exhaled shakily. "Because he went insane."

Lucy clenched her hands in her lap. "Everyone turned against him because of me. He lost everything because of me. He lost his son. He lost Rachel while moving from Riverwood. He lost his wealth because I left him. And when he did, he changed."

"I knew what he was capable of, Jack. I knew. And I was afraid. That's why I left my son with Margaret. That's why I let him continue being the first victim of the silent killer even when he was alive. I thought he would be safer away from me and James."

Lucy watched him carefully, then said something else. Something that made Jack's entire body tense, and this thing she said changed everything.

Jack didn't move for a long time.

Lucy sat frozen in her wheelchair, barely breathing, waiting for him to speak or just do something.

She had just admitted the truth, or at least part of it. She had killed his father. She had left Riverwood not because she was running from Jack, but because she was running from James.

And now Jack stood there, silent. Lucy almost wished he would hurt her. She deserved it, didn't she? She deserved to be punished. To suffer for what she had done.

But Jack only let out a slow breath, shaking his head slightly as if trying to make sense of it all. His hands clenched at his sides, but he never raised them. He wasn't going to kill her.

Lucy felt something like disappointment twist in her chest. All these years of waiting, of wondering when her past would finally catch up to her, and now that it had, it refused to finish her off.

Jack turned away, heading for the door. "Jack," she called weakly. He stopped, but he didn't turn back. Jack didn't say anything. Did he even care?

She wasn't sure. But as he reached for the door handle, Lucy allowed herself one last selfish wish.

"I hope," she whispered, "that before I die, I can see him again."

Jack stood there for a second longer. Then, without another word, he opened the door and stepped out. Lucy listened as his footsteps faded.

And then, another sound. A new set of footsteps. The door didn't close all the way. The breeze pushed it back open slightly so she could see a shadow standing just beyond the threshold.

Lucy's blood ran cold. No, not him. She gripped the arms of her chair, her breath seizing as the figure stepped forward. It wasn't Ben nor Jack. It was someone else. Someone she had been running from for years.

Her mouth went dry and her heart hammered against her ribs. She wanted to scream, but no sound came out. The figure stepped fully into the faint light of her home. Lucy's hands trembled in her lap. Her nightmare had finally found her.

***

Sunset Ridge was too quiet that day when Ronald sat in his car just outside of town, his hand gripping the steering wheel. It was the kind of quiet that came before bad news, and he knew something was wrong, but he just couldn't place a finger on it yet. The radio played low static, he hadn't tuned it to anything. He just needed the noise to keep him from drowning in his thoughts.

His mother's voice played in his mind. The last time she called him. For years, she had been a ghost in his life, she had abandoned him not just with his father and his new wife, but with Margaret. Perhaps foster care was the only thing that made his life a little easier. He thought she had died after she disappeared from Riverwood. Maybe it wasn't a bad thing she was still alive, but did she expect to unite with him just like that.

A million emotions fought for space in his chest, but none of them felt right. He wasn't angry, at least not anymore. He had burned through that rage years ago. He wasn't sad, either. Maybe he should've been.

He could have walked into that house, and listened to what she had to say. To know why she had given up on him. Why she had never come back for him.

He ran a hand down his face, and exhaled sharply. He was glad he didn't. If he was going to, it would not be immediately. He was not ready yet.

The streetlights shone overhead as he turned onto the main road, heading toward the outskirts of town. Maybe some fresh air would clear his head. That was the plan, anyway.

But the second he pulled up to the gas station, flashing red and blue lights painted the pavement in violent color. His stomach turned. Two officers stepped out of a squad car. "Ben Reed?"

His hands went cold. "Yeah?"

The first officer exchanged a glance with the other before stepping forward. "Turn around. Hands behind your back."

Ronald's heart slammed against his ribs. "What?"

"You're under arrest for the murder of Lucy Reed."

The world tilted immediately. "No," Ronald said, shaking his head. "No, that's not-"

Ronald had barely processed the words before the cuffs were on his wrists. He barely heard the rest of the words. He didn't even have time to grieve before they shoved him into the back of a police car, as the sirens screamed through the night.

Now, under the harsh fluorescent lights of the interrogation room, Ronald sat shackled to a metal table, trying to understand how everything had gone so wrong. His mother was dead. And somehow, they thought he did it.

His hands ached from how tightly he had been clenching them. Detective Roderiguz paced around in front of him, a frown on his face, perhaps to intimidate him.

"Tell me again, Ronald…" He grimaced, "Ben…Where were you yesterday?"

Ronald sighed deeply. "Not in that house."

Roderiguz scoffed. "Then how do you explain the witness who saw you leaving? How do you explain someone knowing you went there…"

Ronald clenched his jaw. "I stopped outside. That's it. I never went inside."

"Convenient," Roderiguz said and crossed his arms. "Yet, Lucy Reed is dead. And you -" He leaned in "-have no alibi."

Ronald glared at him. "I didn't kill her."

Roderiguz smirked and flipped through the file in front of him. "You know, you've got an interesting history. You disappeared twenty years ago. People believed it was the silent killer but there is still no record of where you went. No explanation for why you suddenly reappeared. And now, the woman who gave you up is murdered the same day someone sees you at her house?"

Ronald's hands curled into fists. "You think I planned this?"

"I think," Roderiguz said, tapping a pen against the table, "...that you have motive. Abandoned as a child. No closure. A lot of anger, I imagine."

Ronald stared at him blankly. They wanted him to be the killer, they needed someone to blame. But none of it made sense.

"Do you even hear yourself?" Ronald asked in a much calmer way. "You think I'm the Silent Killer? The same person who's been doing this for twenty years?" He let out a short giggle. "I was a kid when this started."

Roderiguz didn't flinch when he said that. "And now you're a man. A man with missing years and no explanation for where you've been."

Ronald shook his head. "I didn't kill her."

Roderiguz studied him for a long moment. Then he shut the file and stood up. "Until you can prove otherwise," he said, "you're our prime suspect."

The door slammed shut behind him as Ronald watched helplessly. He shut his eyes hoping he was dreaming. How did he end up here? His only alibi was probably the one who reported him to the police, Sara. She would not be able to vouch that he didn't walk into that house.

Rodriguez pinched the bridge of his nose as he watched Ronald through the one-way mirror. Ronald was the silent killer's first victim. He was a child when this started. Supposedly if it was truly Margaret who had kidnapped him and kept him hidden for years, then perhaps he learned from watching her?

Something wasn't right. But Ronald was someone convenient, maybe he would explain his way out of this mess. But it really wasn't looking good for him.

Rodriguez ran a hand through his hair. All of it was wrong. But everybody wanted to close the case, wrap it up neatly with a suspect who couldn't fight back.

CHAPTER THIRTY-FIVE

Chaos

Sara stood outside the jailhouse longer than she should have, staring at the door like stepping through it would make everything too real. Part of her was here for the story. After all, it was her job to chase the worst parts of life, write them down, and make strangers care. But this wasn't just another assignment.

Ronald Reed wasn't a stranger. She considered him a friend, if she dared to call it that. Someone she had heard about long before she'd ever met him, a kid lost to Riverwood's cursed history.

Now he was back and in cuffs. Accused of murder. She took a shaky breath and walked in.

The cold smell of metal and bleach hit her instantly. The officer at the front desk gave her a curious glance but didn't stop her. They all knew who she was. Sara had been digging into this Riverwood's secrets for years. She belonged in rooms like this. But this time felt so different.

When she saw Ronald sitting there behind the glass, her chest ached. His face was pale, his hair was a mess and dark circles had begun to haunt his eyes. He didn't look dangerous. He looked tired.

He looked up and smirked weakly. "Took you long enough," he rasped. "Come to write my downfall, Sara?"

She sat down slowly, fingers tightening around her notepad. "No. I came because...because I wanted to hear it from you."

Ronald's gaze darkened as he stared at her. Even if she didn't believe it earlier, those eyes looked like the eyes of a killer. "Ronald. I'm here because... you're my friend. Or... were. I don't even know anymore." She exhaled. "I just needed to hear you say it."

"Say what?"

"That you didn't kill her."

He sighed and said with a straight look. "I didn't."

"But you were there."

Ronald smiled, "you turned me in," he said, his voice flat. "Don't bother denying it. I know it was you." He gave a bitter laugh. "Guess that makes us friends, huh?" He scoffed. "It's a damn good story, right? Ronald Reed, Riverwood's missing kid, returns just in time to kill his own mother. The Silent Killer, full circle. Congratulations, Sara. You got your headline."

"I..." she hated how small her voice sounded. "I didn't know what else to do. You were there, Ronald. You were seen."

His eyes burned into hers. "Outside, Sara. I never stepped inside. Do you really think I could kill her? "

Sara flinched. "You hated her."

"Of course I did," Ronald snapped. "I hated her for leaving me. But hate isn't enough to do this." His shoulders slumped. "You don't know what it's like, Sara. To finally see her again... and realize she's already dead in every way that matters. I sat in my car. I watched that house. That's it."

Sara looked down at her hands. "I thought... after what I found out "

"I know who might have a motive," Ronald whispered.

She looked up at him. "What?"

"Years ago. Before she left Riverwood. She said she couldn't live with what she did. She killed him."

"Killed who?"

"Mr. Harrison. And not because she wanted to, it was an accident but she never paid for it."

"Mr. Harrison…"

"I didn't know what to do with it back then. I was a kid. What the hell was I supposed to do? So, I let her go. She left Riverwood… left me." His voice broke, but he forced himself to keep going. "And then I find out she's dead. And somehow… I'm the one who did it? I never even stepped inside that house."

Sara stared at him. "You think Mr.Harrison did this?"

"Not the dead Harrison, the son. A Haris. A Jack."

"His alibi checks out Ronald, he was not in town when it happened." She sighed. "I don't get it, the body in Margaret's house wasn't her but that of a Jane Doe, you coming out of nowhere to claim Margaret kidnapped you, and everyone believes she's the silent killer but she's not and it's you? And now, no one's asking who the first killer was."

Ronald gave a hollow laugh. "Maybe that's what makes it poetic. The kid who vanished becomes the man everyone's afraid of."

Sara leaned back, staring at him. "If you didn't do it... then who did?"

Ronald shook his head. "I don't know. But you know the thing about Riverwood and towns like it, Sara. Maybe it wasn't any of us. Maybe this town just knows how to kill its own."

For the first time, Sara had no answer. And for the first time... she wasn't sure if she was still hunting the truth or if the truth had finally started hunting them.

Moments later, Ronald sat still, staring after Sara as the heavy door clicked shut behind her. The sound echoed in the small concrete room like the closing of a tomb, and for a second, he could almost feel the finality of it settle over him.

She had left him and she had left with the last shred of hope he didn't even know he'd been holding on to. He slumped back against the cold wall, eyes burning, his throat tight. Maybe he'd thought that if someone, it might change something. But the truth didn't set him free.

Ronald smiled but it was from pain and anger, and slowly it turned to a painful laugh but the sound bounced off the walls. What a joke. They wanted him to be the villain. They wanted him to be the forgotten kid who came back to finish what his mother off. And maybe, in their eyes, that was easier. It could serve as a neat little ending to a story no one wanted to open again.

But as he stared at that door, Ronald knew the truth was uglier than anyone dared to imagine. His mother's death wasn't the end. It was just the beginning .The beginning of the end.

For years, Riverwood's secrets had been kept under lock and key, stitched together with guilt, fear, and silence. And now someone had decided it was time to start cutting those threads and tie off loose ends one by one. Anyone who touched this story, anyone who tried to dig it back up, would be next.

Margaret, Sara, Jack, Roderiguz, the kids all over Riverwood and back, his mother. Now he understood, he was the bait to lure his mother out. And Margaret's death was the bait to lure him out, except she didn't truly die.

All these people thought they could chase the truth, poke around, ask their questions, and walk away. No one walked away from Riverwood. Not even him.

Ronald knew that anyone who got close enough would catch a stray bullet. Not just literally, it was crueler than that. This case ruined and broke people.

Maybe being in here was the safest place for him after all. Ronald looked around the cell, from the gray walls to the thin mattress and the bolted-down sink. It was a cage, but it was still safer than being out there in Sunset Ridge with the killer roaming about.

Out there, the game had pieces moving on a board no one understood. But it was not the same in here. But he knew better than to believe it would last. Because soon, there would be a new death, and they would realize he didn't lie and release him.

Eventually, his past would come knocking and he hoped he would be strong enough to look him in the eye after all he had done.

***

Sara barely remembered driving home. Her mind was caught somewhere between the dead weight of Ronald's words and the haunting way he looked at her through the glass. She had left him there, while he looked as though he had already made peace with whatever fate had in store for him.

The rain had started on her way back. Fine misty drops that blurred her windshield and made the world outside look like it was crumbling. By the time she parked, Sunset Ridge had settled into the the night like it was a cozy blanket to protect it from the cold. There were no lights or sounds on in the neighboring houses. It was just the wind, humming low through the cracks of the buildings around hers. She wondered if she had noticed her surroundings this way or it was just the fear lingering from her visit to the jailhouse.

She dragged herself up to her apartment, locked the door twice out of habit, and tossed her soaked jacket over the couch. The air smelled faintly of dust and something else that was unfamiliar. But it could have been anything, a left over food, the street feral cats that perched by her window sometimes or literally anything. So, she brushed it off and blaming her overworked mind.

Sara couldn't sit. Instead, she pulled out the box of photos she hadn't touched in years. She told herself it was research, maybe there was a clue she missed or a face she had forgotten but deep down, she knew she was grasping for any form of control in a case that was spiraling out of her hands.

Photo after photo passed through her fingers, from images of Riverwood and Sunset Ridge in better days. Families smiling, kids riding bikes and people who were probably dead or gone now. And then she found a picture that had been gnawing at the edges of her mind.

James Reed, Ronald's father. Younger, with that wild smile, his arm around his woman, Rachel, a much younger woman. She had almost forgotten about Rachel, the new wife, but there she was, bright and beautiful , beaming at the camera. A snapshot of a life that had been perfect once.

Sara stared at it, wondering what became of James after Rachel died. Did he lose his mind? Did he blame Lucy? Did he have anything left worth living for? Her fingers hovered over his face like she could pull the answers out from the paper. But with a sigh, she pushed the photo back into the box and shoved the lid closed. And thud. She heard it from somewhere in her apartment, it was soft but distinct.

Sara froze as her breath caught in her throat. There it was again, a soft shift of weight on floorboards. It wasn't the building creaking, no, someone was in her apartment.

For a full ten seconds, her heart thumped painfully in her chest. Then when her instincts finally took over, she grabbed the old baseball bat leaning against her bookshelf and gripped it tight.

"Who's there?" Her voice trembled, but she forced strength into it. "I swear to God, I'll call the police!" But there was no answer.

The loud silence made her ears ring. Still, the prickling at the back of her neck told her she wasn't alone. Slowly, with her bat raised, she moved toward the kitchen where she thought she heard the sound. But she found nothing, thank goodness.

She flicked on the light, just to make sure. But it was the empty kitchen staring back at her paranoia. The cheap clock on the wall ticked mockingly.

"Sara, get it together," she whispered to herself as she slowly laid down the bat. "You're just tired."

She turned around and caught the tail end of a shadow slipping past the hallway and that was the instant her blood ran cold. *No,* her heart dropped. It wasn't her imagination. Someone was here.

Sara didn't think, she ran. Sprinting toward the door, she miscalculated her steps, tripped over the edge of the rug. She slammed hard into the hallway wall as the bat clattered to the floor. Stars burst behind her eyes, and she felt herself sliding down as darkness invaded her vision.

I'm going to die, she thought faintly. *The killer's been here all along.* Were her final thoughts until nothing.

When Sara woke up, it was daylight. Her head pounded, her mouth was dry, and her entire body ached. For a moment, she thought she had dreamed it all. Just a nightmare brought on by stress and fear.

But when she saw the single violet laying by side, fresh and untouched, she didn't know how to react. She didn't know what terrified her more, the fact that the flower was there, or that whoever left it could have killed her but didn't.

It had to be a message or a warning that she was too close and had to walk away. It explained why her photo box had been ransacked and the only picture which was taken was the one she had stared at for a long time the pervious night. Maybe it saved her, or maybe it was part of the warning but it was the first time in her life she would listen.

She packed her stuff. Every piece of clothing, notebook, and every trace of herself and stuffed into suitcases frantically. She didn't stop to call anyone, neither did she care about the articles half-written on her laptop or the boxes of notes. She left it all.

And by the time the sun fully rose, Sara was already driving out of Sunset Ridge, glancing nervously in her rearview mirror. She didn't know what was waiting for her down the road, but she knew what was behind her.

And she wasn't sticking around to find out how this story ended. Not in Riverwood or Sunset Ridge, not anymore. She was done.

CHAPTER THIRTY-SIX

Speak of the Devil

It had been days since Sara stopped picking their calls. At first, Alex told himself it was nothing, people drifted. He convinced himself that maybe, after everything, Sara had simply closed the notebook, packed up her things, and decided the story wasn't worth it anymore. Reporters were like that sometimes. Always chasing the next big headline until something bigger and flashier came along. That's what he told himself and that's what he wanted to believe.

But every day that passed, the bad feeling in his gut only grew worse. By the fifth day, Maya had stopped even trying to reach out. She sat in the library most days, buried in her books, as she prepared for a big exam that would get her out of Sunset Ridge for good. Tyler claimed he was done and said they were idiots for sticking around and acting like characters in a horror movie. He made a joke of it once, "we are gonna end up in the next headline." Even though no one found it funny.

Even Ethan suddenly stopped calling after a while. Everyone was trying to move on.

But Alex couldn't. The house was too quiet these days. His parents had started giving him that look, the one that meant they were waiting and expecting him to start acting like their son again. His mom had even mentioned college applications with careful words the night before like she didn't want to startle him. Like Alex was some wild animal that might bolt if pressed too hard.

"Maybe now that everything's… wrapped up, you can start thinking about your future," her mother had said. "I mean, that kid's in custody now. They closed the case. It's over, son. If I had known it was what you were so interested in, I would have sent you off to the city."

Over? The word echoed in Alex's head as he sat at the kitchen table the next morning, staring blankly at a half-filled application form. Over… As if it were really that simple. As if they could all just pack up the ghosts of Riverwood, shove them into a box, and forget the whole damn thing ever happened.

But he wasn't like Tyler, who could throw himself into sports practice and pretend none of it was real. He wasn't like Maya, who'd made a lot of textbooks and study plans. He wasn't even like Ethan, who had the cold and logical mind of a hacker, someone who could reduce the horror of everything they'd seen into ones and zeroes.

Alex was just Alex. He had no special skills or talents that made him indispensable. He was just a kid who had been in way over his head since the very beginning.

Still, he couldn't stop thinking about Sara. Why had she gone silent now, of all times? Why disappear when they were finally at the end of it all? She wasn't the type to walk away from unfinished business. If anything, she had always been too involved and persistent. And that was what scared him.

He rubbed his hands over his face and groaned softly. The kitchen smelled like coffee and burnt toast. The sunlight streamed lazily through the windows, bathing everything in that soft golden glow that made the world look normal and peaceful.

But peace was a lie. Somewhere out there, something was still watching and waiting. Alex didn't know how he knew but he just did.

The memories came back too easily. That old diner in Riverwood, the crumbling buildings half-eaten by time, the way the townsfolk watched them like they were already picking out their graves. Margaret's twisted smile. And Sara scribbling in that worn-out notebook of hers, determined to uncover every secret no matter what it cost.

Where the hell was she now? The clock ticked. His phone sat silently beside him but there were no new messages or missed calls.

For a second, he thought about calling Emily and how he tried to fix their broken relationship. Maybe he should try and focus on building their relationship and forget all this ever happened. Maybe it was truly time to move on. He could finish this application. Pick a college, follow the path laid out for him like every other kid his age.

He stared down at the form. The blanks felt endless. Name, GPA, extracurriculars, none of it mattered. None of it felt real anymore. He would move on alright, it's not like he had a choice. But only if they found closure to this matter. Because no matter how the police wanted to paint it, Ronald was not the closure.

His phone buzzed suddenly, and he jumped as he grabbed it without thinking. It was Ethan whom he had given a little assignment, to find where Sara lived.

With a shaky breath, Alex swiped to answer hoping Ethan had something tangible for him. "Ethan?"

There was a reluctant pause on the other end. Then Ethan's voice came through, "you sitting down?"

Something cold settled in Alex's chest. He gripped the phone tighter, and stared blankly at the college form in front of him.

"Yeah… I'm sitting."

Ethan exhaled sharply, like he was preparing himself for whatever came next.

"I found her."

"Found who?" he asked, though he already knew the answer.

"Sara."

The name hit him like a punch. Ethan repeated, "I said I know where she lives."

"Oh good," Alex heaved a sigh.

"But-"

"But?"

"She moved out, some days ago. She didn't say anything, she just left."

And just like that, she was gone. He sat there, staring at the phone like it had just delivered his final verdict. Sara was really gone. Of course she was. Why would she stay after everything they'd seen, who in their right mind would choose to stay? Alex couldn't even blame her. He'd wanted to run too more times than he could count. But now that it was real, that she'd actually left, he felt how final it was. Whatever happened that made her leave, she had taken the truth with her. That is, if she had truly left instead of being dead, buried in the dump somewhere.

Alex leaned back in his chair, staring at the ceiling. The walls of his home felt smaller now like the house knew what he was thinking and was quietly agreeing. He thought of Ronald, sitting in a jail cell for a crime Alex wasn't even sure he committed. Of Lucy, dead and buried, the secrets she carried now rotting with her. Of Margaret, the town, the diner, the damned Reed family, and all the pieces that still didn't fit no matter how hard they tried.

They were all fooling themselves, thinking it was over. Maybe it would've been easier to let it go. To finally fold it all up, stuff it deep inside, and move on like others were trying to. Go to college, live a normal life and let the past die.

But as Alex sat there in the silence, he knew he couldn't do that just yet. Maybe he wouldn't even need to, there was still one thing left. There was one place they hadn't checked out because the police were all over it and it made big news. Lucy's home.

It felt ridiculous even thinking it, what could possibly be left there now? But some stubborn part of him refused to let it go. Maybe it was just the need for closure, or maybe it was the desperate desire to understand how everything had gone so wrong. Whatever it was, it pushed the words out of him before he could stop it. "We need to check out Lucy's home," he said to Ethan whom he wasn't sure was paying attention anymore.

If they were really going to walk away from this, they had to stand together first. Face it head-on. Look the past in the eye and finally let it go. He didn't even know why, but somehow, it felt right. And when he told Ethan, he didn't even argue. He agreed.

They gathered that same evening, just as the sky was sinking into a gray orange as the sun struggled to break through heavy clouds. The air felt like the world itself was holding its breath. None of them really spoke as they met outside Lucy's house. Even Tyler, who usually had so much to say just to ease the tension kept his mouth shut. Maya stood with her arms crossed as she stared at the peeling paint of the porch like it might crumble into dust at any second. Ethan was unusually quiet, his eyes darting around. But it was not out of fear, but calculation. Be it about their entry points, escape routes, and cameras they needed to avoid. And Emily stood by Alex, unsure if she had beaten her fear after all they had faced together.

The yellow police tape was still there, fluttering weakly in the breeze like it had given up too. 'CRIME SCENE. DO NOT CROSS' was in faded black. It might as well have said abandon hope, all those who enter here for how heavy it felt.

Alex stood back, to take a good look at the house. It didn't look special, not haunted or cursed, it was just another suburban home trying hard to outlive its secrets.

They weren't supposed to be here. One call to the cops and they'd be hauled away for interfering with an open investigation. It wasn't like Riverwood because a lot of that happened in the past, everything except the moment Margaret disappeared. But Alex knew that the police weren't going to solve this. They weren't interested in digging any deeper. As far as the law was concerned, they had their man, Ronald, case closed.

But for Alex, it didn't sit right. They stood there a little longer, unsure who would make the first move. Then he sighed and began to move toward the side of the house, careful to avoid the obvious line of sight from the street. The others followed, everyone's breath shallow in their lungs.

Alex's heart was pounding by the time they reached the back door. He half-expected it to be locked, but Ethan tested the handle, and to their shock, it creaked open. Either the cops had been sloppy, or someone had been here recently.

Inside, it was worse. The smell of stale air and death clung to the walls. Everything looked normal, like someone had just gotten up and walked out, except for the thin layer of dust that coated the furniture and the faint dark stain on the wooden floor where they knew Lucy had died.

Maya couldn't stop staring at it. Her arms were crossed tight, her mouth pressed in a hard line. Tyler stayed near the door, like part of him was ready to bolt if things got worse. Ethan was already walking slowly, scanning the room like he was documenting it all in his head no while Emily followed Alex closely.

Alex felt the weight of it hit him all over again. Everything they'd learned all ended here. And yet it felt like they were still missing the biggest piece.

He finally spoke in a low voice. "This isn't random," he said. "None of this... Ronald didn't do this. I can feel it. This has Jack written all over it."

The others turned to him waiting for him to explain. Alex took a breath as his eyes drifted over the old photographs still hanging on Lucy's walls. A younger version of her, smiling genuinely, a lie caught on camera. "Jack... Jack comes from Riverwood. And his father owned the old diner that burned down. The one no one ever rebuilt." He looked around at each of them. "What if that's it all Ben Reed was one side of the coin and Jack's father was the other side of the coin? Jack's been playing this game long before we even realized it."

Maya finally found her voice. "You're saying Lucy had something to do with Harrison's death?"

Alex shook his head slowly. "I don't know. But what I do know is we need to find him. We need to confront him. Because none of this ends until we do."

They all knew Alex was right. There were no more theories left, Lucy was dead, Ronald in jail and Sara was gone. There was only Jack now and his story connected so much as from Riverwood's past to Sunset Ridge's present. And it was time to pull it. But first, something was coming.

***

Jack gripped the steering wheel tighter as he drove down town, his knuckles whitening as the memories kept replaying vividly inside his head. He had confronted his father's killer but he had learned something else. "I let Ben stay with Margaret... I thought it was the only way to protect him. From James.."

As he pushed the far harder, the engine groaned under his feet. He didn't remember when he started or why he even got into the car. There was just this pull guiding him down this road. Lucy had painted James as the villain. And maybe he was. A man driven insane by loss, grief and betrayal.

Ben wasn't just a missing boy, he was the center of it all. The secret no one talked about. And Margaret was no innocent bystander. Lucy had trusted her with the only thing that mattered, and that meant Margaret knew. She knew all those years, she sat in that diner spinning stories, smiling, and laughing while the truth rotted just beneath her tongue.

And then there was Rachel. The perfect wife, the one everyone adored. Dead. Another casualty in the Riverwood tragedy.

The truth was, he didn't know what he wanted anymore. Maybe just answers. But answers from who? Lucy was dead. Margaret was dead. Ronald was rotting in a cell for a crime everyone knew he didn't commit. The car slowed as the house came into view. Lucy's house.

It sat in the dark like a corpse. The windows were boarded up now, the grass had grown wild, as if the earth itself was trying to swallow the place. Jack killed the engine but stayed in the car, staring.

He rubbed his face roughly, feeling the stubble scratch against his palm. There was so much he wanted to scream. He remembered

Lucy's voice again, the way it trembled when she spoke about James. He sat there for what felt like minutes, staring at that house, waiting for something but there was only the wind and the dark.

Jack knew then what he had to do. He didn't he would have to rerun to this place after her death but here he was, looking for answers perhaps hidden somewhere the clumsy cops never thought to check. He took a step forward, as the wood creaked under his boots when he pushed open the front door, his gun already resting heavy in his side pocket.

There was a strange chill in the air, it was no just from the cold. Something wasn't right. Jack took a careful step forward, his hand instinctively brushing against the handle of his gun. He didn't know what he was expecting, a raccoon, maybe. The lingering spirit of Lucy, if he believed in that sort of thing. But the second his gaze drifted toward the kitchen, his gut twisted hard. There was someone there. A figure, crouched low, trying to blend into the shadows near the counter.

"Hey!" Jack's voice rang out harsh, breaking the silence as his hand shot toward his gun. He barely had time to react when a blur lunged at him from the side.

The gun flew from his grip, skidding across the floor. "What the-"

"Don't move!" another voice shouted.

Jack staggered back, blinking in shock as his eyes adjusted. There, standing before him, was Tyler, breathing hard. And then the others appeared, Ethan, Maya, Emily and Alex forming a shaky circle around him like kids who'd finally found the monster under their bed but didn't know what the hell to do next.

"Speak of the devil," Alex muttered bitterly.

They looked different now. They were not the curious teens from weeks ago. They looked exhausted. "Where's Sara?" Tyler asked him.

Jack blinked. "What?"

"Don't play dumb!" Maya snapped but her voice trembled. "Where is she? You... You did something to her, didn't you?"

"I don't know where Sara is!" Jack said. "I haven't seen her since the last time she-"

"Stop lying!" Ethan cut in, "You're the only one left! Lucy's dead! Margaret's dead! And Ronald's rotting in a cell! You're the last damn piece of this!"

Jack's lips curled bitterly. "So, what? That makes me guilty? Because I'm still breathing?"

"Because you're from Riverwood," Alex whispered. "Because everything... everything leads back to you."

Jack scoffed. "No it doesn't. Riverwood's a graveyard. Everyone's from Riverwood if you dig deep enough. You think I wanted any of this?" He shook his head. "Lucy... she told me things you wouldn't believe. About your innocent Margaret, Ben. James."

They flinched at the name, James. He was sort of a ghost everyone had forgotten. .

"James went mad because he thought Lucy and the people of Riverwood ruined him. " Jack continued, "You think I killed Lucy? You think I killed Margaret? I was just as lost as you."

The kids exchanged weary glances. The fear was still there, but doubt was creeping in. "I didn't kill Lucy, neither did Ronald but I think we all know who did…"

Then the all froze as the door creaked open. It could have been the wind, it had been rainy these past few days. But it wasn't windy and no one had touched it.

Every head turned as they heard something cream. But it wasn't the door, something had walked in, a shadow filled the doorway, tall, wide, faceless, just standing there. And in that second, they all knew the real monster was here.

Before anyone could speak, a soft pop echoed. It was almost silent, but louder than any gunshot to their ears. Someone gasped and fell.

But it was getting too dark for them to know who it was, but no one dared to move anymore, as the shadow raised a hand. And they saw themselves staring at a gun. And that's when they smelt the sweet scent of flowers.

"Run," someone whispered.

But no one did. They all knew the moment that gun fired, the game changed. The Silent Killer was here in the house. And none of them were walking out the same. If at all.